Quality Measurement in Economics

Dr Steven Payson is an economist with the US Department of Agriculture. This work is based on his doctoral dissertation, which he completed while at Columbia University, New York, in 1991. The views expressed here are attributable to the author alone, and not to Columbia University or the US Department of Agriculture.

Quality Measurement in Economics

New Perspectives on the Evolution of Goods and Services

Steven Payson
Economic Research Service
United States Department of Agriculture, Washington, DC

Edward Elgar

© Steven Payson 1994

Published by
Edward Elgar Publishing Limited
Gower House
Croft Road
Aldershot
Hants GU11 3HR
England

Edward Elgar Publishing Company
Old Post Road
Brookfield
Vermont 05036
USA

British Library Cataloguing in Publication Data
Payson, Steven
    Quality Measurement in Economics: New Perspectives on the Evolution of Goods and Services
    I. Title
    338.5

Library of Congress Cataloguing in Publication Data
Payson, Steven, 1957-
    Quality Measurement in Economics: New Perspectives on the Evolution of Goods and Services / Steven Payson.
        p.   cm.
    Based on the author's doctoral dissertation, Columbia University, New York, 1991.
    Includes bibliographical references.
    1. Quality of products—United States—Cost effectiveness-
-Econometric models. 2. Technological innovations—United States-
-Econometric models. I. Title.
    HF5415.157.P39 1994
    658.5'62—dc20
                                 93-28612
                                   CIP

ISBN 1 85278 926 3

Printed and Bound in Great Britain by
Hartnolls Limited, Bodmin, Cornwall.

To Vyviahn and Mikhail

Time series of prices and of quantities . . . are . . . among the most familiar of economic data. Familiar, too, are the difficulties encountered both in the construction and interpretation of such series because of the qualitative changes over time in the products which compose them. It is not necessary, then, to argue for the existence of such changes. What is necessary is to recognise them as variations of vital importance in themselves, rather than as disturbing elements in the problem of price and quantity indexes. We know next to nothing about the history, even the recent history, of the qualitative improvement or deterioration of products, either individually, by classes, or in general. There is a limitless field for investigation here.

Edward H. Chamberlin (1953)

Contents

List of Figures

List of Tables

Preface

The importance of technological change in human society is unquestionable. Yet, little progress has been made in our ability to understand it. In order to do so, we must first explore new avenues of thought, and go out on a limb in our efforts to develop and test new hypotheses. Consequently, readers will quickly find that this book is not, by any means, another standardized, homogenized, sanitized and purified collection of state-of-the-art essays in economic formalism. In fact, its lack of formality may well disappoint some readers. Its mathematics are by no means impressive, the economic theory presented is not complex, and the text does not build heavily upon previously-established theoretical structures. In short, it is not a theoretical work, but what I would call a scientific exploration into the meaning and measurement of quality change. While this book does draw upon the existing literature, its purpose is to develop a new set of guidelines in the assessment of how goods and services change over long periods of time. Of course, once these guidelines are recognized, then theoretical economists will be free to formalize about them to their hearts' desire.

The reader may also find the structure of the book to be somewhat idiosyncratic. Chapters are not arranged strictly by the similarity of their subject matter, but are arranged in a manner that builds up the argument for a specific perspective on quality measurement. Furthermore, the discussions do not evade criticism or controversy — quite the contrary, they embrace them. This is not done to ruffle anyone's feathers, but to facilitate useful and progressive discourse.

The first three chapters provide a background on the subject of quality measurement. Chapters 4-6 then present a new framework, based on the 'representative good approach' to quality measurement, and on the distinction between quality improving and cost reducing technical change. The remaining three chapters address the broader issues of quality measurement which relate to many other areas of economic thought.

I would like to express my gratitude to several professors at Columbia University, especially my dissertation advisor, Kelvin Lancaster, and reader, Richard Nelson. I would also like to thank Philip Cagan for his helpful advice, and Phoebus Dhyrmes and Duncan Foley for their valuable comments. I am extremely grateful to Sears Roebuck and Company for allowing me to use photographs from the *Sears Catalog*, and in particular, I would like to thank Mary Lou Bilder and Al Mathes for their courtesy and generosity. I greatly appreciate the support I received from Malcolm Abrams and Harriet Bernstein in allowing me to use information from their book *Future Stuff*. I truly appreciate the excellent assistance I received from Rhonda Franklin in preparing the graphs and from Jane Wertz in editing the final text. I am grateful for the useful comments I received from Mark Blaug, George Frisvold, Robert Gordon, Lutz Kilian, Francis McFaul, Montague Lord, Michael Ollinger, Steve Vogel and Michael Weiss. Finally, I would like to express my appreciation to Carol Kramer, Fred Kuchler, Biing-Hwan Lin and John Miranowski at the Economic Research Service, United States Department of Agriculture, for their encouragement and interest in my research.

1. The meaning of quality

The least of things with a meaning is worth more in life than the greatest of things without it.

Jung (1953)

INITIAL CONSIDERATIONS

Looking beyond the Creation of Price Indices

Outside the world of economic theory, the term 'quality' is an extremely important concept. Advertisers, politicians and the news media are incessantly bombarding us with the term. We are told, literally, that 'quality is job one'. It defines our ability to produce, to compete in world markets, and to pride ourselves on our labour and management. It legitimizes us as providers of goods and services. It is, in some sense, our *raison d'être* as economic beings.

Within the world of economic theory, on the other hand, quality is very different — it is not an end in itself. Rather, it is merely a device, or trouble-shooter, that economists use in building price indices. In essence, economists study *quality* in order to figure out *quantity*.[1] Hence, while businesses, political organizations and research institutes are continually struggling to *foster* quality improvement, the economic community is passively, and somewhat complacently, finding new ways to *measure it*.

In contrast, the small group of economists who study technological change and evolutionary economics does have a strong interest in the forces that *cause* quality improvement.[2] However, their interest in quality improvement is often subtle, because they refer to it by a different name — 'product innovation'. As a practical matter, their use of different terminology is desirable, for three reasons: (1) it allows them to focus on the causal forces of quality change without being distracted by methodological aspects of price indexing; (2) it enables them to emphasize their interest in the behaviour of firms, especially in relation to industrial organization and R & D activities; (3) it lets readers avoid confusing their material with material on price indices.

This dichotomy in the study of quality change, between price-index research and technical-change research, has been convenient to both groups of economists. It has enabled each to delve deeper into its own paradigms, and to consolidate its own small niche in the spectrum of economic literature. Thus, the dichotomy has been created, in large part, as a by-product of the psychology and sociology of the economics profession.

Yet, in terms of the pursuit of useful knowledge, the dichotomy is extremely wasteful, and perhaps even irresponsible. The study of the causes of product innovation is weakened enormously by the fact that such innovations are not weighted by their relative economic importance, which would be based on prices. Conversely, the classification of goods and the generation of indices by price-index economists would be much more meaningful if the underlying causes of quality change were also addressed. In short, the two branches of thought have a great deal to learn from each other. Therefore, one of the main goals of this work is to encourage an interchange between them. If such an interchange takes place, then the 'whole' would be much greater than the sum of the parts.

The Word 'Quality'

When economists use the word 'quality' they often mean something different from what a layman would normally consider. Surely, a term can have a technical meaning in economic literature that differs substantially from its common meaning. The terms 'chaos', 'stability' and 'sterilization' are just a few of many examples. However, unlike these terms, quality is addressed quite often by the public in reference to the economic system. Moreover, the economic term itself, has a great deal in common with its public counterpart. Thus, it will be worthwhile for one to explore what the economic term and the public term have in common.

Within economics itself, there is considerable variation in the meaning of quality. An examination of the similarities and differences among various meanings could be quite useful, and could lead to improvements in the description and measurement of quality. It could also lead to important observations about economic thought itself.

More precisely, when one investigates quality in economics, one is asking, in effect, 'what is it about a good or service that makes it more desirable?' This question could be empirical, requiring the study of actual physical properties. In the case of consumer goods, the empirical question would also encourage the study of relevant components of human perception that influence a consumer's willingness to purchase a product. Conversely, quality can be studied on a purely theoretical basis where, for example, hypothetical 'widgets' are assumed to possess hypothetical 'widget characteristics'.

Before quality can be discussed, a specific perspective must be established with regard to its meaning. The perspective that will apply here is that a *good's quality is an inherent aspect of the good itself, whether or not one can actually measure it*. Quality is a function of a good's physical characteristics, or in the case of services, the physical activities that are carried out. Quality is not, by any means, a formula that is applied to a set of prices. Formulas may be used to estimate or measure quality, but not to define it.

On the other hand, quality must remain an economic concept — it cannot serve as an ultimate measure of value. The value of a life-saving medicine or medical operation, for example, would depend on the ultimate value of human life itself. Such a determination would go well beyond the scope of economics. Ultimate value, in other words, could be understood as a subjective concept, while quality (or at least 'economic quality') is an objective concept. Put simply, quality is *not* 'in the eyes of the beholder'. As it is dealt with in this study, *it is a measure of the typical consumer's willingness to purchase a good or service*.[3]

Quality is a 'relative' concept in the sense that one cannot actually measure the 'quality of good A', but rather, the 'quality of good A relative to good B'. On the other hand, one could also consider an 'absolute quality change' when the quality of the same good is compared at different points in time, in reference to a base period.

Whether the subject of quality change is approached empirically or theoretically, it will always challenge the economist to look deeper into what goods and services actually are. Otherwise, a good or service would be seen as an indivisible, elementary element, like a cell in biology or an atom in chemistry. Yet, just as progress in chemistry has allowed biologists to study the inner workings of the cell, and progress in nuclear physics has allowed chemists to study the inner workings of the atom, progress in the measurement of quality will allow economists to study the 'inner workings' of goods and services.

Along these lines, there appears to be a crucial need in economics for a better understanding of the characteristics of goods and services. 'Characteristics', for now, may be regarded as aspects, or qualities, of a good, that are relevant to a consumer's preferences. (Characteristics are discussed extensively in subsequent chapters.)

As an example, a great deal of economic research in recent years has looked into the rapid rate of quality change in computers. Yet, in this research there appears to be no mention of one of the primary ideas that could explain, at least at a scientific level, why computers have been able to increase in quality as rapidly as they have.

Suppose that one conducted a survey of economists and physicists, and asked them to explain why the quality of information processing has improved enormously relative to, for instance, the quality of transportation. Many economists would be at a loss to provide such an explanation, while many others would provide some kind of explanation, but not the correct one. Physicists, on the other hand, *would* come up with the right answer. The answer involves the differences between information processing and transportation in terms of physical requirements: A basic property of information is that it can be contained in objects of extremely small size, such as microfilm. More precisely, there is no physical quantity restriction on information, except at the molecular level (e.g., DNA) where information can be stored in terms of the positioning and selection of different molecules. At the same time, the speed at which information can be processed is constrained only by the speed of electrical impulses, which is the speed of light (186,000 miles per second).

Hence, the storage of information can be carried out at a molecular level, while information processing can be carried out at the speed of light. Indeed, at 186,000 miles per second, an electrical impulse can traverse an extremely large number of molecules!

In contrast, the transportation industry experiences much greater physical constraints. The energy expended in transporting any object will always be at least $\frac{1}{2}mv^2$ where m is the object's mass and v its velocity. Of course, the actual energy expended could be much greater than this, depending on air resistance, friction, the additional energy to slow down and stop, the maintenance of an environment within the vehicle, etc. These energy constraints will always exist. Thus, unless and until energy becomes extremely inexpensive, the quality of transportation is not likely to change in the near future in terms of time-saving, the spaciousness of passenger vehicles, etc.

Another example may also be illuminating. It is a well-known fact that chemical elements and specific chemical compounds, such as aluminum, pure sodium chloride (table salt) and pure sucrose (sugar), in a specified physical state (e.g., crystallized), cannot improve in quality. This follows from the fact that molecules of the same chemical composition and physical state will always be indistinguishable from each other.[4] Yet, this fact appears to be blatantly absent from discussions among economists on quality improvement among primary commodities, many of which are chemical elements or compounds.

One might ask what the relationship is between these two examples and economists' interest in quality change. The answer is that they illustrate that quality change is, ultimately, a natural or scientific phenomenon. As such, a minimum of basic scientific knowledge could be extremely useful in helping the economist understand how and why goods change in terms of quality. Conversely, by ignoring the natural sciences, economists may have considerable difficulty in understanding the true causes of quality change.

Definition or Classification of Goods and Services

In economics a 'good' is defined as something that is bought and sold in a market, and there is usually little need to expand on that notion. However, when one is dealing with technical change, the boundary line that separates one good from another is ambiguous in many circumstances, which creates problems in the measurement of quality.

For example, consider relative changes in the qualities of two goods: (1) films (or the service of showing a film to an individual) and (2) radios. Suppose further that the analysis is conducted for the time interval 1920-1993. One might suspect that both goods would undergo considerable quality improvement, as well as cost reduction over the 73-year period. One would have a great deal of difficulty, however, in reconciling what should be included in the category of 'radio'. One would ask whether modern audio systems, with their receivers, speakers, equalizers, etc. should be placed in the category. Moreover, perhaps televisions should be placed there as well. In the 1920s when the analysis begins, radios did not have a picture, and films did not have sound (other than accompanying music). It is somewhat arbitrary, then, that 'talkies' continued to be called 'films' while televisions were never called 'picture radios', or 'lookies'. Hence, one could argue that televisions are as much 'improved radios' as 'talkies' are improved films.

If televisions represent a quality improvement over radios, then so must the television/VCR combination. Yet, the television/VCR combination also shows films, and so one is faced with a dilemma. The comparison between quality improvements in radios and films has nearly become meaningless, because one does not know which innovations to attribute to which goods.

Recent speculation in the news media about future products suggests that this problem is likely to become worse. For instance, one prediction is that the television, telephone, audio system, personal computer and modem, will all become components of a single good, in which optical telephone lines will be used for communication, entertainment and computer operations.[5]

Of course, one could avoid this issue entirely, and simply measure quality changes on the basis of existing labels. For example, one could measure changes only in items called 'radios' and 'films'. But that would not lead to a higher understanding of the tendencies of certain goods to undergo quality improvement. Whatever it accomplishes would be primarily a function of circumstantial semantics.

There is certainly a great potential for confusion with regard to the distinction between one good and another when long-term quality changes are being considered. In a sense, it is quality differences themselves that allow one to distinguish among different goods. Thus, when one studies 'quality change', in the context of individual goods, one can no longer rely on 'quality differences' to help distinguish among them. One must look for inherent aspects of the goods themselves, even though those 'inherent' aspects cannot be determined in any absolute sense. For instance, if the function or purpose of the good is its most notable feature, then one could consider metal bookshelves and wooden bookshelves as being different forms of the same good. If one is more inclined to focus on physical composition, then one would treat 'wooden furniture' as one type of good and 'metal furniture' as another.

A Theoretical Framework for Categorizing Goods

When first approaching quality change, one need not rely on any standard definitions of goods. One could say, from the outset, that there is a continuum with regard to how specific or stringent the classification of goods should be. At one edge of this continuum is the most stringent classification scheme possible, in which there is one good for every economic transaction. For instance, one quart of milk bought at Joe's Grocery Store is a different good from the quart of milk bought at the same store one minute later. Of course, one could say that such a hypothetical break in the continuum contradicts the definition of a 'good' in economics, in that both quarts of milk are sold in the same 'market'. But such a concern would not be relevant to the analysis at hand, because one would simply be left with the same problem of defining separate 'markets'.

The purpose of this 'extremism' is simply to start from a particular perspective of the economic system. In this perspective, all goods and services could be seen as a massive pool, or 'gas' metaphorically speaking, of minute elementary elements — those elements being the most narrowly defined 'goods' that one could possibly think of, such as the specific quart of milk described above. The number of dimensions in this analysis depends only on what one chooses to study about those goods or their related transactions. For example, goods could be thought of as lying in dense clusters, or clouds, in a multi-dimensional characteristics space (see Lancaster, 1971).

Thus, if one of the characteristics of the good is its colour, another is whether or not it can be drunk, etc., then surely millions of points in characteristics space will be clustered tightly together, and the resultant cluster would be understood as 'quarts of milk'. If economic dimensions were also considered as part of the 'universe', the cluster would have a location in, say, price and quantity space. There could be a 'purpose space' as well, with dimensions on how the good is used, e.g., for food or recreation.

Chamberlin expressed similar ideas in a less geometric context in his article, 'The Product as an Economic Variable':

> In view of the generally sanctioned procedure of studying price-quantity relationships for *given* products it is of the utmost importance at the outset to realize that there is literally no such thing as a given product. Products are actually the most volatile things in the economic system — much more so than prices. To begin with, almost every 'product' has a variable element at least in the circumstances surrounding its sale: convenience of location, peculiarities of shop environment, personalities, service, methods of doing business, etc. These factors are, of course, of varying importance in the individual case. (Chamberlin 1953, p. 114)

In economics in general this framework is not necessary, because goods are assumed to maintain their positions in characteristics and purpose space.   In the study of quality, however, goods are moving[6] in these spaces. How one interprets their movements will definitely depend on how one locates their positions, that is, on how one initially chooses the dimensions of the universe to be studied. Equally important, one must determine what size of clusters to examine. Small clusters, like quarts of milk, may move as part of a larger cluster like dairy products. Still another consideration is the availability of data, which could place important constraints on the 'dimensions' and 'clusters' that could be used in an empirical study.

These basic notions could be made more concrete through the consideration of the physics and chemistry of goods. For example, one might argue that 'chemicals' cannot undergo quality improvements while 'electronic equipment' can.   However, while *individual* chemicals cannot improve in quality, new chemicals of higher quality are constantly being discovered. In the framework described above, individual chemicals such as 'concentrated sulphuric acid' remain as stationary clusters in characteristics space, but clusters for new chemicals are continually being produced, so that the larger cluster of 'all chemicals' is continually expanding. Thus, 'all chemicals', and even subgroups such as 'adhesives' or 'cleaning fluids', are consistently improving in quality. Indeed, in terms of quality measurement, one could say that *the whole is greater than the sum of the parts*.

There is the additional issue of how one measures and compares the movement and expansion of clusters. Each cluster, to begin with, is a distribution of points in characteristics space. Suppose, hypothetically, that radios and televisions are the only kinds of electronic equipment in existence, and neither can improve in quality — all that can change are the numbers of each in the economy. Suppose further that in year *A*, shortly after the television is invented, there are one million radios, but only one thousand televisions. Subsequently, in year *B*, there are one million of each. One would then be inclined to say that from year *A* to *B* the quality of electronic equipment rose. In order to make that observation concrete, one would need to say that the ratio of televisions to radios has gone up, therefore the *average piece of electrical equipment* has improved in quality.

However, now suppose that later on, in year *C*, the typical household that previously owned one radio and one television is able to buy additional radios for other rooms of their homes. The total number of radios in year *C* increases to three million, while the number of televisions remains at one million, and the ratio of televisions to radios declines. It would be counter-intuitive for one to say that the quality of electronic equipment falls between years *B* and *C*, since neither the quality of radios nor the quality of televisions declines. On the other hand, such a conclusion would follow directly from the method that was used previously to assess the quality change from year *A* to year *B*.[7]

These are serious problems, but they are not insurmountable, because quality has definite intuitive content. That is, there is no reason why the term cannot be used in a variety of contexts, as long as it provides useful information. For instance, 'chemicals' could be examined in two contexts, where: (1) each individual chemical is a single good (or cluster), and (2) the composite of all chemicals is a single good. For an economy that produces several different chemicals and conducts a significant amount of research and development in chemistry, the future prospects for its chemical industry might best be revealed by an analysis of 'all chemicals' as a single good. For an economy that has little or no R & D in chemistry, and processes a small set of specific chemicals, the analysis of each chemical as a separate good would be more useful.

Hence, the interpretation, measurement, and policy implications of quality change depends greatly on the initial context in which quality is defined. Unfortunately, the importance of this initial context is not often recognized in the economic literature, as will be demonstrated throughout this text.

QUALITY AS A FUNCTION OF COMPONENTS

One of the greatest sources of confusion in the subject of quality change is the distinction between quality, itself, and its measurement. As an example, let us consider four hypothetical definitions of quality: (1) *'user-value'* where quality is monotonically related to utility; (2) *'user-component'* where quality is a reflection of the quality of components that make up the good, e.g., the quality of a car is based on the quality of its motor, suspension system, heating system, etc.; (3) *'cost-component'* where the quality of a good is a function of the costs of its components; (4) *'total-cost'* where quality is a reflection of the total production cost of the good. One could argue that the last two of these definitions, which are based on costs, need not contradict the notions of quality discussed in the previous sections, under certain economic conditions (see the discussion below).

The user-component definition is not the same as a 'hedonic' definition based on the characteristics of a good. While the user-component definition refers to specific physical pieces, or parts, of the good, a hedonic, or characteristics-based definition could also include properties of the good as a whole, such as, for a car, its make and model, horsepower, interior space in cubic feet, etc.

Among these four definitions, the user-component and cost-component definitions raise serious concerns. Both ignore the nature of the good in its entirety, independent of the components that make it up. In the case of a package of items, such as a computer system, these component definitions could serve as adequate approximations to the user-value and total-cost measures. In the case of most art work, on the other hand, they would not. One must ask if they offer, in any sense, a more meaningful definition than their corresponding user-value and total-cost definitions. In terms of actual meaning alone, these component definitions are weaker, for three reasons:

1. The set of all information about a good contains, as a subset, the set of information about that good's component parts. Consequently, if all the information about the good is properly assessed, then an analysis of quality in this sense would be at least as thorough as an analysis of the good's component parts.
2. If quality is defined as a function of the qualities of component parts, then it follows that the 'qualities' of *those* component parts are defined as a function of *their* component parts. When taken to the extreme, one would conclude that the user-value quality of a good is defined as a function of the user-value qualities of its raw materials. Similarly, in the case of the cost-component definition, a good's quality would be a function of the *costs* of its raw materials. Both of these ultimate outcomes would be highly counter-intuitive for most goods.
3. If quality were a function only of component parts, then the consumer would have no inclination to purchase the good in its entirety, and would be indifferent with regard to purchasing, instead, the separate component parts.

Although these arguments may appear obvious, confusion does exist when people have preset notions about the quality of components. For instance, most people would correctly expect a gold bracelet to be higher in quality than a comparable silver bracelet of the same weight. On the other hand, some might not realize that gold and silver are much higher in quality when they are items of jewellery than when they are raw pieces of gold and silver metal. Thus, while the component definitions are sometimes useful as operational devices for approximating quality, they are not useful for defining it.

Naturally, the user-value definition is consistent with the meaning of quality as it appears in common language. The total-cost definition, then, can be regarded as an operational definition, used to measure user-value quality. That is, assuming perfect competition, in which marginal utility equals marginal cost, information on marginal cost could serve as a proxy for information on marginal utility, and could thereby validate the cost-based definition. Much work has been done that justifies the total-cost approach, which has generally required the conditions of perfect competition and market equilibrium. This topic will be discussed in considerable detail in the remainder of this chapter and in the chapters that follow.

THE THEORETICAL DEFINITION OF QUALITY

In most theoretical treatments of quality, the concept is defined within an elaborate framework. Several of these frameworks, such as price indexation, characteristics theory and household production are addressed in Chapter 3. In this section an alternative, 'generic' definition of quality is explored, that captures its basic meaning in economic thought.

In studying quality change, one studies, in effect, the difference between two states of nature: the state before the change took place, and the state afterwards. This aspect of quality change has two important implications: First, there will always be ambiguity as to whether the first state should be evaluated relative to the second state (e.g., in terms of prices that exist in the second state), or vice versa; and second, a comparison of the values of particular variables in each state may not be a good reflection of the difference between the states, because many other variables could have changed as well, and in different directions and magnitudes. For example, if a good improves in quality, then a comparison of its prices before and after the change could be irrelevant, if supply-side shifts, unrelated to quality change, also had an effect on prices.

With these reservations in mind, the discussion that follows will be based on quality change in a single good, while all other goods remain the same. In addition, the change in quality is interpreted as occurring at time $t = 1$, relative to the initial situation at time $t = 0$. The reverse analysis, in which the change is interpreted relative to time 1, is considered at the end of this section.

The basic principle that underlies most treatments of quality change in economic theory is the principle of 'compensating variation'. Layard and Walters describe it as follows:

> The compensating variation (CV) is the amount of money we can take away from an individual after an economic change, while leaving him as well off as he was before it. (For a welfare gain, it is the amount he would be willing to pay for the change. For a welfare loss, it is *minus* the amount he would need to receive as compensation for the change.) (Layard and Walters 1978, p. 151)

Thus, if the 'economic change' under consideration is a change in quality, then the compensating variation would be the amount of money with which one could 'bribe' individuals into not purchasing the improved product. In this sense, there is a direct, one-to-one relationship between the magnitude of that bribe, and the magnitude of the quality improvement.

Algebraically, one could define compensating variation, *CV*, as follows:

$$CV = C(p^0, u^0) - C(p^1, u^0) \qquad (1.1)$$

where p^0 and p^1 are the vectors of prices at times 0 and 1, u^0 is a fixed level of utility that was obtained at time 0, and C is the consumer cost function, i.e., the minimum cost to the consumer for obtaining a fixed level of utility, given a fixed vector of prices (Layard and Walters, 1978, p. 152).

An example of compensating variation is presented in Figure 1.1, in which there are two items in the economy: (1) a specific food item, which is simply called *X*, and (2) *all other* goods in the economy, including other types of food. *X* is measured in units of pounds, while all other goods are measured in units of dollars. Consequently, at time 0 the consumer's budget constraint is defined by the points Q_0, A and Q_0/P_0. In this context, Q_0 indicates: (1) the total quantity of all other items which the consumer could purchase if he purchases 0 units of *X*, and (2) the consumer's total nominal income at time 0 and at time 1. Moreover, for any budget constraint displayed in Figure 1.1, the vertical intercept equals the nominal income.

In the example shown in Figure 1.1, the change that occurs would

*Figure 1.1 Example of compensating variation: a reduction in the
price of food item X*

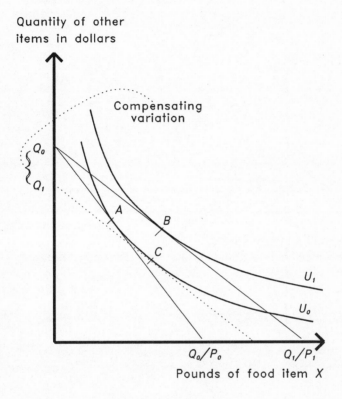

not normally be described as a change in quality. Rather, it is a
price shift, in which the price of X falls from P_0 to P_1, which enables
the consumer to move from Point A to Point B, and from utility
curve U_0 to U_1.   Given the price structure in time 1, the
compensating variation would be based on the reduction in the
amount of total income that would put the consumer on his original
indifference curve. In Figure 1.1 that reduction is shown as the
difference between Q_0 and Q_1, in which the consumer would now
purchase at point C.

   Suppose that instead of a price change, the nutritional content of
X, per pound, improved. For simplicity, assume nutritional content
can be measured on a linear scale. This change *would* be a quality
change. In Figure 1.2, the horizontal axis is now expressed in units

*Figure 1.2 Quality measurement on the basis of a change in
          characteristics*

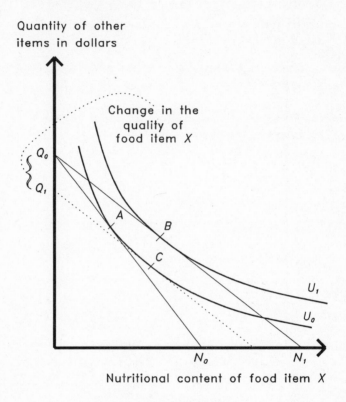

Nutritional content of food item *X*

of nutrition, which increases by a ratio of N_1/N_0 between periods 0
and 1. As in the previous figure, the compensating variation of the
economic change would be given by Q_0 minus Q_1, which would now
be called the *change in the quality of X*.

Note that the structure of Figure 1.2 is identical to that of Figure
1.1. The only difference is that the horizontal axis of Figure 1.2 is
in units of a *characteristic* of *X*, rather than in units of *X*. In fact, if
units of nutrition were normalized to equal units of *X* at time 0, then
the price change in Figure 1.1 could be translated into a change in
the shadow price of units of nutrition. It would then follow that the
compensating variation of a change in the shadow price of nutrition
units would be equivalent to the quality change in *X*, in which the
nutritional content of *X* increases in the same proportion.

It is also worth noting that, even though the nutritional content of X increases by the proportion $(N_1$ minus $N_0)/N_0$, the quality of X increases by a different proportion, $(Q_0$ minus $Q_1)/Q_1$. That is, quality change is not, in general, proportional to changes in the magnitudes of characteristics. If it were, then quality would be arbitrary, because it would then depend on arbitrary conventions in the measurement of characteristics.

One could also consider quality change when the characteristics cannot be measured. In Figure 1.3, the consumer starts at point A,

Figure 1.3 Example of a quality measurement in which characteristics are not evaluated

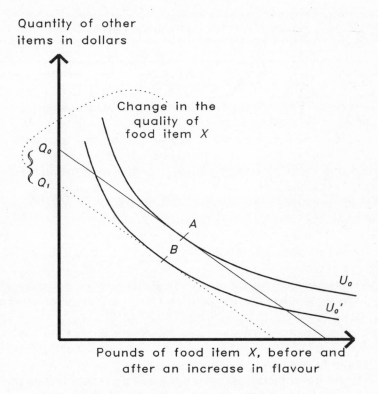

where the horizontal axis is, again, pounds of X, and the utility curve is U_0. In the next period, X improves in flavour, causing point A to be at a higher level of utility, though it would no longer be at the optimal level of utility (given the budget constraint), because a new set of utility functions would now apply. U_0' would be one of the new utility curves in period 1 which would correspond to the same utility that the consumer received in period 0. That is, the consumer would be indifferent between consuming at point *A before* the improvement in the flavour of *X*, and consuming at point *B after* the improvement in flavor. It follows that the compensating variation and the change in quality are Q_0-Q_1, as shown in the Figure 1.3.

In the absence of any explicit measurement of characteristics, Fisher and Shell (1972, pp. 2-9) have called the type of change displayed in Figure 1.3 a change in tastes, as opposed to a change in quality. In other words, because the change is not measurable as a function of units of characteristics, the mathematics involved is indistinguishable from a change attributable to tastes alone. Specifically, Figure 1.3 would be identical to the situation in which the consumer changes his mind and prefers *X* at time 1 more than he did at time 0, even though *X* itself did not change. However, Fisher and Shell (1972, p. 8) make the distinction between two types of 'changes in taste': *embodied* versus *disembodied*, where a disembodied taste change 'is independent of any change in the qualities' of a good.

This terminology reflects a highly theoretical perspective on quality change. Under an alternative, empirical perspective, one would argue that, if a good actually does change in some manner that affects people's preferences, then that change is a quality change, regardless of whether one happens to have explicitly measured the change in characteristics. Conversely, if the good does not change, but people change their perception of it, and/or desire for it, then only that situation would constitute an actual change in tastes.

One could argue, in other words, that the appropriate terminology should describe the *objective reality* underlying the phenomena being observed. In contrast, the Fisher/Shell definition of 'taste change' embraces the perspective of *idealistic reality*, where, as the cliché goes, a tree falling down in a forest only makes a sound if someone is around to hear it.

As will be argued throughout this study, one must adopt an objective, or scientific perspective on quality change, if one is to identify and understand important trends in the evolution of actual goods and services. Without such a framework, one could be constrained to explore the theory of quality measurement only for theory's sake.

Furthermore, if information does exist that establishes the fact that a new good is physically different from a former good, then it would be incorrect for one to interpret the consumers' reaction to the new good as a 'change in tastes'. In so doing, one would be ignoring the distinction between physical change and consumer discretion, and would thereby make consumer perception, and consumer reasoning, irrelevant. As will be discussed throughout this study, consumer perception and reasoning are key factors that account for many evolutionary changes in the quality of goods and services.

The example shown in Figure 1.3 is actually a special case, because after the improvement, the original item X no longer exists. If both X and X' exist at the same time in period 1, which is more likely, then the above discussion on taste change versus quality change becomes virtually irrelevant. The reason is that now one could talk about a more general good, such as X-like food, which would include both X and X'. In this case, whether a particular X-like product is X or X' could be interpreted as a 'characteristic' of that X-like product.

This kind of characteristic — the distinction between brand X and brand X' — is different from a 'characteristic' that reflects specific physical attributes of a good. Nevertheless, as long as there are identifiable, physical differences between X and X', the change should be understood as a quality change rather than a change in tastes.

Figure 1.4 provides an illustration of the quality change from X to X'. To minimize the number of needed dimensions in the Figure, the original food item X is included among *all items at time 0*. Thus, at $t=0$, the consumption point is along the vertical axis, at point Q_0. The utility at this point is U_0, which is the same utility that would be obtained if income were only Q_1, but X' were available.

At time 1, when X' is made available, utility rises to U_1, and consumption moves to point A. Thus, the compensating variation, or the increase in quality, is Q_0 minus Q_1. This increase in quality could be interpreted as an increase in the quality of all goods, but is more appropriately seen as an improvement in the quality of 'X-like food'.

The above examples are designed to provide an understanding of quality change as a basic phenomenon in itself, which need not depend on a particular economic model for its definition. Nevertheless, these examples suggest that, even in the simplest cases, the issue of quality change can raise important and difficult

Figure 1.4 An interpretation of quality change when a new variety is introduced

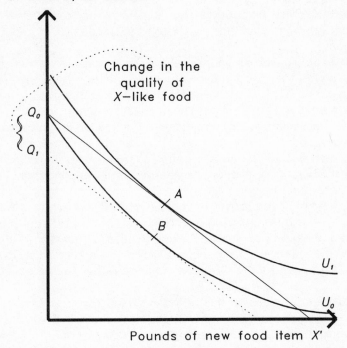

questions.

    The above cases were based on the evaluation of a new situation in terms of the former situation. Alternatively, one could evaluate the former situation on the basis of the new one. The two evaluations will not be the same, except under special conditions or by coincidence. The latter is termed 'equivalent variation,' as opposed to compensating valuation. In terms of consumer cost functions like those in Equation 1.1, equivalent variation, *EV*, is defined as:

$$EV = C(p^0, u^1) - C(p^1, u^1) \qquad (1.2)$$

which is essentially the same as Equation 1.1, except with u^1 instead of u^0 (Layard and Walters, 1978, pp. 150-54). They describe equivalent variation as follows:

> The equivalent variation is the amount of money we would need to give an individual, if an economic change did not happen, to make him as well off as if it did. (For a welfare gain, it is the compensation he would need to forego the change. For a welfare loss, it is the amount he would be willing to pay to avert the change.) (Layard and Walters 1978, p. 151)

Figure 1.5, which is comparable to Figure 1.2, provides an illustration of the difference between compensating variation and

Figure 1.5 Illustration of the difference between equivalent variation (EV) and compensating variation (CV)

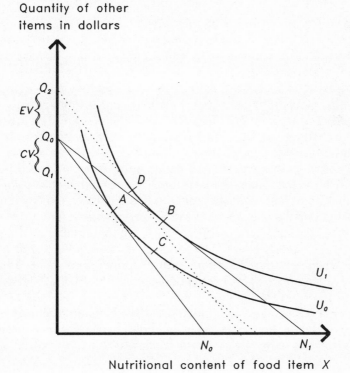

equivalent variation. All of the above discussions on compensating variation as a basis for measuring quality would also apply to equivalent variation. However, because of the similarity of the two concepts, a detailed examination of equivalent variation would tend only to replicate the previous findings on compensating variation.

THE DEBATE ON 'COSTLESS QUALITY CHANGE' AND ITS IMPLICATIONS

The idea of 'costless quality change' is presented as an argument against the 'resource-cost' definition of quality change, in favour of the user-value definition. It states that technological change could lead to a substantial reduction in production costs, while the actual physical features of the good remain unchanged. Consequently, the cost-based method of measuring quality change would be arbitrary, and thus, only the user-value measure would be appropriate.

An opposing viewpoint, however, favours the resource-cost method. As an example, let the computer be the good in question, whose initial factor requirements schedule is F_1 in Figure 1.6.[8] This schedule plots an 'output characteristic' variable, 'computations', against a single input used to produce the computer, labour. In this framework, the number of computations is an indicator of a computer's quality.[9]

We begin the analysis at point A, in time 0, where each computer can yield calculations of C_0 (per time unit), and L_3 units of labour are required to produce that computer. One could argue that 'costless quality change' could reflect either an existing property of the production process, or change in the process. In the former, the factor requirements schedule is flat at point A, as indicated by the line A-L_0. In this case, costless quality improvement would be a static phenomenon, and, according to this argument, quality change would not entail any changes in factor requirements. Triplett (1983) is correct in stating that this property is highly unrealistic. He goes on to say, 'A better characterization . . . is to suppose a shift of the factor requirements function (corresponding to cost-reducing technical advances in producing computers)' (p. 302). That shift is reflected in F_2 in Figure 1.6.

Assuming market equilibrium and perfect competition, the market price will equal both the marginal utility and marginal product. Consequently, under these circumstances the amount of labour at points A and B are proportional to the price of a computer. For

Figure 1.6 Triplett's argument on 'costless' quality change

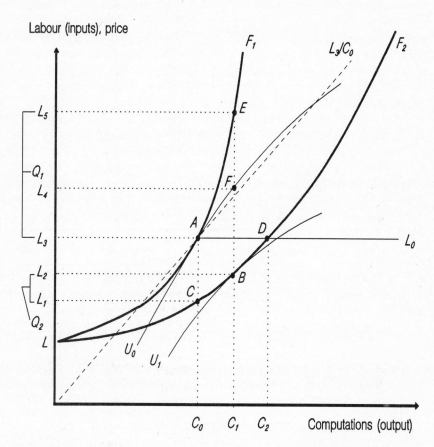

simplicity, let labour and prices be measured in equivalent units.

Utility could be included, as shown by the curves U_0 and U_1. For example, let utility be a function of computations, C, and a composite of all other goods, X, and assume that the individual purchases one, and only one, computer. Then, if Y equals total income and P the price of a computer, utility can be interpreted as $U = U(C,X) = U(C,Y \text{ minus } P)$. In this case, U_0 and U_1 are utility curves in C,P space.[10]

We see automatically from the figure that the computer at B is, simultaneously, lower in price and higher in quality than the original one at A. Triplett (1983) states, 'Obviously, direct comparison of labour inputs for A and B adjusts the [quality] index in the wrong direction, whether by user-value or resource-cost criteria.' However, the operational definition of user-value in this remark is the price that consumers are willing to pay for the good. This operational definition is useful in many instances, but not here. An alternative user-value definition would be based on the actual variable that *is* directly relevant to the consumer's desire to purchase the good — namely, computations. Technically speaking, this would entail a 'hedonic', or 'characteristics' approach.

One could simply observe that the computer at point B accomplishes C_1 calculations in comparison to C_0 calculations for the computer at point A. Therefore, quality improvement *in terms of calculations* can be unambiguously defined in reference to the change from C_0 to C_1. Nevertheless, as suggested in the previous section, the key to the determination of the quality change lies in the difference between U_1 and U_0. Thus, the best measurement of the quality change would be the vertical distance between points F and B, or L_4-L_2. That is, the price of the computer in the latter period would need to be raised to L_4 in order for the consumer to be as well off, in terms of utility, as he was in the initial period.

In contrast, Triplett recommends two possible resource-cost measures of quality adjustment: Q_1 and Q_2. At the same time, though, he acknowledges:

> Usually, neither requirements function is known. If any information is available at all, it may consist only of cost data for two points, such as A or B . . . that lie on different functions. That is, there may be data on the cost of the old machine under the old technology and the cost of the new machine under the new technology, but no data at all on the cost of both under comparable technologies. (Triplett 1983, pp. 302-3)

Triplett goes on to say that, in spite of the empirical difficulties that may arise in practice, the problems that occur in the measurement of quality during costless change 'have nothing whatever to do with the feasibility or conceptual appropriateness of . . . resource-cost alternatives for making quality adjustments' (p. 302). This last remark is highly disputable, on several grounds. First, it is evident from the figure that Q_1 and Q_2 could each be very different from the theoretically correct measure of L_4-L_2 (not to mention being very different from each other). Thus, there is, in fact, a conceptual inappropriateness to the use of Q_1 or Q_2. That inappropriateness stems from the fact that points C and E are not points at which demand equals supply — they are merely points of feasible production. Consequently, the equivalence of marginal productivity with marginal utility, which is the necessary criterion that justifies the use of production costs as an indicator of quality, does not exist. Therefore, at these points, there is absolutely no theoretical justification for the use of resource requirements in the measurement of quality.

Fisher and Shell (1972) express the same criticism of the resource-cost approach. In their discussion of the compensating variation associated with a new good, which was unavailable in the base period, they remark:[11]

[T]he demand reservation price measures (locally) the value to the base-period consumer of the relaxation of the constraint stating that the good in question is unavailable. . . . It is thus the demand reservation price which affects how much income the consumer would be willing to give up to relax that constraint. How much income he would in fact be technologically required to give up to accomplish such relaxation (the supply reservation price) is not directly germane to a theory which runs in terms of indifferent positions. If the demand reservation price is known, the supply reservation price is not relevant. (Fisher and Shell 1972, p. 25)

Triplett, himself, expressed the same position in his earliest writings on the topic. In his doctoral dissertation in 1966, he states:

Total factor costs, or production costs, must be rejected as a standard for quality measure. . . [I]n equilibrium the costs and value of quality differences must be equal, at least at the margin, so that one would apparently get the same quality measure whether derived from a cost or value criterion. However, . . . if we admit the possibility of technical change and product innovation, a new variety may be introduced that makes it possible to obtain the same utility from a smaller amount of resources, in which case the total factor cost criterion will not be equivalent to a value criterion (and . . . will be inferior to a value criterion). (Triplett 1966, p. 5)

What appears to have happened since the 1960s is that the use of cost-based quality estimation has become so routine, and so widely accepted, that it has taken on a life of its own, independent of the original concept of quality that it was first designed to estimate. Hence, the 'costless' quality change argument (which Triplett himself advocates in the above quotation) could be interpreted as a valid attempt to challenge the high acceptance that the cost-based method has achieved. In defence of the resource-cost method, one could always demonstrate that *some* methodology could be used to measure quality change based on costs, even after a 'costless' quality change. Nonetheless, the fact that *some* method could be used is hardly an adequate defence of the cost-based approach — one must show that a *correct* method could be used.

The lack of a theoretical rationale for using Q_1 or Q_2 in Figure 1.6 as a measure of quality change is further evidenced by the arbitrary positions of points E and C. For example, it would not be difficult to find circumstances for which point E would exist only at $L = \infty$. Other examples might be easy to find in which point C, in the second period, requires nearly the same amount of resources as point B, in which case Q_2 would be negligible in spite of a substantial quality change.

In fact, going back to computers, one could regard the horizontal axis in Figure 1.6 as being computations per second, on a logarithmic scale, while F_1 and F_2 represent typical computers for 1987 and 1993. In this case, Q_1 would, in all likelihood, be enormous, while Q_2 would be minuscule. This pattern of technological change is not unusual, and would actually be expected to occur whenever there is a technological breakthrough.

As another example, consider the service of sending information, where the horizontal axis is the log of the speed at which a message is sent. Let F_1 exist before the telegraph was established, i.e., when the fastest mail carriage was by Pony Express, and let F_2 exist soon after the telegraph was established. Under these conditions, it is easy to envision the same kind of problems in quality measurement.

There is, in actuality, a more basic flaw in the defence of resource-cost quality measurement under costless quality change. That flaw is a philosophical one. As already implied, the essential, underlying theme of cost-based quality measurement is that *one can estimate quality change on the basis of information about production*. In addition, one of the basic ideas embodied in cost-based quality measurement is that direct estimates of user-value *are not necessary* for the measurement of quality.

However, the horizontal axis of Figure 1.6 is, in fact, a variable that relates directly to user-value. This variable could be couched as an 'output characteristic' as opposed to an 'input characteristic' but that distinction is peripheral to the concerns addressed here (see Chapter 3). The computations that a computer can perform is a relevant variable because, and only because, it bears directly on consumers' willingness to purchase the computer.

The consumer himself could be a producer, and his willingness to purchase the computer would then be based on a formula for profit maximization. This would not change the fact that the computer has some intrinsic value which is directly related to its number of computations. In an abstract sense, all buyers are 'producers', with the final product being their own happiness. Thus, the distinction among buyers between consumers and producers has little or no bearing on the relevance of the user-value concept.

Consequently, the utilization of Q_1 or Q_2 in Figure 1.6 as a cost-based measurement of quality is, in fact, reliant upon a user-based variable — the number of computations. That is, both Q_1 and Q_2 rely upon C_0 and C_1 for their existence, which, in turn, *ultimately rely upon an implicit appeal to a user-based definition of quality*. Hence, if the analysis of Figure 1.6 is a 'proof' of the validity of the cost-based method of quality measurement, then that proof is logically flawed. The flaw is that one cannot prove the irrelevance of a concept (in this case the concept of user-value), if the proof itself requires the assumption of that concept. A classic example of this type of flaw is in the statement, 'God cannot do everything, because He cannot build a rock that is too heavy for Him to lift'. The statement is logically flawed because one cannot agree with it without implicitly assuming its opposite.

In conclusion, whatever Q_1 and Q_2 happen to measure, they are dependent on user-value, but are not user-value itself, or even a close approximation to it, unless by coincidence. One could call Q_1 and Q_2 'resource-cost quality measures'. However, doing so would be erroneous. Thus, the costless quality change argument, which states that cost-based measures are irrelevant when there are 'costless' technological improvements, does hold up.

Triplett (1983) is certainly correct in his remark that the only points in Figure 1.6 that may be observable are points A and B, and that it would be wrong to use a resource-cost comparison of these points. However, support for the resource-cost criterion, primarily at a theoretical level, could have had the policy effect of promoting the use of resource-cost quality measurement at points like A and B. That is, the greater the use of resource-cost measurement in actual practice, the more likely points A and B would, in fact, be compared in the measurement of quality. The result would be an observed quality decline, when there is actually a quality improvement.

At first glance, the erroneous interpretation of an actual quality improvement as a quality decline may seem absurd. Yet, one must bear in mind that, in the reality of quality measurement, the horizontal axis of Figure 1.6 may not exist. That is, the only data that one may have are the prices of the two computers and their resource-cost requirements. Moreover, in terms of nominal prices, the price of the second-period computer could be much higher than the price of the first, and the true rate of inflation may not be known.

Furthermore, the fact that point B is located at a lower labour requirement than A gives at least some hint that production technology has changed. If, on the other hand, point B coincided with point D, then such a technology shift could go completely undetected, in which no quality change would be observed.

Hence, the error in considering points A and B in cost-based quality assessment is a very real one. The chance of that error occurring in actual practice is only enhanced, indirectly, by the theoretical support for the cost-based method currently offered by theorists and administrators.

It could be argued that a user-value quality measurement would be equally likely to make the same error. That is, rather than using labour requirements, a user-value approach might use prices, which would be equivalent to labour requirements in the framework of Figure 1.6. Yet, in actual practice, it is highly unlikely that any user-value methodology would compare nominal prices alone. Realistically speaking, inflation has been in existence for too long now for it to be ignored. A user-value approach, therefore, would compare the prices of two different kinds of computers only if those computers exist at *the same point in time*. In this way, errors of the kind mentioned above would be minimized.

In the absence of two different kinds of computers existing at the same time, a hedonic, user-value approach could be employed. If no better information were available, the line L_3/C_0 could be used to reflect the value per calculation in the first period. Thus, the quality of a computer that provides C_1 calculations could be estimated as $C_1(L_3/C_0)$, which would be the price at which the L_3/C_0 line intersects the $C=C_1$ line. In Figure 1.6, and given the way the curves are drawn, that price would be quite close to L_4, which would be the true quality change in economic theory.

In addition, one could consider the situation in which perfect competition does not exist. For example, a possible scenario is that one firm invested considerable resources in research to move from F_1 to F_2, and developed a patent on the new process. Other firms will move to F_2 as well, but only after the patent has expired. In this case, while most of the firms are producing at A, the firm producing on F_2 will produce at point C, and earn economic rents which will help it to cover its initial research costs.

Economic rents in return for successful research throws another monkey wrench into the works of the cost-based approach to quality measurement. In the chapters that follow, it will be argued that *cost reduction* is a process that is distinct from quality improvement, and therefore, cannot be measured on the same scale.

QUALITY IN TERMS OF SOCIAL, RATHER THAN PRIVATE, BENEFITS

In contrast to the conventional theory on quality change, one could raise the issue that perhaps quality *can* improve without a corresponding increase in utility. Under the simple assumptions that 'quality improvement' reflects physical changes that are beneficial,[12] while 'utility' reflects what is desired by an individual or household, one might be able to draw a distinction between the two by finding something that is beneficial but not desired, or vice versa. Griliches finds such an example in 'antipollution devices in automobiles', on which he remarks:

> There may be changes that cost more, such as antipollution devices for automobiles, which are 'quality changes' in some sense, but not the relevant one. *From the point of view of the individual consumer, if he were not willing to buy these devices on his own, their introduction by law represents a form of tax (in kind) rather than a rise in his utility.* This should be recorded as a rise in price, not a fall. It may lead to externalities, possibly to an overall improvement of his environment . . . and hence to an indirect rise in his utility, which then could be perhaps represented by a decline in the 'real price' of air, but this is a different matter. (Griliches 1971b, p. 14)[13]

Griliches's assessment here of antipollution devices ignores the main reason for the consumer's unwillingness to purchase the device on his own, which is that he is facing a 'prisoner's dilemma'. That is, if he buys the device and no one else does, then he spends more money but gains virtually nothing in terms of cleaner air. The consumer's unwillingness to purchase the device, therefore, does not mean that he thinks the device is not worth having — it simply means that he thinks the device is worth having as long as others think so as well.[14]

Moreover, the consumer is willing to 'pay' for the device, in terms of the time and effort he is willing to spend to lobby for such pollution devices, and/or vote for politicians who support them, knowing that these devices will lead to an increase in the prices he pays for an automobile. Hence, in a broader sense, and in the sense of society as a whole, antipollution devices do represent a quality improvement and an increase in utility. At the very least, the typical consumer acquires utility from knowing that he is complying with a law that he favours.

Any argument over what 'utility' includes, or does not include, would be confined to the area of semantics. Moreover, the operational definition of 'utility' by economists is not at issue in the above discussion on air pollution devices. The main issue is whether public decisions that influence the costs of goods reflect what consumers regard as beneficial. If they do, then those costs, or more precisely the physical changes associated with them, should be regarded as quality improvements.

Rosen (1974) examines a similar issue: the question of whether mandatory seat belts or air bags in automobiles represent a quality improvement or a price increase. Like Griliches, he takes the position that they are not a quality improvement, but a price increase, 'because choices are restricted' (p. 53). His evaluation of how the price index should be adjusted is based solely on the willingness of consumers to pay for the safety device. Yet, what is absent from his analysis is the wide range of economic benefits that would result from reduced injuries and fatalities. Furthermore, he ignores the fact that people who prefer to wear seat belts are often passengers in other people's cars, and thus, even if the car owner does not use his own seat belts, some of his passengers may.

In his article, 'Cost-Benefit Analysis: An Ethical Critique,' Steven Kelman analyses public decisions involving health risks. He argues such decisions should be interpreted as being *desired by* consumers, and not *imposed on* consumers, in contrast to Griliches's and Rosen's analyses. His argument is worth quoting in full:

[S]ocial decisions provide an opportunity to give certain things a higher valuation than we choose, for one reason or another, to give them in our private activities. . . . [O]pponents of stricter regulation of health risks often argue that we show by our daily risk-taking behavior that we do not value life indefinitely, and therefore our public decisions should not reflect the high value of life that proponents of strict regulation propose. However, an alternative view is equally plausible. Precisely because we fail, for whatever reasons, to give life-saving the value in everyday personal decisions that we in some general terms believe we should give it, we may wish our social decisions to provide us the occasion to display the reverence for life that we espouse but do not always show. By this view, people do not have fixed unambiguous 'preferences' to which they give expression through private activities and which therefore should be given expression in public decisions. Rather, they may have what they themselves regard as 'higher' and 'lower' preferences. The latter may come to the fore in private decisions, but people may want the former to come to the fore in public decisions. They may sometimes display racial prejudice, but support antidiscrimination laws. They may buy a certain product after seeing a seductive ad, but be skeptical enough of advertising to want the government to keep a close eye on it. In such cases, the use of private behavior to impute the values that should be entered for public decisions, as is done by using willingness to pay in private transactions, commits grievous offense against a view of the behavior of the citizen that is deeply ingrained in our democratic tradition. It is a view that denudes politics of any independent role in society, reducing it to a mechanistic, mimicking recalculation based on private behavior. (Kelman 1981, p. 38)

In developing an understanding of quality in the context of externalities, one must draw a distinction between (1) the reasons for ruling out externalities in mathematical modelling, namely, simplicity and convenience, and (2) how consumers actually behave and what they actually regard as desirable. Quality should be based on what is ultimately desired by consumers, regardless of the technical circumstances associated with how those desires are implemented.

One could then ask how to go about analysing the additional components or features of goods that conform to these additional desires by consumers, such as pollution control devices, compliance with safety standards, etc. That question, however, would presume that such additional components or features are not already accounted for when the analysis begins. In an empirical study that uses actual prices, it is likely that such prices would already reflect the demand by society for these additional components or features. Actually, the price mark-ups for socially desirable characteristics could be more a function of additional production costs than of society's true willingness to pay for these characteristics. Yet, if no other information is available, perhaps one could treat the additional costs as a lower bound on that willingness-to-pay measure, depending on how one interprets the market for the characteristics in question and how one evaluates the concordance between regulation and consumer preferences.

In finding a method for measuring quality change, one could be at a total loss if no prices exist, as in the case of 'public goods'. A good or service is a 'public good' if it meets the following criteria:

1. *Nonexcludability*. A person cannot be prevented from deriving

the benefits of a good or service even if he does not pay for it.
2. *Nonrivalrous consumption.* One person's consumption of the good or service does not impair another person's ability to consume it (except at extreme levels in which there are crowding effects).[15]

The classic example of a public good is the lighthouse, because sailors can see the lighthouse without having to pay for the service, and when sailors in one ship see it they do not impair the ability of others to see it.[16]

Measuring a change in the quality of a public good could be a rather formidable task for economists. To begin with, economists often have a great deal of trouble determining whether certain types of public goods are worthwhile at all. In addition, in cases in which no prices exist, it is quite tempting for economists to fall back on the cost-based definition of quality change. This 'fall back' position could be justifiable in some cases in the absence of any better sources of information.

On the other hand, the quality of (or benefits from) public goods may not be quantifiable in economic terms, as suggested in the above-mentioned positions taken by Griliches, Rosen and Kelman. As described above, Griliches and Rosen would exclude socially-desired externalities from quality estimation. Kelman, who does not address quality measurement, makes a strong argument in favour of societal preferences having influence in public decisionmaking, independent of the influence of individual preferences. One must also observe that Griliches and Rosen do not actually refer to public decisionmaking in the above references, but stick to the topic of quality measurement in economics. Consequently, it is quite possible that Griliches and Rosen (and others of the same school of thought) are not opposed to Kelman's (and others') emphasis of the importance of social criteria. That is, they simply separate social criteria from quality measurement as a matter of definition.

Nevertheless, as argued above, a definition of quality measurement that excludes social concerns is a weaker, and less useful one. As also mentioned, in many cases this narrower definition could actually be more difficult for economists to estimate.

In certain instances, however, the idea that social benefits should be excluded from quality estimation does have validity if the social benefits in question are non-quantifiable, or more precisely, if social benefits cannot be translated into pecuniary concepts. (This idea relates back to Kelman's argument about different types of preferences.) The key to whether social benefits are translatable depends on whether the social benefits are, in essence, economic. For example, if people could attribute an economic value to clean air, then antipollution devices in automobiles could have measurable economic benefits, even though the issue would be treated as an 'externality' in the automobile market. In contrast, if the social benefits in question involve inalienable rights, like the right to a fair trial, then the quality of these benefits could easily be unmeasurable, as well as irrelevant. Of course, grey areas exist with regard to the distinction between economic benefits and inalienable rights, e.g., some might argue that individuals have an 'inalienable right' to clean air. Often the distinction can be determined as a matter of degree, i.e., below a certain hazardous pollution level, clean air is an economic variable, and above that level it is a matter of human rights.[17]

In the case of public goods, quality measurement may or may not make sense, depending on the nature, or character, of the public good. A useful method of classifying public goods is on the basis of how it meets the nonexcludability condition. In general, the condition could be met in three ways:

1. *Physical nonexcludability*. Because of the character and circumstances of the physical world, excludability is impossible. For example, excludability is impossible in the lighthouse example, because of the physical nature in which light is dispersed and perceived.
2. *Transaction-cost nonexcludability*. Excludability could be carried out, but the costs of administering and enforcing payment are infeasible. For example, if a small bridge is built in a rural environment, and is crossed by only a few vehicles per day, it would not be cost-effective to have a toll booth established there.
3. *Ethical nonexcludability*. A medical facility in an impoverished area could charge an admission fee to patients requiring immediate medical attention, but does not do so as a matter of ethical policy.

A good example of the distinction between economic science and economic rhetoric would be in the way in which the last condition, ethical nonexcludability, is interpreted. Many would consider this concept to be irrelevant to economic thought, because it contradicts the philosophy of utilitarianism, upon which neoclassical economic analysis is based. This position would be rhetorical, in the sense that it is based on what *should* exist as opposed to what *does* exist. In the physical world, ethical nonexcludability does exist. It exists in the physical structures of the institutions that promote it, in the living human beings who advocate it, and in the electrochemical impulses that occur when people think about it. In juxtaposition to the economic actions of economic agents, ethical nonexcludability is no less physical than 'physical nonexcludability'. Hence, from a purely scientific perspective, ethical nonexcludability is as important as physical nonexcludability in the identification of public goods.

Public goods and services that exist by virtue of ethical nonexcludability, as opposed to physical or transaction-cost nonexcludability, cannot be measured in terms of economic quality, since they are designed to meet noneconomic objectives. This conclusion is similar to the position upheld by Griliches and Rosen, but the 'line' is drawn further out — to include economic, but not ethical, externalities.

One could argue that quality measurement could be applied to goods and services that meet ethical objectives, based on characteristics. For instance, the quality of police protection could be approached through a hedonic analysis of convictions per arrest, absence of police brutality, etc. However, economists would not be qualified to perform this type of quality measurement. In such cases, economists should admit to the limitations of their framework, and pass the ball to other social scientists and public policy analysts.

NOTES

1. This general rule does have exceptions. Perhaps the most notable is the recent book by Steenkamp (1989).
2. See, for example, Dosi et al. (1992), Dosi et al. (1990), Nelson and Winter (1982) and Rosenberg (1982).
3. See Steenkamp (1989) for additional discussion of alternative perspectives on the concept of quality.
4. The case of isotopes is left out of the discussion for reasons of simplicity.
5. See, for example, Abrams and Bernstein (1989), pp. 67-80.
6. Or, more precisely, constantly being erased and then created in slightly different positions.
7. This type of problem may be called an 'index-number problem'. Some economists have tended to regard index-number problems as 'uninteresting'. However, the fact that this problem can be easily understood and/or easily classified should not be an excuse for ignoring it.
8. Most of this figure was taken directly from Triplett (1983).

9. For a more detailed discussion of this framework, see Rosen (1974). The graph reflects the simplifying conditions in Rosen's model, which he discusses on pages 44-5.

10. These curves could also be called value functions, bid functions, or the marginal rates of substitution between the characteristic and money. For example, see Rosen (1974), pp. 38-9.

11. In the Fisher/Shell terminology, the change they discuss is a 'taste change' — but that is merely a difference in semantics. The actual effect to which they are referring is illustrated in Figure 1.4, which is being called a 'quality change' in this study. (See pages 16-18.)

12. The assumption is somewhat tautological, since 'beneficial' has yet to be defined. However, what is meant by beneficial becomes clearer in the discussion that follows.

13. My own italics used here for emphasis.

14. For a thorough discussion of the 'prisoner's dilemma' see Leibenstein (1980).

15. For a detailed explanation of these concepts, see Cowen (1992).

16. For more on this topic of lighthouses as examples of public goods, see Coase (1974).

17. To add to the confusion, there is an emerging literature in natural resource economics (or more generally, agricultural economics) on 'non-use value'. This term refers to the value that consumers would place on resources like clean air which they, as individuals, use very little of in relation to the rest of society. Contingent valuation methods are often used to estimate non-use value, see Larson (1992).

2. Quality change in the context of economic evolution and scientific inquiry

The transition from one mode of thought to another is difficult, since it involves abandoning a beautiful sailing ship — the equilibrium price-auction model — that happens to be torn apart and sinking in a riptide. So a raft must be built to catch whatever winds may come by. That raft won't match the beauty or mathematical elegance of the sailing ship, although it has one undeniable virtue — it floats.

Thurow (1983, p. 237)

INTRODUCTION

Goods and services *evolve*. That is, they change systematically over time in terms of their physical characteristics, the technologies used to produce them, and the perception, or demand, that consumers have toward them. This 'mixed bag' of effects associated with evolutionary change could be studied in a variety of ways. For example, in Chapter 6 a formal economic model is presented, where the focus is on relative prices and the distinction between quality improvement and cost reduction. In the present chapter, the focus will be on the meaning and interpretation of economic evolution as it pertains to quality change.

The evolution of goods and services has, thus far, received relatively little attention in economic thought for two basic reasons:

1. As a long-run phenomenon, changes in goods and services are usually overshadowed by faster, and frequently more dramatic, institutional and political effects. These short-run effects often capture much of the attention in applied economics, especially when decisionmaking is carried out for the purpose of meeting short-run objectives. In theoretical economics, on the other

hand, actual patterns of evolutionary change cannot, in general, meet the standard steady-state and stability conditions.

2. When evolutionary effects are studied, the focus is primarily on a single area: *hedonic price indices* in the case of quality change, *technological change* in the case of process innovation or product innovation of capital goods, the *microeconomics of consumer behaviour* in the case of changing tastes, and *the net barter terms of trade* in the case of long-run price movements. Thus, the concept of evolutionary economic change as a global phenomenon in itself has generally not been explored — there simply appear to be too many factors to be accounted for in a single model.

Nevertheless, these problems can be overcome. The first problem — the lack of attention to long-run effects — is fading away on its own, while the importance of long-run strategies for economic growth is receiving greater recognition, as are long-run resource and environmental issues. Furthermore, if long-run growth is what is now being sought, then, eventually, it may be recognized that the study of evolutionary effects could play an important role in policy decisions.

The second problem, the discontinuity among different evolutionary effects, which creates considerable difficulty in the development of a comprehensive economic model, cannot be addressed as easily. However, if important systematic patterns of change do occur, then an attempt should be made to observe them, regardless of the modelling difficulties.

QUALITY CHANGE AS AN EVOLUTIONARY PROCESS

Evolutionary Economics

'Evolutionary economics' could be considered a relatively new area, even though it has roots that trace back to certain classical theoreticians, such as Schumpeter and Marshall. In a nutshell, the theory of evolutionary economics is analogous to Darwin's Theory of Evolution, where economic institutions and economic activities, especially at the level of the firm, undergo a process of mutation, or innovation, and natural selection. The process of selection occurs as firms compete for limited markets, where the best managed, and/or most successfully innovative firms have a greater chance for survival and expansion.

There are three features of evolutionary economics, which are strongly interrelated and which distinguish it from conventional neoclassical theory. First, it relies heavily on the idea that technical changes made by firms occur as a result of variation, much the same way that Darwin's theory relies on variation among organisms. In and of itself, this perspective on economic change represents a substantial departure from the 'deterministic' qualities of conventional theory. Secondly, because evolutionary theory allows for, and in fact focuses on, unsystematic or 'random' changes over time, it is not preoccupied with the theoretical search for some ultimate state of nature, such as the 'steady state'. This relieves the evolutionary economist from the burdensome mathematical obligations often associated with achieving a general equilibrium theory, and instead, gives him more leeway to explore the behavioural and institutional causes of economic change. Finally, evolutionary economics opens up a new area of economic thought, that creates a need for the economist to look underneath the old economic variables in order to understand economic change. In essence, the theory is scientific, not because of any 'imitation' of a theory in biology, but because it calls upon a search for a new set of elementary components — components which could explain the causality of how economic institutions and processes change over long periods of time.

According to Nelson and Winter (1982, pp. 16-19) firms perform three types of activities: standard operating activities, investment planning decisions, and decisionmaking whereby 'people within the firm may engage in scrutiny of what the firm is doing and why it is doing it, with the thought of revision or even radical change'. Not surprisingly, it is this third type of activity that is the major focus of evolutionary economics. Viewing technical change in this context, evolutionary economists regard it as endogenous, in contrast to its common treatment in neoclassical economics.

The idea that technical change is endogenous is also a central theme of this study — but there is a notable difference: instead of it being regarded as a function of the characteristics and/or behaviour of the firm, it is regarded as a function of the particular good (or group of goods) in question.

As already suggested, there is a tendency for evolutionary economists to draw an analogy between evolutionary economics and Darwin's Theory of Evolution. For instance, Nelson and Winter state:

[P]rofitable firms will grow and unprofitable ones will contract, and the operating characteristics of the more profitable firms therefore will account for a growing share of the industry's activity. . . . The selection mechanism here clearly is analogous to the natural selection of genotypes with differential net reproduction rates in biological evolutionary theory. And, as in biological theory the sensitivity of a firm's growth rate to prosperity or adversity is itself a reflection of its 'genes'. (Nelson and Winter 1982, p. 17)

This analogy is quite useful, and implies the following notion: the forces that maintain balance in the economy, like the forces that maintain balance in the ecosystem, may have little to do with the forces that govern long-term, or evolutionary, change. For instance, the number of rabbits and the number of foxes in a forest may vary over time according to systematic balancing forces, such as the tendency for rabbits to multiply rapidly when there are few foxes, and the tendency for foxes to starve when there are few rabbits. Similar balancing forces exist in the economy with regard to supply and demand. Yet, balancing forces in themselves may tell little about the characteristics of future generations. They do not explain why rabbits have a tendency to hop greater distances with each passing generation, nor why certain goods have a tendency to increase in quality while others have a tendency to decline in cost. *Thus, what evolutionary theory adds, to both biology and economics, is the idea that long-run change can be explained in terms of very different phenomena than the balancing forces that maintain equilibrium in the present.* Thus, evolutionary theory calls for a new set of considerations, or variables, for understanding long-term change.

To fully appreciate this principle, let us step back and consider any type of evolutionary process, be it the evolution of organisms, societies, institutions, or in our case, goods and services. In the study of evolutionary change in general, there are two major areas of inquiry. One addresses the question of 'how' and the other the question of 'why'. For organisms, the question of 'how' organisms evolve would be explained in terms of the bio-molecular processes whereby genetic material changes from generation to generation, and the factors that enable genetic material to be manifested in the phenotypes that one observes. The question of 'why' organisms evolve is a separate matter. It requires an explanation about population pressure and limited food supplies, and about other forms of competition among organisms whereby only the 'fittest' can survive and multiply in the long run.

The questions of 'how' and 'why' are important aspects of any evolutionary process, and they support, and perhaps validate, one another. However, as argued above, they are also independent of each other. Their independence is supported by the fact that Charles Darwin formulated his theory of biological evolution, explaining the 'why', long before the discovery of DNA, explaining the 'how'.

In the evolution of goods and services, the question of 'how' involves production processes and research and development activities. The question of 'why', is answered by the notion that goods and services evolve to compete for the consumer's budget, not unlike the way that organisms evolve to compete for limited food supplies. *In this competition for survival, the goods, like organisms, are the active players; the firms, like genes, are the passive players that accompany the winners and losers.*

Of course, the successful firm will be the one that has the properties to allow it to invent and market successful new products. In this sense, the firm is not passive, and the evolution of goods has much in common with the evolution of firms in the Nelson/Winter framework, which also focuses on research and development.

Nevertheless, in terms of the evolution of the economic system, it is more appropriate for one to think of goods and services as being the entities that evolve, rather than firms. For example, there are countless cases in which the firm that first develops a new and useful good is not successful, while later on other firms are successful at selling the same good. In contrast, it is rare to find a firm that has been successful in the long run, in spite of it selling products that are relatively low in quality. Furthermore, a particular good or service is often a concrete and unambiguous concept, while a firm is often partially owned by other firms, which makes it difficult for one to determine where one firm ends and another begins. Finally, large firms are diversified in a wide variety of products. Therefore, the success of a large firm can be seen as a weighted average of the success of all of its products.

Chance does play an important role in the evolution of goods and services, as it does in biological evolution. Specific events that occur by chance are relevant to the extent that they are an aspect of a general force toward change, just as random mutations of organisms are an aspect of the process of biological evolution, and the random movements (or 'Brownian motion') of molecules are an aspect of many phenomena studied in chemistry and physics.

Quality Improvement versus Product Innovation

Product innovation is generally treated as an activity (or a consequence of activities) carried out by the firm. However, quality improvement need not be — it is a joint activity carried out by the firm *and* the consumer, in the sense that the consumer is the agent who actually evaluates the quality of a good or service. Furthermore, innovation is not as general a concept as quality improvement in the sense that innovation refers to an item which is uniquely different *in terms of easily-defined physical characteristics*, while quality improvement can refer to any physical differences at all so long as it renders a difference in perception. Hence, the changes that occur with regard to product innovation are a proper subset of the changes that occur with regard to quality improvement.[1]

The distinction is subtle, but nevertheless, important. For example, the compact disk is, without question, a product innovation in that it is unique and physically different from records and cassette tapes. By the same token, it is a quality improvement. However, a new best-selling song on a compact disk, by a specific musical artist, can also be a quality improvement over previous songs by the same or different artists, while it would not be regarded as a product innovation.

The distinction between product innovation and quality improvement gives rise to a very broad question that, at some point, must be addressed by evolutionary economics. That question is: which of the two, product innovation or quality improvement, is the more relevant concern with regard to the evolution of goods and services, or with regard to the evolution of the economic system in general?

One can always answer that the choice of quality improvement as a topic, or product innovation, should depend on the framework of the study being conducted. None the less, the question that must be raised, from the beginning, is: what makes quality improvement and product innovation *important* with regard to the economic system? Quality improvement is important because it is a measure of how important the good or service is to the consumer. Taken collectively, the quality improvements of all goods and services reflect the quality of life in a society. Furthermore, to the extent that quality improvements coincide with price increases, or increases in value added (all else being equal), the prevalence of quality improvements in certain industries will reflect the expansion of those industries in terms of market share, or, in a more general sense, in terms of economic significance.

Product innovation has much less to offer. As a proper subset of quality improvement, it is a weaker indicator of long-term changes in the economic system. Its only advantage might be that, because of its focus on the development of new, and uniquely different, goods and services on the basis of easily-defined physical characteristics, it may somehow lead to discoveries that do not apply to the broader notion of quality improvement.

The Concept of a Trajectory

An important concept in the literature on innovation is the 'technological trajectory', which Dosi describes as:

> [T]he activity of technological trade-offs defined by a paradigm. . . . Thus, for example, technological progress in aircraft technology has followed two quite precise trajectories (one civilian and one military) characterized by log-linear improvement in the trade-offs between horsepower, gross takeoff weight, cruise speed, wing loading, and cruise range . . . In microelectronics, technical change is accurately represented by an exponential trajectory of improvement in the relationship between density of the electronic chips, speed of computation, and cost per bit of information. . . . More generally, there is growing evidence that specific 'innovation avenues' are a widespread feature of the observed patterns of technological change. (Dosi 1988, pp. 1128-9)

However, the basic concept of a 'trajectory' need not be restricted in this manner. For example, the Chinese restaurant industry could be regarded as a trajectory, in the sense that it provides a unique service which has grown and evolved in the economy. One could speculate that if, by some strange set of circumstances, culinary arts had come to be regarded as a branch of chemistry, then economists, especially agricultural economists, would already be studying the evolution of different cuisines in the economy in terms of technological trajectories. By the same token, the 'horror film' could be regarded as a trajectory in the entertainment industry. It involves the continual use of new technologies in film making, which, it could be argued, are associated with one or more technological paradigms in the areas of photography, computer graphics, and certain branches of psychology (e.g., perception and abnormal psychology). In this sense, there exist 'artistic trajectories' and 'cultural trajectories' that could be just as important as technological trajectories in terms of quality improvement and economic change.

In essence, the study of product innovation has been confined largely to the areas of conventional science and engineering. As such, it may be useful for monitoring the development of science and engineering in various industries. However, it is not useful in general for drawing inferences about quality improvement across the wide spectrum of goods and services in the economy.[2]

To expand on this point, one could identify three types of quality improvement:

1. *Product innovation*. The development of a 'new' good which can be distinguished from any other good preceding it in terms of easily-identifiable physical attributes or characteristics, or any new 'service' which is characterized by unique, easily-identifiable activities.
2. *Artistic creation*. This source of quality improvement would not involve the development of a 'new good' or 'new service', which would have a different name, but would involve quality improvements in individual items 'within' the category of a single good. Such quality improvements would be associated with differences in the characteristics of individual items, or the specific events associated with a service.
3. *Intellectual achievement*. This source of quality improvement would not involve any identifiable differences among items in terms of easily-definable physical characteristics (in the case of goods) or activities (in the case of services). Rather, the quality of items improve (or worsen in some cases) in terms of the *ideas* which those items convey.

For example, oil paintings could be regarded as a single good, and there is no research and development involved. Nevertheless, oil paintings can surely improve, or worsen, in terms of quality. The same may be said of virtually any type of artistic, and/or entertainment, medium. Similarly, a mathematics textbook could be improved by providing more information, or improved in the way that it explains a particular point. There may be virtually no change in its physical appearance, and thus, its improvement would be one of intellectual achievement rather than artistic creativity. In addition, one could easily see how cases could arise in which there are various combinations of the above sources of quality improvement: a theatrical performance could embody both artistic creativity and intellectual achievement, for example. Perhaps the small pieces of the Berlin Wall, which were commonly sold in 1991 in department stores, embody all three sources of quality improvement.

Aside from ignoring improvements due to artistic creativity and intellectual achievement, the study of product innovation also downplays discoveries that are not 'scientifically interesting', or that are not associated with the R & D departments of firms. (See Chapter 7.) Moreover, it places greater emphasis on capital goods, rather than consumer goods, which in many respects is associated more with the topic of 'process innovation' (for the firm that will utilize the capital good) than product innovation.

In some of the literature, in fact, consumer preferences are regarded as peripheral, or even contradictory, to the process of product innovation. For example, Freeman writes:

> [G]eneralizations about the benefits of technical innovation do need to be heavily qualified outside the area of capital goods. Most innovation studies have been concerned with the more spectacular 'break-through' innovations and have hardly considered the type of 'annual model' changes which are more characteristic of many consumer products. . . . Several . . . examples may be cited to illustrate the extent to which innovators and designers may neglect the interests of users and simply pursue their own fashions and enthusiasms. . . . These examples demonstrate the extent to which the values and preferences of designers and innovators may be *imposed* on the consumer, whether through private firms or public authorities. (Freeman 1982, pp. 203-5)

Others, like Schmookler (1966 and 1972), have argued in favour of a 'demand-pull' model, in which consumer interests do contribute to product innovation. However, in many of these discussions on the causes of technological discoveries, and in Schmookler's work in particular, there is considerable emphasis on a separate topic. That topic addresses the broad philosophical question of whether scientific discoveries 'just happen' or whether they occur as a direct result of human motivations toward specific goals. This philosophical concern is peripheral to the much simpler question addressed here, which is whether *consumer* motivations are as important as *producer* motivations in the evolution of goods and services.

In some respects, product innovation, as it is commonly studied, may imitate a 'scientific' approach toward analysing the topic of quality improvement, by focusing on the kind of innovations that can often be physically measured. However, if one is to be scientific about studying any phenomenon, one must study *all* types of factors that have an important influence on that phenomenon, not simply the types that are most easily measurable. For example, in clinical psychology the anxiety that people sometimes get from their dreams is given as much attention as, say, their fear of height, even though dreams are not physically measurable[3] while height is. This aspect of clinical psychology does not make it any less scientific. In fact, it makes it more scientific, because the scientific phenomenon of human anxiety is being studied more thoroughly when dreams are included.

One could argue that, ultimately, all aspects of quality improvement are scientific. All are associated with human perception, and the cognitive process whereby evaluations are made of that perception. That process does not occur in the realm of metaphysics, but in the realms of psychology and neurophysiology. Surely, a scientist may not know how a particular intellectual or artistic improvement in a good gets translated into the particular patterns of neurological transmissions which, in turn, determine the consumer's desire for that good. Nevertheless, as a scientist, one must acknowledge that some sort of translation does occur. Scitovsky writes:

> Although economists have never analysed the nature and origin of consumer preferences, others have, so we need not start from scratch. Psychologists have done a lot of work on the motivation of man's behavior, of which consumer behavior is a part. Moreover, the scientific method of at least some psychologists — mostly those who are known as physiological psychologists — is very similar to the economists; they too observe behavior and from that infer its motivation. The main difference is that while economists observe man's market behavior in real-life situations, physiological psychologists observe many more kinds of behavior, mostly under carefully controlled experimental conditions, and they do not confine themselves to man. (Scitovsky 1976, p. 7)

It follows that the study of artistic and intellectual contributions to the quality of goods are as much a part of 'economic science' as product innovation. As all scientific concepts, they support the objective of science itself, which is to achieve a greater understanding of the causal relations that exist in objective reality.

One observes, however, that the study of product innovation has focused heavily on data pertaining to R & D activities. These data generally refer to formal scientific and engineering activities, and not to the types of activities associated with other forms of quality improvement. Consequently, the limited focus of product innovation economics may be due, in part, to the wide availability of these data, as opposed to other types of data. This problem — the absence of useful data on other forms of quality change — is addressed in Chapter 4.

A SCHEMATIC REPRESENTATION OF THE EVOLUTION OF GOODS AND SERVICES

Figure 2.1 displays a schematic representation of the interrelationships among various aspects of evolutionary change. Starting at the upper left-hand corner of the figure one begins with the block 'Possibilities for discovery', which represents, in broad terms, the concept of 'nature' or 'physical reality', but restricted to what man is capable of perceiving under current circumstances. For example, the night-time sky first provided the possibilities for discoveries in astronomy. Research into optics, and specifically the invention of the telescope, then led to an expansion of those

Figure 2.1 The evolution of goods and services

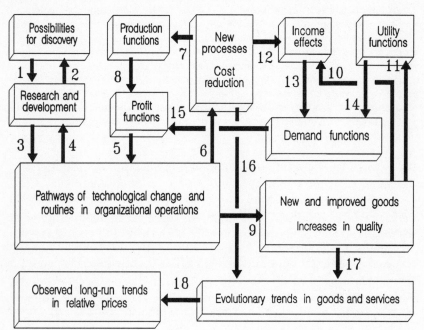

possibilities. Thus, interaction occurs between the possibilities for discovery and R & D, as indicated by Connections 1 and 2 in the figure.

R & D, in turn, interacts with the block entitled 'Pathways of technological change and routines in organizational operations', as shown by Connections 3 and 4. In many respects these factors play a central role in the evolution of goods and services. Pathways of technological change involve two general categories of discovery: invention and the acquisition of broader-based knowledge (Nelson and Winter, 1982, p. 249). With regard to routines in organizational operations, Dosi (1988, pp. 1132-3) remarks that they embody, 'heuristics on "how to do things" and "how to improve them" . . . which, through practise, repetition, and more or less incremental improvements make certain firms "good" at exploring certain technological opportunities and translating them into specific marketable products'. Along similar lines, Nelson and Winter (1982, p. 104) remark that routines are 'remembered' by organizations by way of individuals 'knowing their jobs', and by way of evolving feedback mechanisms through which signals are sent and interpreted.

Pathways of technological change and routines in organizational operations have been placed in the same block because they are highly interrelated. As Nelson and Winter (1982, p. 104) remark, 'skills, organization, and "technology" are intimately intertwined in a functioning routine, and it is difficult to say exactly where one aspect ends and another begins'.

Pathways and routines, in addition to being influenced by R & D, are influenced by the profit functions of firms (Connection 5). The outcomes of technological and organizational changes, in turn, are broken down into two types of economic effects: the development of new or improved production processes, or equivalently, 'cost reduction', as indicated by Connection 6; and the creation of new and improved goods and services, or 'quality improvement', as indicated by Connection 9.

'New processes and cost reduction' can be interpreted economically as particular changes in the production functions of firms (Connection 7), which then affects the profit functions of firms (Connection 8), feeding back into pathways and routines (Connection 5). The loop defined by Connections 5-8 could be seen as lying entirely within the supply side of the economic system, except for the influence of production costs on real income (Connection 12).

In contrast, the other effect of pathways and routines, 'New and improved goods; increases in quality' feeds into the demand side of the system. The utility functions of consumers can be thought of as accounting for goods which have not yet come into existence, where such goods — at the present time — could be seen as having an infinite price. In this sense, the utility functions come into play in the establishment of the demand for new and improved goods, as shown by Connections 11 and 14. Furthermore, as goods improve in quality real income rises, which then affects patterns of demand, as indicated by Connections 10 and 13.[4]

The demand functions represent the final stage in the demand side of the framework, which feed into the supply side by way of the profit functions (Connection 15). Taken together, the boxes discussed thus far, and their interconnections (1-15) represent a system. That system can be seen as being three-sided, containing a research side, a supply side and a demand side. At the heart of the system is the block representing technological pathways and organizational routines.

The two bottom blocks in Figure 2.1 are not operating components but by-products of the system. Evolutionary trends in goods and services could be studied in a variety of ways, as there are many 'trends' that one could observe. For example, if one is interested in the applications of new scientific discoveries, then one could have trajectories and routines as the block that feeds into 'evolutionary trends'. If it is real income that one is most interested in, then the 'income effects' block would provide the link. In the present study the focus is on quality change and relative prices, and therefore, the two blocks that apply are 'new processes, cost reduction' and 'new and improved goods, increases in quality'.

If cost reduction and quality improvement occur in a random fashion, then there would be no trends or patterns in prices as goods and services evolve. On the other hand, if there are observable, systematic tendencies for particular types of goods to undergo particular patterns of change in their relative prices, then the discovery of these systematic tendencies could contribute to an understanding of the evolution of goods and services.

There is a difference between systematic tendencies in the evolution of goods and services, and the particular observations that we might happen to make about them. Thus, the final block, 'Observed long-run trends in relative prices' is what we can, and actually do, observe.

Figure 2.1 serves to demonstrate the vast range of considerations that are relevant to the topic at hand. In contrast, Figure 2.2 illustrates a simplified picture, displaying those parts of Figure 2.1 that are addressed in the present study. Needless to say, all of the factors shown in Figure 2.1 that are not present in Figure 2.2 (as well as all other factors that may be relevant but are not shown in *either* figure) are components that lie underneath the components shown in Figure 2.2.

Figure 2.2 Simplified scheme, representing the focus of the present study

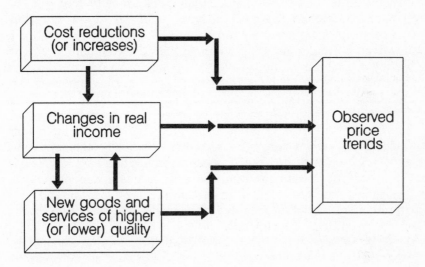

The main feature of Figure 2.2 is the dichotomy between cost reduction and quality improvement, suggesting that some goods and services could be more inclined toward one or the other of these effects. This dichotomy among goods and services has been discussed in the economic literature in a variety of contexts. For example, Rosenberg (1982) remarks:

> A central problem in examining technical progress . . . is that it takes many different forms. . . . Perhaps the most useful common denominator . . . is that it constitutes certain kinds of knowledge that makes it possible to produce (1) a greater volume of output or (2) a qualitatively superior output from a given amount of resources.

However, in order to understand this dichotomy fully, a distinction must be made between what Rosenberg calls 'a qualitatively superior output' and 'a greater volume of output'. This distinction is discussed in the next section.

THE 'GREY AREAS' OF QUALITY MEASUREMENT

Quality versus Quantity

In many contexts, whether a good undergoes a quality improvement or a cost reduction depends on how quantities of the good are measured, or more precisely, on how a unit of the good is defined. However, a 'true' quality improvement, i.e., one that conforms with the most basic notions of quality improvement as opposed to cost reduction, will always be measured as a quality improvement regardless of how units are defined.

For example, suppose, through the miracles of modern agricultural science, a new variety of pineapple is produced. This variety yields pineapples which weigh twice as much as ordinary pineapples, all else being equal. Is this a quality improvement or a cost reduction? In terms of the current literature, the answer would depend on how the pineapples are sold. If they are sold by the pound, the improvement would be regarded as simply a cost reduction on the part of the supplier (given the simplifying assumption that each plant requires the same space and the same quantity of nutrients). On the other hand, if the new pineapples are sold with a single price per pineapple, then the price of the new, larger pineapple would naturally be higher, because of greater demand and greater handling costs. In this second case, then, the new pineapple could only be interpreted as a quality improvement, because it is an improvement per unit. Thus, from this simple example, one can see that whether a change is a 'quality improvement' or a 'cost reduction' might only depend on how the good is sold, which, in turn, might only depend on historical or cultural circumstances.

If, however, economists are to make any useful distinctions between quality improvement and cost reduction, they cannot allow circumstance to make the distinction for them. The distinction must be given greater meaning. Specifically, it must be based on what people generally have in mind when they think of the difference between cost reduction and quality improvement. *More precisely, if any reasonable definition of the unit of a good could be made that*

would translate the change to a change in terms of cost reduction,
then that change should be regarded as a cost reduction. In the
above example of a pineapple, a reasonable unit of measurement,
the pound, is quite plausible. Thus, the change should be regarded
in broad terms as a cost reduction, even if pineapples happen to be
sold in units which, on a simplistic level, would imply a quality
improvement.

In general, if a change could easily be regarded, by the consumer,
as a cost reduction, depending on how units are defined, then it
should be regarded as a cost reduction regardless of how units are
defined. Let us refer to this idea as the *'principle of unitless quality*
change', because, under this principle, all changes identified as
quality improvements will be independent of the particular units used
to measure the good in question.

Ultimately, economists should strive for a greater understanding
of quality improvement and cost reduction as two distinct
phenomena with their own inherent characteristics. As already
suggested, in order to achieve this greater understanding, thought
must first be given to the appropriate units of measure. For
example, Griliches remarks:

> The economist . . . does not have to restrict himself to the particular form in
> which the data come to him. For example, a farmer may be buying 'all-
> purpose' fertilizer in 100-pound sacks and paying a price that is quoted 'per
> sack'. Both we and the more intelligent farmer know that what he is
> interested in is not total poundage but the 'plant nutrient content' of it. From
> this it is only one step, and a feasible one at that, to translate the 'fixed per
> sack transaction' into prices paid per plant nutrient unit and perhaps to
> complicate it further by distinguishing different plant nutrients (nitrogen,
> phosphoric acid and potash) and assigning different units to each one of
> these. (Griliches 1964, p. 400)

Yet, one often finds in the literature 'superficial' quality
improvements that are, inherently, cost reductions — this situation
is often referred to as the 'repackaging case'. In reality, those
products that are 'improved' in this superficial sense often do not
replace their earlier counterparts, but rather, enter into their
counterparts' markets in the form of a new differentiated product.
For instance, there may be two types of pineapples on the grocery
store shelf, the 'giant pineapples' selling for $5.00 each, and the
'regular' ones selling for $2.50 each. If this is the case, the
repackaging type of quality improvement, which would have the
larger pineapple as being of 'higher quality' than the smaller one,

could create substantial difficulties to any researchers making a
serious attempt to measure actual quality improvement.

Along similar lines, Lancaster remarks:

> What about quality as quantity, the simple repackaging case? If a box of
> crackers or a candy bar contains 10 percent less content this year than last,
> it has been the practice among economists to refer to this as a quality
> change. If the term is appropriate, the quality change would be truly
> measurable. But it would seem likely that a hypothetical consumer would
> regard the change, correctly enough, as a mere change in the quantity units
> having nothing to do with quality in the proper sense. (Lancaster 1977, p.
> 158)

In other words, in the simple repackaging case consumers and
suppliers are actually thinking in terms of a price per unit of weight,
in spite of whatever numbers or symbols they might happen to see
on the grocery store shelf. This means that, in reality, it is the
broader notion of *unitless quality* that actually enters into the
considerations of consumers, once they have solved the repackaging
calculations that may be required.

One might ask, what would then constitute a better 'quality'
pineapple? The answer is a pineapple that tastes better, that spoils
less, that looks more attractive, etc. Basically, a better quality
pineapple is one that would be better *regardless of how each unit is
measured*, be it by the pound, the fruit, or the cubic foot.

The above appeal for a workable distinction between actual
quality improvement and actual cost reduction may appear to be
somewhat obvious, and hardly a point worth disputing.
Nevertheless, there is no consensus among economists on this
issue, and, in fact, radically different ideas have often appeared in
the literature. For example, Fisher and Shell wrote the following on
the distinction between 'a taste change' and 'a quality change':

> [S]uppose that consumers suddenly learn to use a certain fuel more
> efficiently, getting a certain number of BTUs out of a smaller quantity of fuel.
> If the relevant axis on the indifference map is the amount of fuel purchased,
> then there has been a taste change; if it is the number of BTUs gained from
> such fuel, there has not been a taste change but a quality change — a change
> in the opportunities available to them. (Fisher and Shell 1968, p. 24)

The above quotation is clearly an exercise in the semantics of
theoretical economic modelling. As such, it correctly examines how
an economist could make references to the various operations he
could perform with indifference maps. However, as is often the·

case with economic theory, its application to actual consumer behaviour could be misleading. For instance, the consumer would be highly irrational to base his purchasing decisions on how much fuel he receives independent of how much heat that fuel produces.

It should be noted, however, that the broader framework presented here for analysing unitless quality is not free of conceptual problems, nor measurement problems. There will always be grey areas in the distinction between actual quality improvement and actual cost reduction. Nevertheless, this is a problem that exists in the classification of all things that are real. The bottom line will always be whether the classification scheme is useful and/or enlightening, in spite of its ambiguities and imperfections. Surely the concepts of 'liquid' and 'solid' are quite useful, in spite of the fact that one often finds ambiguous mixtures of both.

The Continuum between Quality Improvement and Cost Reduction

Whether a change is a quality improvement or a cost reduction will depend on how narrowly, or broadly, goods are defined. Consequently, the distinction between the two could be approached with greater analytical precision if the 'broadness' of a good's definition is held constant. Consider four levels, or categories, of goods (and services) on the basis of the breath of their definitions:

Category I.   Each good is so narrowly defined in terms of characteristics that any innovation to it, or basic change in its composition would cause it to be categorized as a different good. Examples are: sulphuric acid, copper, distilled water, table salt, 14 carat gold and other specific chemicals and minerals. Other examples would include plant or animal products of a specific quality or 'grade' and/or a specific origin, such as particular grades of cotton, coffee and tea; particular strains of rice and wheat; and other well-defined agricultural and natural resource commodities.

Category II.   These goods can have somewhat different forms, but are defined too narrowly for the inclusion of any dramatic changes in an existing member of the group, such as changes that would normally be associated with historically-notable inventions (in the case of manufactures) or distinctly different animal or plant species (in the case of livestock or produce). Examples are: horses, automobiles, flashlights, compact disk players, chairs and wallpaper. Other examples would be the broader counterparts of the commodities in Category I, such as: coffee (of all grades and types), lettuce (of all varieties) and sweetcorn (fresh, frozen and canned).

Category III. These goods are defined broadly enough to include dramatic inventions, or different species of plants or animals, but could also have much in common in terms of their use and their physical characteristics. Examples are: meat, vegetables, musical instruments, fuel, office supplies, motor vehicles and toys.

Category IV. These goods are associated with a very general use or purpose.   Examples include: food, recreation, transportation, household durables, housing and medical care.

With these four type of goods, and with the recognition of the continuum that they reflect, one can avoid a great deal of confusion that might otherwise exist in the study of cost reduction and quality improvement.

To elaborate on the continuity between cost reduction and quality improvement, one could conceive of a spectrum of cost reduction and quality improvement possibilities, which could apply to a particular good. Figures 2.3 and 2.4 provide illustrations of this spectrum, and demonstrate how the spectrum could be interpreted, alternatively, as a spectrum of change in the context of Categories I-IV.   The goods chosen for these illustrations were telephone services and chicken eggs.

From these considerations, one has some additional tools to address many of the old arguments on quality change. For example, one could re-examine the classical debate over whether primary products undergo more cost-reducing, and less quality-improving, technical change than manufactured goods.   (See Chapter 7.) Certain disagreements in reference to that argument may be interpreted as purely semantic involving one's definition of 'quality'. For instance, Spraos (1980, p. 117) argues that there is evidence that many primary products have undergone quality improvement in recent times, and he presents as one of his examples, 'In 1950 one-third of iron ores exported worldwide . . . had a Fe content of more than 60%, but by 1964 more than half did'. By his use of this example, he is implicitly assuming that iron ore is measured in units, like tons, that are independent of its iron content.   But, if one interprets the *unitless quality* of iron ore to be proportional to the *quantity* of actual iron that it contains, then this change in iron ore could be regarded, in broader terms, as a cost reduction rather than

Figure 2.3 A spectrum of cost reduction and quality improvement changes in telephone services

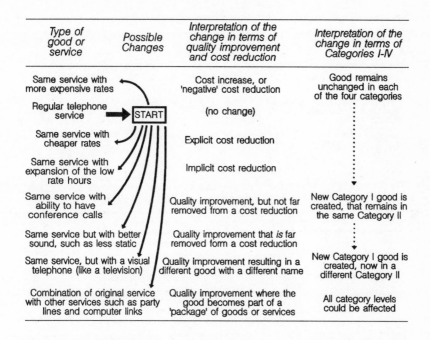

Type of good or service	Possible Changes	Interpretation of the change in terms of quality improvement and cost reduction	Interpretation of the change in terms of Categories I-IV
Same service with more expensive rates		Cost increase, or 'negative' cost reduction	Good remains unchanged in each of the four categories
Regular telephone service	START	(no change)	
Same service with cheaper rates		Explicit cost reduction	
Same service with expansion of the low rate hours		Implicit cost reduction	
Same service with ability to have conference calls		Quality improvement, but not far removed from a cost reduction	New Category I good is created, that remains in the same Category II
Same service but with better sound, such as less static		Quality improvement that *is* far removed form a cost reduction	
Same service, but with a visual telephone (like a television)		Quality Improvement resulting in a different good with a different name	New Category I good is created, now in a different Category II
Combination of original service with other services such as party lines and computer links		Quality improvement where the good becomes part of a 'package' of goods or services	All category levels could be affected

a quality improvement.

Nevertheless, except for the problem of where to draw the line, quality-improving technical change and cost-reducing technical change are two distinct phenomena. Cost reduction exerts its influence in the production of the good, and thus, can be viewed as leading to downward shifts in the supply curve. Quality improvement, on the other hand can be seen as exerting its influence, in an abstract sense, on *utility*. That is, even though one generally regards quality improvement as a change that is initiated by suppliers, that change is only recognized and acted upon by demanders. This view of quality change is discussed in the chapters that follow.

The Equivalence between Characteristics Space and Goods Space

Using the four categories of goods defined above, let us simplify the discussion by distinguishing between two types of goods,

Figure 2.4 A spectrum of cost reduction and quality improvement changes in chicken eggs

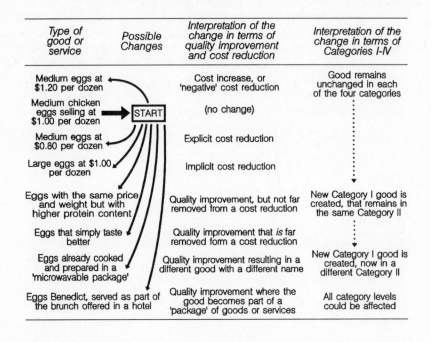

Type of good or service	Possible Changes	Interpretation of the change in terms of quality improvement and cost reduction	Interpretation of the change in terms of Categories I-IV
Medium eggs at $1.20 per dozen		Cost increase, or 'negative' cost reduction	Good remains unchanged in each of the four categories
Medium chicken eggs selling at $1.00 per dozen	START	(no change)	
Medium eggs at $0.80 per dozen		Explicit cost reduction	
Large eggs at $1.00 per dozen		Implicit cost reduction	
Eggs with the same price and weight but with higher protein content		Quality improvement, but not far removed from a cost reduction	New Category I good is created, that remains in the same Category II
Eggs that simply taste better		Quality improvement that *is* far removed form a cost reduction	
Eggs already cooked and prepared in a 'microwavable package'		Quality improvement resulting in a different good with a different name	New Category I good is created, now in a different Category II
Eggs Benedict, served as part of the brunch offered in a hotel		Quality improvement where the good becomes part of a 'package' of goods or services	All category levels could be affected

'subgoods' and 'sectors', where the former represents a narrower definition than the latter. One could envision a characteristics space, in which every characteristic of every subgood is a separate dimension. One could regard future subgoods as existing in the present but in zero amounts, thus adding still more dimensions to the space. In this framework, technical change for an entire sector could then be understood as the set of changes in the frequencies and locations of subgoods within the sector's own characteristics space.

If all the information on a sector is contained in the amounts of its subgoods, then one could transform the space from characteristics space to subgood space. In this new space, each single unit of a specific subgood would lie on a specific axis (or dimension) for that subgood, and the number of dimensions would equal the number of distinct subgoods. Of course, if there are more subgoods than characteristics, then such a transformation would lead to an increase in dimensions, and vice versa if there are more characteristics than subgoods. In this 'subgood space', there is no reason why the amounts of different subgoods in a sector could not, themselves, be considered as different 'characteristics' of the sector.

For instance, let the sector be 'food', defined as the total amount of food consumed per capita and per annum. Let subgoods be different types of food, and let the initial characteristics of subgoods be nutrients.[5] In characteristics space, food would be described by the quantities of protein, complex carbohydrates, essential lipids, fibre, vitamin B, etc., that it contains. In subgood space, food would be characterized by the quantities of chicken, broccoli, french fries, etc., that are consumed in a hypothetical, year-long meal. Thus, the subgoods themselves also serve as characteristics of the sector. This principle will come up again in later chapters.

NOTES

1. In some contexts, especially in economic theory, 'product innovation' may, indeed, be a function of consumer preferences. For instance, Pearce (1983) defines 'product innovation' as 'A change made by a firm in its saleable product and which can arise due to an addition to technology, or a change in relative prices where the latter may be a consequence of a change in consumer preferences' (p. 354). However, as argued below, the *effective* definition of product innovation, in terms of the literature, is rather different.
2. For a review of some of the literature on technological change, see Dosi (1988).
3. For simplicity, I am leaving out the possibility of measuring dreams in terms of rapid eye movements, electroencephalograms, etc.
4. Regardless of the changes in the nominal prices of goods and services per constant unit of quality, real income will always be best understood as the product of the quality of goods and services and the volume of goods and services. Thus, if quality improves overall per unit, while volume, in the same units, remains unchanged, then income rises, *a priori*.
5. See Lancaster, 1971, pp. 15-19.

3. Microeconomic foundations and empirical approaches

> Literally hundreds of learned papers have been written on the subject of utility. Take a little bad psychology, add a dash of bad philosophy and ethics, and liberal quantities of bad logic, and any economist can prove that the demand curve for a commodity is negatively inclined.
>
> *Samuelson (1983, p. 4)*

QUALITY AS IT RELATES TO PRICE INDICES, VERSUS QUALITY AS AN END IN ITSELF

In the literature on price indices, the issue of quality arises when there is a change in utility, or the willingness of a consumer to purchase a product, that *cannot be explained by a change in income, prices, or tastes*. In this sense, quality is a residual concept — something designed to explain what other economic variables cannot. Conversely, one could adopt the perspective that any change in the physical characteristics of a good could represent a change in quality. Lancaster (1977, p. 121) has referred to this framework as 'quality change as an objective in itself'. For ease of presentation, it will be called the 'quality change framework', in contrast to the former case, which will be called the 'price index framework'. Models affiliated with these two perspectives will be examined in the sections that follow.

An important difference between the two frameworks is that the price index framework would pay as much attention to the repackaging case as it would to the case of unitless quality change. In contrast, the quality change framework pertains primarily to unitless quality change.

As another example of the difference in perspectives, suppose a society exports a product that it does not consume, and all the products that it does consume are imports. (This construct allows one to avoid the complications that would otherwise arise in a

56

typical general equilibrium model.)   Further suppose that, for whatever reason, the relative price of the export rises, and thus, income levels rise. The society may then purchase more expensive, or 'higher quality' items. In this situation, there is no improvement in the quality of goods according to the price index framework, because the prices of goods per unit of quality has not changed. In contrast, according to the quality change framework, quality has, in fact, been altered, because the goods purchased now have different characteristics and a different effect on utility. In short, quality change could be important in itself, even if there is no need for price adjustment.

Another important division in the literature on quality measurement, already discussed in Chapter 1, is between the user-value and resource-cost interpretations of quality. This division lies entirely within the price-index framework; in the quality change framework only the user-value interpretation applies.

MODELS UNDER THE PRICE INDEX FRAMEWORK

Measuring the Unmeasurable

As discussed in Chapter 1, current support for the resource-cost method of quality measurement is often expressed in terms of an argument against the concept of costless quality change. According to this line of reasoning, the notion of costless quality change is invalid — therefore, a resource-cost approach is appropriate. Yet, ironically, the resource-cost definition of quality change was originally based on precisely the opposite argument. The previous argument was: *costless quality change does occur, but cannot be measured; therefore, one is forced to measure the other type of quality change — based on resource costs*.

For example, Gilbert and Kravis referred to the costless type of quality change as 'noneconomic' and the resource-cost type as 'economic':

> A product may be of a higher quality in the sense of being more attractive to the purchaser for one of two reasons. The one is that there is a more advanced state of the arts or state of technical knowledge which enables a better product to be made without requiring the use of more resources. The other is . . . that the purchasers . . . are willing . . . or able . . . to pay for a product that requires more resources to produce it. The first type of higher quality is cost free, and hence is non-economic. The second type requires

higher cost, and hence is economic. (Gilbert and Kravis 1954, p. 80)

Their justification for resource-cost quality measurement is then based on the following argument:

> It does not matter that the ultimate benefits to the consumer from the non-economic differences in quality may be greater in some sense than those from the economic differences . . . a qualitative measure of relative production cannot be constructed in terms of ultimate satisfactions of the users of the goods, but must be limited to the relative quantities of the goods and services they command. (Gilbert and Kravis 1954, p. 80)

There are certain fallacies in this viewpoint. First, the use of the terms 'economic' and 'non-economic' are rhetorical — they are merely semantic devices to lend support to the framework. If one were focusing on the demand side of the economic system rather than the supply side, one could equally well call the effect of a good on utility as the *economic quality* of the good, and the resource-cost effect as *'non-economic' quality*.

Secondly, the resource-cost definition appears to break down when one looks underneath what is meant by 'resource costs'. Gilbert and Kravis's assertion that the replacement of less appealing goods by more appealing goods could be 'cost free' is hardly the case when one considers the research and development expenditures that are often required. Furthermore, there is the matter of wages and returns on capital. For example, wages are likely to be adjusted by a cost of living index, which, in turn, would be based on resource costs, if, in fact, resource-cost advocates get their way. As a result, real wages in the overall economy, in terms of the utility of workers, would rise due to costless quality change occurring at the same time. But, if real wages are, themselves, a 'resource cost', then this component of resource costs rises when costless quality change occurs. Moreover, in the industry in which costless quality change occurs, the productivity of labour increases, because the same amount of labour can now be used to produce more desirable goods which command higher relative prices. Equilibrium in the labour market would then require a bidding-up of these labour inputs, thereby raising 'resource costs'. Needless to say, similar arguments are equally applicable to capital and the return on capital.

Moreover, as discussed in Chapter 1, the resource-cost definition breaks down when one takes it to its extreme, where the quality of a good would depend only on the natural resources exhausted in its production, plus all of the labour and capital utilized. If, for example, a technically more efficient machine can be produced with the same resources as a previous model, then that technical efficiency would go undetected. Ultimately, each new generation of better machines could have its quality defined by the quality of previous machines, plus (or minus) any changes in labour and natural resources used in its production. Yet, that would leave out exactly what is most important about new machines — their innovations. In other words, patents, trademarks and copyrights; research and development; and entrepreneurial ability would become, in effect, valueless in the resource-cost framework.

Nevertheless, Dennison is correct in taking the position that the resource-cost method of quality measurement is simply a device that has been used for purposes of convenience, ease of interpretation and conformity with convention. The last of these attributes has allowed for intertemporal and international comparisons, which is probably the most desirable aspect of the resource-cost approach. However, as logic would dictate, Dennison is quick to point out:

> Clearly, the estimates do not take into account either the improvements made in a great range of products without a corresponding change in their production costs or the vastly greater range of choice open to today's consumer. He can, if he wished, choose to buy antibiotics that will cure his illness rather than spend the same amount on remedies that will not; to buy a television set rather than spend the same amount for radios; or to cross the continent by plane in hours rather than by train in days. (Dennison 1962, pp. 156-7)

Hence, the original rationale for the resource-cost measurement of quality was rather simple: it was believed at the time to be the only feasible measure of quality. Utility-based quality measurement was not considered feasible, primarily because ideas on consumer preferences and the characteristics of goods had not yet been formalized in economic theory, and hedonic methods of measurement had not yet received wide recognition. However, once utility-based quality measurement came into being, the old defence of the resource-cost approach, based on feasibility, was no longer appropriate. In order for the tradition, or momentum, of the resource cost method to be maintained and justified, a new theoretical foundation had to be invented. That theoretical foundation has been called the 'output-based' measure of quality change, which is the topic of the next section.

Output-based Measures of Quality Change

An important aspect of the theory of output-based quality measurement is the distinction between 'input' and 'output' characteristics. The characteristics that have been discussed in previous chapters would fall under the input category,[1] because they are inputs for a utility function. In contrast, output characteristics are aspects of a good that are associated with how the good was produced. They are characteristics of the ingredients or resources that have been exhausted in the creation of 'output'. These characteristics are not necessarily needed or wanted by anyone — that would qualify them as 'input' characteristics. More precisely: 'Something is an output characteristic if it accounts for, or partly accounts for, the unexplained variation in resource usage occasioned by changes in the varieties of nonhomogeneous goods produced. . . . This definition of an output characteristic says, in effect, that an output is something that uses resources' (Triplett, 1983, p. 294).

There is a strong symmetry between the mapping of utility curves in input-characteristics space and the mapping of production possibility frontiers (PPFs) in output-characteristics space. Similarly, there is a symmetry between the plot of an input characteristic of a single good against the quantity of all other goods, and the plot of an output characteristic of a single good against the quantity of all other resources. In the former, one has a utility curve and a price line, as was shown in Figure 1.2. In the latter, one has a PPF and a price line, as shown in Figure 3.1. In both Figures the vertical axis represents an aggregate of all other entities — goods in Figure 1.2 and resources (or 'ingredients') in Figure 3.1.

In the analysis of Figure 3.1, assume, for simplicity, that food is the only type of good produced; the ingredients that make up all food are the only scarce resources, and only one food item contains vitamin C. Also assume that no significant resources are expended in the making of the food item that contains vitamin C, except vitamin C itself.[2] Of course, the vitamin C content of the food item could, just as well, be seen as an input characteristic, but this dual role of vitamin C would not contradict its relevance as an output characteristic. As Triplett (1983, p. 294) states, 'Normally an output is not produced unless someone wants it, so in most cases an output characteristic will also be an input characteristic.' In this case, one's focus is on vitamin C as a reflection of the resources used in the production of the good.

Figure 3.1 Output-based quality measurement

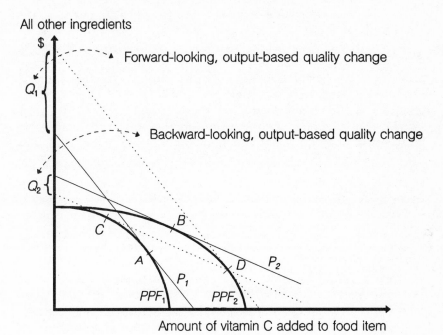

Amount of vitamin C added to food item

In Figure 3.1, one begins at point *A*, in output-characteristics space, which lies on the production possibility frontier (in terms of output characteristics), PPF$_1$. Point *A* also lies on the price line *P*$_1$ which reflects the shadow prices of output characteristics. Because the vertical axis is in dollar units, the vertical intercept of the price line reflects total revenue. This property is analogous to the vertical intercept of Figure 1.2 reflecting total expenditure by the consumer.

In the context of output-based quality measurement, a quality improvement is defined as a change in the output characteristics of a good, in the absence of any compensating change in the definition of the good's units. An example would be the expansion of the PPF in Figure 3.1 to PPF$_2$, and the corresponding movement from point *A* to point *B*, at the new price line *P*$_2$. The quality change from A to B is then defined as 'the value of the resources required to move the set of output characteristics . . . back to the same production possibility curve' (Triplett, 1983, p. 299). One could measure the quality change on the basis of the original price line or the new price line. According to the original price line that change would be given by Q_1, while according to the new price line it would be Q_2.[3] Since Q_1 is based on the first period's prices, it could be categorized as a 'forward-looking' measure of quality change, while Q_2, based on the second period's prices would be a 'backward-looking' measure.

Notice that Q_1 is analogous to equivalent variation, and Q_2 is analogous to compensating variation, if one were to replace the production possibility frontiers by utility curves. (See Chapter 1, Figures 1.1 and 1.5, and the corresponding discussion.) More precisely, if one now assumes that these output characteristics are also input characteristics for a utility function, then the relationship between Q_1 and equivalent variation would be illustrated by Figure 3.2. For ease in the comparison of concepts, we could also call the

Figure 3.2 Output-based quality measurement versus equivalent variation

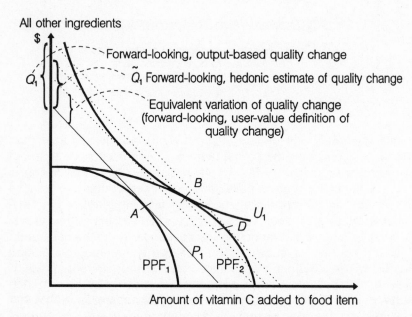

All other ingredients

Q_1 Forward-looking, output-based quality change

$\tilde{Q}_1$ Forward-looking, hedonic estimate of quality change

Equivalent variation of quality change (forward-looking, user-value definition of quality change)

B

A U_1

D

P_1

PPF$_1$ PPF$_2$

Amount of vitamin C added to food item

equivalent variation the 'forward-looking, user-value' measure of quality change. As also shown in Figure 3.2, one could have a forward looking, 'hedonic estimate' of quality change, based on point *B*, the equilibrium point for the second period. The term 'hedonic' is applied here because the quality measure makes use of the observed levels of characteristics.

As suggested in the figure, under the normal assumptions that utility functions are convex and PPFs concave, the forward-looking, output-based quality change will be greater than the forward-looking, user-value quality change. Moreover, the forward-looking, hedonic estimate would lie in between these two measures.

Figure 3.3 presents the alternative case of backward-looking

Figure 3.3 Output-based quality measurement versus compensating variation

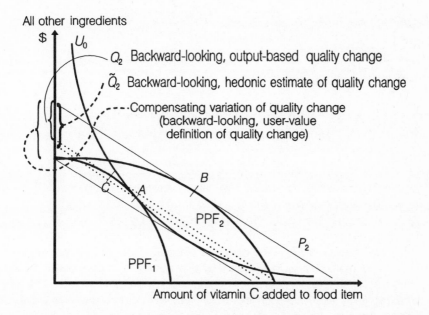

measures, which are based on shadow prices in the second period. A reversal in the size of the effects is now apparent, in that the user-value measure (compensating variation) is largest, the output-based measure is smallest, and, again, the hedonic estimate lies between them.

In the economic literature on these measures, there has been a strong association between the concept of forward-looking measures, especially the output-based and hedonic estimate measures, and the Laspeyres price index. Similarly, backward-looking measures have been associated with the Paasche price index. However, other than the fact that the Laspeyres index is forward-looking and the Paasche index is backward-looking, the relationship between these price indices and the quality measures described above is quite weak. Specifically, suppose one stretches the definition of these price indices, so that they are now functions of characteristics (i.e., their quantities and shadow prices) rather than goods. Let x_{ij} and p_{ij} be, respectively, the quantity and shadow price of characteristic j at time i. The Laspeyres (L) and Paasche (P) price indices from time i to time $i+k$ would be given by:

$$L = \frac{\sum_j x_{ij} p_{i+k,j}}{\sum_j x_{ij} p_{ij}} \;;\quad P = \frac{\sum_j x_{i+k,j} p_{i+k,j}}{\sum_j x_{i+k,j} p_{i,j}} \;. \tag{3.1}$$

In contrast, the forward-looking hedonic estimate (H_F) and backward-looking hedonic estimate (H_B) would be given by:

$$H_F = \frac{\sum_j x_{i+k,j} p_{i,j}}{\sum_j x_{ij} p_{ij}} \;;\quad H_B = \frac{\sum_j x_{i+k,j} p_{i+k,j}}{\sum_j x_{i,j} p_{i+k,j}} \;. \tag{3.2}$$

Hence, the Laspeyres index is a ratio of prices weighted by first-period quantities, while the forward-looking hedonic estimate is a ratio of quantities weighted by first-period prices. Similarly, the Paasche index is a ratio of prices weighted by last-period quantities, while the backward-looking hedonic estimate is a ratio of quantities weighted by last-period prices. The potential for overstating the relationship between the price and quality indices may arise when one implicitly assumes homothetic PPFs, which would create a one-to-one correspondence between relative shadow prices and relative quantity ratios.[4]

   As argued in Chapter 1, there are several limitations in the output-based definitions of quality measurement. The most appealing aspect of the output-measurement framework is that it demonstrates a symmetry between utility-based quality and quality defined in terms of productive capability — i.e. a symmetry between utility curves and production possibility frontiers. However, while symmetry, in itself, may be appealing to some economists because of their interest in mathematical principles, it is not relevant to the issue of *usefulness*.

Moreover, the use of the term 'output' to describe resource-cost quality measures is, in itself, highly misleading. The actual quantity of output produced is, to begin with, a function of *quality*. Hence, the user-value definition of quality, or any other measure of quality, could equally well be termed an 'output' measure. The distinguishing feature of the above-mentioned 'output' measure is that it is based on optimal productive capability. More precisely, the production possibility frontier maps out productive capability; consequently, its relevance to quality measurement must be based on the relevance of productive capability to quality measurement, regardless of the presence of any symmetries or other mathematical 'niceties'. Yet, the concept of productive capability, unlike the concept of utility, is much different from the basic notion of 'quality'.

Furthermore, while tastes, which form the basis of utility, have tended to evolve slowly over time, productive capabilities have frequently undergone rapid transformations. Consequently, quality based on optimal productive capability would often be circumstantial, and would therefore be limited in terms of its contribution to useful knowledge. (See the discussion of costless quality change in Chapter 1.)

In essence, there is only one main distinction between input and output characteristics: the first is related to wants or desires, and the second need not be.[5] But, one is then inclined to ask what is it about an output characteristic that makes an economist desire to study it, instead of studying any other 'non-desired' physical characteristic associated with the good. Even though output characteristics are more closely associated with resource costs, one is still left with the task of resolving the relationship between resource costs and the true meaning of quality.

The essential flaw in the resource-cost perspective is that it presumes that 'quality' is simply a function of whatever characteristics one happens to regard as important, for whatever reasons, as long as they relate in some way to production. However, if one is free to choose any arbitrary set of characteristics that one considers relevant, and then define a function of these characteristics as 'quality', then quality itself has no meaning. The quality of good, for instance, could be a function of the assortment of sounds that emanate when the good is dropped down a flight of stairs. In the end, one must conclude that if quality is to be described as a function of characteristics, then it can only be described as a function of *those characteristics that are, to begin with, pertinent to the inherent concept of quality.*

The current dilemma in the theory underlying the resource-cost perspective of quality measurement is reflected by the riddle: 'How many legs does a sheep have, if we call a tail a leg?' The correct answer is four, because calling a tail a leg does not *make* it a leg.[6] By the same token, calling changes in resource-costs 'quality changes' does not make them quality changes. *Actual* quality changes must depend on what 'quality' actually means. As Griliches remarks:

> Most economists . . . would like the 'price' index to be a 'price-of-living or of utility' indicator. Many government statisticians . . . will reply that they cannot achieve this and . . . should not even try, but should concentrate instead on some more 'objective' index of 'transaction' prices and/or allow only for those 'quality' changes which are based on 'production' costs. The fact that 'truth' cannot be achieved doesn't mean that one shouldn't strive to do so, though I sympathize with the position that it is better to measure well something definite than to do a very poor job on a more interesting but also more nebulous concept. Nevertheless, I would deny the contention that 'transaction' units or 'production' costs are much more definitive concepts. In general, they too make little sense without some appeal to utility considerations. (Griliches 1971b, p. 14)

As mentioned above, in reference to Figures 3.2 and 3.3, resource-cost measures of quality tend to be inversely related, in terms of size, to their corresponding user-value measures. That is, forward-looking output-based quality change is greater than its corresponding user-value measure, and vice versa for backward-looking measures. As a result, measures that are estimates based on observed quantities and prices, such as $\tilde{Q}_1$ and $\tilde{Q}_2$ in Figures 3.2 and 3.3, respectively, end up lying somewhere in between the theoretical resource-cost and user-value measures. This situation has enabled resource-cost advocates to suggest, though somewhat rhetorically, that their measures are not necessarily any more 'biased' than user-value measures, but are simply 'biased' in the opposite direction.[7] This line of reasoning is erroneous, however, because 'bias' in this context would be in reference to the hedonic methods of quality measurement. The 'bias' of a quality measure should, instead, be in reference to compensating or equivalent variation, which is, in fact, the very basis upon which the user-value measure has been established.

The Household Production Model

In studying the household production model one finds many similarities with the model presented above on resource-cost quality measurement. In fact, in some respects the household production model helped sow the seeds of the resource-cost model. It derives its name from the idea that households purchase *inputs*, x, which they, themselves, utilize to produce *goods*, z_1 and z_2 (Muellbauer, 1974). These households solve a two-stage problem of minimizing the cost of producing each combination of z_1 and z_2, and maximizing utility subject to a budget constraint.

That is, households:

$$Minimize \; L_1 = \sum p_i x_i + \phi[F(x; z_1, z_2)] \qquad \text{(M.1)}$$

where $F(x,z)$ is the joint production function normalized to equal zero, ϕ is a Lagrangian multiplier, and p is the vector of input prices.[8] By solving for x in the above equation, one derives a cost function,

$$C = C(p,z) \; . \qquad \text{(M.2)}$$

In the second stage, utility is maximized, i.e.,

$$\max \; L_2 = U(z) + \sigma[y - C(p,z)] \qquad \text{(M.3)}$$

where y is income (Muellbauer, 1974). From these stages, x and z are solved, from which an expenditure function can be established, which calculates the minimum expenditure required for a given level of utility:

$$E = E(p,U) \; . \qquad \text{(M.4)}$$

After a change in input prices from p to p', the *constant utility price index* is defined as:

$$I = \frac{E(\boldsymbol{p}',U_0)}{E(\boldsymbol{p},U_0)} \qquad \text{(M.5)}$$

where U_0 is the utility level in the initial (or 'base') period (Muellbauer, 1974).

This price index, I, does not reflect adjustments in the actual prices of inputs (p). Rather it is a single number, or scalar, that serves as a deflator, such as the GNP implicit price deflator, which is designed to reflect the value of common monetary units (e.g., the purchasing power of a dollar in real terms). In this sense, it is a cost of living index.[9]

One may notice that this cost of living index is closely related to the notion of compensating variation — the cost of living index being the ratio between $E(\boldsymbol{p}',U_0)$ and $E(\boldsymbol{p},U_0)$, and compensating variation being the difference (see Chapter 1).

Figure 3.4 provides an illustration of these concepts in goods (z)

Figure 3.4 Household production model: changes in the prices, or quality, of inputs

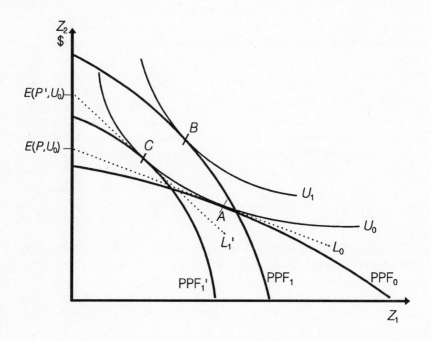

space. The initial income y, input prices p, and joint production function F, map out the initial production possibility frontier, denoted by PPF_0 in the figure. The maximization of utility is achieved at Point A, where the highest utility curve, U_0, intersects PPF_0. A shift in the prices of inputs, all else being equal, would generally lead to a uniquely different production possibility frontier, as indicated by PPF_1. After the shift, a new point of intersection is reached, B, at which a new level of utility is achieved, U_1.

In the context of Figure 3.4, the price indexing question, or compensating variation question, asks what the level of income should be that would bring the PPF back to the original utility curve. In other words, it asks for the level of income, given the new input prices, that would render PPF_1', where the new point of intersection, C, lies on the original utility curve. Hence, if the good z_2 is measured in dollar units, the expenditure levels appearing in Equation M.5 would correspond to the vertical intercepts of the shadow-price lines L_0 and L_1', as shown in Figure 3.4.

In the discussion thus far, no changes in quality have occurred. However, one could now use the same analysis to study the cost of living index when the quality of inputs change, instead of their prices. For instance, quality changes in the inputs could cause the same shift from PPF_0 to PPF_1, and consequently, render the same measurement of the cost of living index, but this time attributable to these quality changes. The connection between this household production model and the resource-cost definition now becomes more apparent. Since $E(p,U)$ is, in fact, the expenditure on inputs, and $I = E(p,U_0)/E(p',U_0)$ is the cost of living index, there is a one-to-one relationship between resource costs and the price index, or equivalently, a one-to-one relationship between resource costs and 'quality', if 'quality' is a measure of *the required change in the cost of living index that cannot be accounted for by changes that have occurred in prices*.

Of course, the quality measurement of a single input in this case would require that all other inputs remain the same in terms of quality, since the cost of living index is a single number. However, this *ceteris paribus* requirement is no different from the same *ceteris paribus* requirements that exist in other methods of quality measurement.

The key feature of the model that allows for the direct relationship between quality and resource cost is the absence of any 'intermediate utility' in the production process itself. That is, the producer has no utility, or psychological preferences, that extend beyond the pure maximization of profits. In many contexts, especially if actual households are the producers, this simplifying assumption is unrealistic. Nevertheless, in several instances it *is* realistic, as, for example, the situation in which an input that is basically a 'black box' in the eyes of the user becomes a *new and improved* black box.

On the other hand, there is an enormous difference between the household production model of quality measurement and the conventional resource-cost model. Surprisingly, this difference appears to be absent from the literature on quality measurement. In the household production model, changes in resource costs are associated with quality changes in inputs. In the conventional resource-cost model, *changes in resource costs are attributed to quality changes in outputs*. Not only does this distinction reflect different interpretations of quality change, but it implies completely opposite effects on the cost of living index. For example, if the quality of an input increases, all else being equal, then, according to the household production model, the cost of living index has gone down — a dollar is now worth more than it had been worth before, because more output can now be produced per dollar. Moreover, a change of this kind could be viewed as a costless quality change, as discussed in the first chapter. Yet, in the resource-cost method, suppose the same quality improvement of an input coincides with a superficial change in the name of the output, which calls for an assessment of the new output's quality. For example, a new, higher-quality tomato that contains less water per unit weight is developed and used in the production of tomato sauce; and the sauce itself is sold as a new type of specialty product. Due to the lower resource costs of producing the output (i.e., fewer tomatoes per unit weight), the resource-cost method would conclude that the quality of the output is *lower* than the quality of other goods of the same type! The cost of living index would then be adjusted *upward*, based on the conclusion that one now receives less quality per dollar spent, under the assumption that the new tomato sauce is of lower quality.

In conclusion, the household production model lends considerable support to the concept that quality can, under special circumstances, be measured on the basis of resource costs. However, that change in quality refers to the quality of inputs, not the quality of outputs. In this sense, the household production model contradicts, rather than supports, the conventional resource-cost approach to quality measurement.

Quality versus Changes in Taste

Fisher and Shell (1972) make several important contributions to the theory of quality measurement under the price index framework. One of them is their work involving the idea that quality, relative prices and the cost of living index, cannot be measured accurately between two time periods, at least in theory. The reason is that tastes could change over time, making the measurement of any such changes ambiguous. They conclude that all questions involving quality, prices and the cost of living index must be raised in reference to a single set of preferences existing at a single point in time (Fisher and Shell, 1972, pp. ix-6). Another important contribution of theirs is a discussion of the ambiguity of quality change when the quality of one good depends on that of another (Fisher and Shell, 1972, pp. 26-8) (see Chapter 7).

Their greatest contribution, however, may be their theoretical treatment of quality change and taste change. For changes in tastes, Fisher and Shell (1972, pp. 8-12) define a 'good augmenting' taste change as occurring 'if and only if the preference maps can be represented by a utility function whose i^{th} argument is a function of the amount of purchases of the ith good and of the level of some taste change parameter'. That is, utility is defined as:

$$U = U(bz_1, z_2, \ldots, z_n) \qquad \text{(F.1)}$$

where z_i is the quantity of good i consumed, and b, which equals 1 at time 0, represents a taste change.

With y_m denoting the minimum income required to maintain a constant level of utility, U_0, Fisher and Shell explore how y_m changes in relation to U_0. They prove that under standard conditions:

$$\left(\frac{\partial y_m}{\partial b}\right) = \frac{-p_1 z_1}{b} \qquad \text{(F.2)}$$

where p_1 is the price of the first good.

As mentioned in Chapter 1, however, the Fisher-Shell definition of taste change could include actual changes in the characteristics of the good, and at the same time, not include changes in people's preferences toward goods with identical characteristics. Normally, one would think of this type of change as a change in *quality*, rather than *tastes*, whereas in the theoretical framework of Fisher and Shell (1972, p. 8) the determining factor would be 'the relevant axis on the indifference map'.

Consequently, under an alternative perspective, if the change reflected by the parameter b does reflect a physical change in the good, rather than a cognitive change in the consumer, then the negative of the left-hand side of Equation F.2 could serve as a measure of the change in *quality*. In this sense, $-(\partial y_m/\partial b)/z_1$ would represent quality change per unit of z_1 and per change in b, and:

$$-\left(\frac{\partial y_m}{\partial b}\right)\left(\frac{1}{z_1 p_1}\right) = \frac{1}{b} \tag{F.3}$$

would represent the *proportional* quality change per unit, i.e., the quality change per unit as a proportion of the value of each unit. Quite simply, the larger b is, the smaller the proportional quality change per change in b, as one would expect (see Chapter 1).

In addition, Fisher and Shell provide a more general, and quite useful, formulation for what they, themselves, regard as quality change. In this case, the 'b' parameter, now an indicator of quality, lies outside the individual quantities of goods in the utility function:

$$U = U(z_1, z_2, \ldots, z_n, b) \ . \tag{F.4}$$

Again, $b = 1$ represents the initial condition of no quality change.

Fisher and Shell examine the idea of measuring quality change as the change in the price of the first good, p_1, to p_1^*, such that:

$$y_m(p_1^*, p_2, \ldots, p_n, 1) = y_m(p_1, \ldots, p_n, b) \ . \tag{F.5}$$

In other words, an increase in b would be associated with a decrease in p_1^*, and the change in quality would be viewed in terms of the difference (or quotient) between p_1 and p_1^*. However, the difference between p_1 and p_1^* would not reflect the usual definition of quality change, but rather, an approximation to quality change that would tend to be an underestimate. The reason is that an important aspect of quality improvement is that consumers will tend to purchase more of the improved good. Therefore, the compensating variation of the quality improvement will be greater than the product of the initial amount of the first good times the difference in the compensating price. For example, looking back at Figure 1.2 in Chapter 1, the difference between p_1 and p_1^* would reflect the difference between Points A and B. However, quality improvement in the usual sense would measured as the difference between Points B and C.

Nevertheless, their interpretation, or approximation, of quality change is worth considering. In particular, Fisher and Shell (1972, pp. 28-31) focus on the relation:

$$\frac{\partial p_1^*}{\partial b} = \frac{\partial y_m / \partial b}{\partial y_m / \partial p_1^*} . \qquad \text{(F.6)}$$

They find that, at $b = 1$,

$$\frac{\partial p_1^*}{\partial b} = \frac{-p_1 u_b}{z_1 u_1} . \qquad \text{(F.7)}$$

However, within this construct, the derivative of utility with respect to b, u_b, is extremely difficult to interpret intuitively. Unlike the placement of b in Equation F.1, the placement of b in Equation F.4 gives little meaning to what the parameter actually does, or reflects. In fact, it is said to reflect quality improvement in the first good, but nothing in terms of the mathematics precludes it from reflecting quality improvement in any other good, or in any combination of goods.

Fisher and Shell remedy this problem by determining the 'necessary and sufficient condition for $\partial p_1^* / \partial b$ to be independent of $x_2, ..., x_n$':

$$U(z,b) = F(g(z_1,b),z_2,...,z_n) \equiv F(g^*(z_1,b)z_1,z_2,...,z_n) \qquad \text{(F.8)}$$

where '$g(z_1,b) \equiv g^*(z_1,b)z_1$ for ease of interpretation'.[10] Note the similarity between Equation F.8 and Equation F.1. This similarity between the equations mirrors the conceptual similarity between quality change and changes in tastes. As already discussed, quality change will always be associated with an actual, physical change in the good or service. Nevertheless, certain taste changes, such as those based on the reinterpretation of the benefits of a good, could be equivalent to actual quality changes in terms of their effect on consumer behaviour.

On the basis of Equation F.8, Fisher and Shell develop a formal definition of the condition known as the 'pure repackaging case' (see Chapter 2). This condition applies if $\partial p_1^*/\partial b$ is independent of all z_i, including z_1, which occurs when:

$$g(z_1,b) = z_1 h(b) \qquad \text{or} \qquad g^*(z_1,b) = h(b) \qquad\qquad \text{(F.9)}$$

for some function h. This definition is entirely consistent with the intuition underlying the repackaging case.

Current Methods of Quality Measurement for Price Indices

Many conventional methods of quality estimation are employed by the US Department of Labor, Bureau of Labor Statistics (BLS) in its calculation of the Consumer Price Index (CPI) and Producer Price Index (PPI). These measures also serve as input into the calculation of the GNP Implicit Price Deflator, by the US Department of Commerce, Bureau of Economic Analysis (BEA). Because the present study is conducted on consumer goods, the focus of this discussion will be on the CPI.

The CPI is not designed to measure quality change, *per se*, but serves as a cost of living index. In theory, a cost of living index 'reflects the ratio of the wealth required to attain a given indifference curve of the intertemporal utility function in alternative price situations' (Pollak, 1989, p. 53). However, in practice, the sensitivity of that indifference curve to actual changes in goods may be difficult for one to ascertain, and this difficulty has direct bearing on the measurement of quality.

For instance, if the average loaf of bread improves in flavour, this change should theoretically be interpreted as a quality improvement, because, all else being equal, less wealth would then be needed to maintain the same level of utility. On the other hand, there is a tendency for the CPI to remain unchanged in this case. The reason is that changes in the price of bread would tend to be recognized only when the price per pound changes. In this way, for example, the CPI would better reflect the ability of minimum-wage earners to afford a loaf of bread in general, regardless of any improvement in flavour. Otherwise, the CPI would be adjusted so that less bread (and/or other items) would be purchased, to compensate for the added utility of its improved flavour.[11]

In the CPI calculation, BLS employs one of five approaches in accounting for new items: direct comparison, deletion, direct quality adjustment, linking with an overlap price, and linking without an overlap price. In direct comparison, the characteristics of a new item are considered to be close enough to those of an old item so that no quality change is warranted (US Dept of Labor, 1989, p. 169). Similarly, in deletion the price of a new item that is similar to an old item, and not considered to possess any quality improvements, is 'deleted', i.e., removed from the sample (Gordon, 1990, pp. 85-6).

In direct quality adjustment, standardized methods are employed, such as the evaluation of food prices on a per ounce basis, and adjustments of apartment rents to account for changes in the utilities paid by landlords. It is in this group of methods that resource-cost measures are applied. For example, for cars, direct quality adjustment is based on 'costs in manufacturing plus the established manufacturer and retail markup' (US Dept of Labor, 1989, p. 169). However, BLS also states, 'Quality adjustments . . . exclude changes in style or appearance, . . . unless these features have been offered as options and purchased by customers. Also, new technology sometimes results in better quality at the same or reduced cost. . . . In such cases, it is ignored' (US Dept of Labor, 1989, p. 169).

Hence, from a policy perspective, the resource-cost interpretation of quality change has been used to justify the current utilization of resource costs as indicators of quality by the Bureau of Labor Statistics, under the advisement of the Bureau of Economic Analysis. In effect, the resource-cost approach has been well established in the governmental bureaucracy, which could account for much of the support (either direct or indirect) that the approach has currently received in the literature.

In price-linking, BLS calculates the base-period price of a new item, P_a^*, where 'a' denotes the base period and '$*$' a new item. The base-period price is an indicator of quality, in the sense that it is a price that has been adjusted to account for pure price effects. This price is calculated as the product of its current price, P_t^* and the ratio of the base price to the current price of an old item that can serve as a substitute, P_a/P_t (US Dept of Labor, 1989, p. 169). In linking without overlap prices, the same method is employed, except that P_t is not available and is estimated from the prices of similar items.[12]

THE THEORETICAL DEFINITION OF QUALITY UNDER THE QUALITY CHANGE FRAMEWORK

Lancaster regards quality as inherently an ordinal measure. He does suggest, however, that under the right conditions a cardinal measure of quality can be developed, and can be useful depending on how it is applied. He writes:

> We shall take the initial step of assuming that the ordering of . . . goods in terms of quality is a well-defined operation for an individual consumer . . . However, we can also presume that an individual would be unable to answer . . . 'By how much is the quality of one variety greater than that of the other?', and thus must regard perceived quality as inherently ordinal . . . we conclude that . . . the terms 'measuring quality' or 'measuring quality change' refer to the construction of some numerical index with the following properties:
> 1. that it correctly ranks goods varieties in terms of quality whenever an unambiguous ranking exists,
> 2. that it measures something well-defined and useful in the context to which the index is applied.
> (Lancaster 1977, pp. 157—8)

Given this definition, Lancaster presents an illuminating model on quality change, based on consumer preferences and the set of characteristics associated with goods in a particular group. He assumes that goods that are not in this group do not share any of the same characteristics. He also assumes that the utility function is separable between the group of goods with specific characteristics and the composite of all other goods.[13] That is:

$$U = U[u(z), v(s)] \tag{L.1}$$

where z is an m-vector of characteristics $(z_1, ..., z_m)$ of the goods in the group and s is a scalar that represents the sum of all other goods. Relative prices are assumed to be constant outside the group, with P representing the total price (or expenditure) for goods outside the group. By substitution, utility can then be expressed as:

$$U = U[u(z), v(I-P)] \tag{L.2}$$

where I is total income.

Now suppose there is a change in the vector of characteristics of the goods in the group, from z to $z+dz$, and one could find a new expenditure level for the group, $P+dP$, which would leave utility unchanged. In this framework, if the change in z increases utility, then dP would be negative in order to bring utility back to its original value. One now has:

$$dU = U_1 \sum u_i dz_i - U_2 v' dP = 0 \tag{L.3}$$

which implies,

$$dP = \frac{U_1 \sum u_i dz_i}{U_2 v'} . \tag{L.4}$$

Lancaster (1977) refers to dP/P as a measure of quality change, on the basis of an 'expenditure equivalent index'. In addition, if y is the vector of shadow prices on the characteristics of goods in the group ($y'z = P$), then before the quality change occurred the consumer had solved the problem:

$$\text{Max } U[u(z), v(s)], \quad \text{subject to} \quad y'z + s = I . \tag{L.5}$$

By differentiation for each element of z, and then substitution, Lancaster finds the final 'expenditure-equivalent index of quality change', or $\mathcal{L} = dP/P$ to be:

$$\mathcal{L} = \frac{\sum u_i dz_i}{\sum u_i z_i} . \tag{L.6}$$

As one might expect, the change in quality is proportional to the hypothetical change in expenditure that would be required to maintain the same level of utility. That hypothetical change in expenditure is proportional to the relative change in utility, which is the sum of the 'utiles' attributable to each of the characteristics.

Note that the separability of the utility function led, eventually, to a final equation that does not involve any goods that are outside the group.

One aspect of the above analysis that might appear limiting is the fact that the quality change does not involve any new characteristics, only a different set of weights placed on the same characteristics. On the other hand, there is nothing in the analysis that precludes there being a zero weight on characteristics in the first period. In that sense, new characteristics are allowed.

A greater and more obvious limitation in the analysis is its reliance on a utility function that could be difficult to estimate empirically. In fact, given that individuals have different utility functions, the very meaning of quality change in the context of an entire population becomes cloudy. Perhaps a 'population utility function' could be employed which would represent the sum of the utility functions of individuals weighted by their incomes. The maximization problem, however, would no longer be straightforward, especially in view of the fact that quality change would now be a function of the distribution of income. These issues are brought out by Rosen's (1974) model, which is discussed below.

On the other hand, the notion of quality change being based on some average of individual tastes, weighted by income, should not be particularly surprising. As remarked earlier, quality will be regarded as an economic concept that is quite distinct from any notions of 'ultimate value'. Hence, the quality of a good will always have to depend on the circumstances surrounding it. For instance, the quality of a house and an acre of land would be meaningless without any consideration given to its location. Similarly, the quality of a lake that is perfect for sailing would depend on the number of people in the area who can afford (and would buy) sailing boats.

Lancaster (1977) shows that the expenditure-equivalent index in Equation L.6 is also a 'quantity-equivalent' index. That is, he first considers the original specification of characteristics to be magnified by $d\beta$, i.e., $dz = z \cdot d\beta$. He then finds that, if the additional utility derived from that magnification is equal to the additional utility derived from the new specification, then $d\beta$ would represent a quantity-equivalent index. In other words, equal changes in utility imply:

$$\sum u_i dz_i = d\beta \sum u_i z_i \qquad \text{(L.7)}$$

which implies,

$$dβ = \frac{\sum u_i dz_i}{\sum u_i z_i}$$ (L.8)

which is equal to $\mathcal{L}$ in Equation L.6. In addition, he notes that his measurement of quality change is also 'identical with that given by a fixed-weight index of characteristics with weights proportional to the $u_i's'$ (pp. 164-5). Thus, the quality change index first shown in Equation L.6 and again in Equation L.8 is, simultaneously, an expenditure-equivalent index, a quantity-equivalent index, and a fixed-weight index.

Nevertheless, Lancaster (1977, pp. 164-5) cites several problems that could arise in the use of the index in actual practice. One of these has already been discussed — its reliance on identical preferences. Another reflects the real-world limitations of analyses based on first derivatives: '[t]he change in characteristics per unit of the good should be small (but characteristics need not change in the same ratio).' However, two other problems that he mentions are particularly troublesome:

[1] We are concerned with a single good which changes in specification and which is consumed by itself without cooperating inputs or combinations with other goods. . . . The good belongs to a separable group, one that is separable both in terms of the consumption technology . . . and the utility function.[14]
[2] The prices of goods outside the group do not change, nor is there quality change anywhere except for the good under investigation. (Lancaster 1977, pp. 164-5)

In contrast, one advantage of Lancaster's framework is that *it need not apply to explicitly defined characteristics*. Rather, in an economy in which there are several different goods, each one of those goods could be interpreted as being an implicit characteristic of the larger group. For example, if there are a variety of food products, then each type of product, such as beef, chicken and vegetables could also be thought of as characteristics of the 'typical meal', which could be derived as the aggregate of all food products, divided by the total number of meals (see Chapter 2). Hence, if z^g denotes a vector of the quantities of particular goods in a group, and $u(z^g)$ is the same as $u(z)$ above except that it is a function of z^g, then a symmetric analysis would imply:

$$\mathscr{L} = \frac{\sum u_i \, dz_i^g}{\sum u_i z_i^g} \qquad\qquad (L.9)$$

where $\mathscr{L}$ continues to reflect proportional changes in the quality of the group. As shown in Chapter 6, this extension of Lancaster's quality change index could be useful as a tool for studying evolutionary trends in goods and services.

Along similar lines, Griliches (1971b, p.6) estimates a change in the 'quality-of-characteristics index', defined by:

$$\frac{dQ}{Q} = \sum w_j \frac{dq_j}{q_j} \qquad\qquad (G.1)$$

where 'q_j is the level of the jth characteristic, and w_j is the value share of that characteristic in the total price'. This measure of quality change can then be related to price indexation where the 'pure price change' for good i, $d\pi_i/\pi_i$, can be defined as the difference between the observed price and the change in quality, i.e.,

$$\frac{d\pi_i}{\pi_i} \equiv \frac{dP_i}{P_i} - \frac{dQ_i}{Q_i} \,. \qquad\qquad (G.2)$$

Hence, the pure price index for an entire class of commodities can be calculated as:

$$\frac{d\pi}{\pi} = \sum v_i \frac{d\pi_i}{\pi_i} \qquad\qquad (G.3)$$

where v_i is the value share of the ith model. Griliches's approach is classified here as being within the quality change framework, rather than the price index framework, because of his application of hedonic methods for solving Equation G.1. Examples of these hedonic methods are described below.[15]

HEDONIC MODELS UNDER THE QUALITY CHANGE FRAMEWORK

Much has been written on the topic of hedonic price indices, although there appears to have been considerably more interest in it in the 1950s and 1960s than between 1970 and the present. Griliches explains the topic as follows:

> The 'hedonic,' or, using a less value-loaded word, characteristics approach to the construction of price indexes is based on the empirical hypothesis (or research strategy) which asserts that the multitude of models and varieties of a particular commodity can be comprehended in terms of a much smaller number of characteristics or basic attributes of a commodity such as 'size,' 'power,' 'trim,' and 'accessories,' and that viewing the problem this way will reduce greatly the magnitude of the pure new commodity or 'technical change' problem, since most (though not all) new 'models' of commodities may be viewed as a new combination of 'old' characteristics. (Griliches 1971b, p. 4)

He remarks that the hypothesized relationship between characteristics and prices need not be linear, and that '[m]ost of the investigators settle after some experimentation for a semi-logarithmic relationship . . . implying a rising supply price per characteristic unit' (pp. 5-6).

Differences across Consumers and Producers

Rosen (1974) presents a thorough and illuminating analysis of quality change when consumers and producers differ among themselves. The model is similar to Lancaster's in the sense that it involves two groups of goods. The first, z, is described by the vector of characteristics $(z_1, ..., z_n)'$, and the second represents the composite of all other goods. As in the Lancaster model, no symbol is needed for the quantity of the second group, whose units are normalized so that the quantity purchased is equal to expenditure. That is, quality change is allowed only in the first group of goods, as reflected by its vector of characteristics. In addition, the consumer is assumed to purchase only one unit of the quality-changing good, although Rosen later relaxes this assumption.

In the model, the consumer maximizes:

$$U = U(I\text{-}P,z) \tag{R.1}$$

where I is income, and P is expenditure *on the quality-changing good* (as opposed to the composite good in Lancaster's model). If consumers differ in their levels of income, but have the same utility function, then a bid function for the ith consumer would be given by:

$$B(z^*, U^*, I) = P(z^*) \qquad \text{(R.2)}$$

where B is the maximum amount that consumer is willing to pay for an additional unit of z, and the asterisk denotes optimal levels of U and z when U is maximized. Rosen (1974, p. 38) notes that B is concave in z, following from strict concavity of U.

If one of the characteristics, such as z_1, is now allowed to vary, then the bid function for a given level of utility would be represented by a curve in P, z_1 space. In effect, this function would constitute a utility curve that maps out equivalent tradeoffs (in terms of utility) between (1) a higher cost of purchasing a unit of z and (2) a greater quantity of z_1 acquired in that purchase, all else being equal (including the prices of the other characteristics). Across individual consumers, U^* would vary monotonically with I, and thus, the existing diversity in income could be translated into a diversity in U^*. This enables us to write the indifference curve:

$$B^j = B^j(z_1, z_2^*, ..., z_n^*; U_j^*) \qquad \text{(R.3)}$$

for the jth consumer at utility U_j^*.

As Rosen (1974, pp. 38—9) states, in this context $\partial B^j/\partial z_i$, 'is the marginal rate of substitution between z_1 and money, or the implicit valuation the consumer places on z_1 at a given utility index and income'. It follows that utility is maximized when consumers purchase goods for which their B^j curves are tangent to the curve $P(z_1, z_2^*, ..., z_n^*)$, which is the market price for the good as a function of z_1. (See Figure 3.5.)

As shown in Figure 3.5, an analogous situation exists on the supply side, where $P(z_1, z_2^*, ..., z_n^*)$ can be interpreted as the envelope of the offer curves for the differentiated products of individual firms. This envelope traces out the minimum marginal prices of the good with respect to z_1, and the marginal rate of transformation among different product varieties. Each offer curve, represented in the figure as G^1 or G^2, is a function of z_1, optimal levels of the other characteristics $(z_2^*, ..., z_n^*)$, and an expected profit

Figure 3.5 Rosen's model of unequal consumers and unequal producers

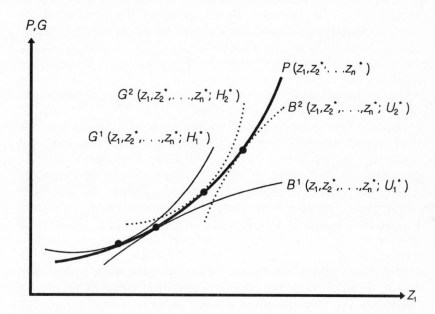

level for that firm, H^*.

Rosen uses this framework to raise important suspicions about the relevance of 'hedonic prices'. He writes:

> *What Do Hedonic Prices Mean?* . . . In equilibrium, a buyer and seller are perfectly matched when their respective value and offer functions 'kiss' each other, with the common gradient at that point given by the gradient of the market clearing implicit price function $P(z)$. Therefore, observations $P(z)$ represent a joint envelope of a family of offer functions. An envelope function by itself reveals nothing about the underlying members that generate it . . . Hence, estimated hedonic price-characteristics functions typically identify neither demand nor supply. In fact, those observations are described by a joint-envelope function and cannot by themselves identify the structure of consumer preferences and technologies that generate them.[16] (Rosen 1974, pp. 44-54)

This interpretation of his theoretical results is highly relevant, and does raise a legitimate concern regarding the use of hedonic methods in quality measurement.

On the other hand, one should be careful not to read too much into the above findings. As argued extensively in this and other chapters, the 'underlying structure' of the technologies of production have limited bearing, to begin with, on the *quality* of goods and services, if one adopts the user-value perspective on quality change. As for the structure of consumer preferences, one should note that the 'bid function', which is based on the marginal substitution of goods at a constant level of utility, is simply one aspect of the 'structure of consumer preferences' — hedonic prices reflect other aspects of that structure.

It should be obvious that hedonic prices do not capture the kind of information that would be required for one to understand fully the supply and demand for a particular product. Yet, this is not their purpose. What Rosen refers to as 'the structure of consumer preferences' could, conceivably, be analysed through an analysis of survey data on consumer behaviour. However, consumer behaviour would be meaningless in the measurement of quality unless it could be linked to the physical characteristics of goods.

Furthermore, in all areas of scientific inquiry, there are strong reasons for rejecting the idea that, because an 'envelope of curves' represents only an infinitesimal amount of information about certain underlining phenomena, that envelope itself is unimportant. One could argue that all aspects of observed human behaviour, of which economics is a part, are, themselves, circumstantial aspects of much more complex processes. In particular, observed economic trends could be described as merely 'envelopes' in the space of variables that influence behaviour. What is important, then, is not whether something is circumstantial — ultimately everything is circumstantial. The question that must be answered is what is meant by *quality*, and only from there can a determination be made of the relevance of hedonic prices.[17]

Empirical Regression Analyses using Time Series Data

As early as 1939, Court combined cross sectional data on the characteristics of a good with time series data on prices, in order to separate the pure price effect from the price changes attributable to differences in characteristics. In this approach, a regression equation is considered of the form:

$$\ln p_{it} \; = \; a \; + \; \sum_k b_k x_{kit} \; + \; v_t \; + \; e_i \tag{E.1}$$

where x_{ikt} is a measure of the kth characteristic of good i, at time t. The time dummy, v_t would be estimated for each time period, where observations would be made across time, t, different goods, i, and different characteristics, k. The parameter e_i is a separate constant for each good, and is called by Griliches (1971b, pp. 7-8) the 'model' effect[18], in that it is 'the effect of other left-out qualities, assumed to be independent of calendar time and the other xs'.

Another empirical approach to the measurement of quality change involves the prices of used goods.[19] For example, Cagan considers a model, j, of a good (a car in particular), and the vintage, or 'model year', v. He then has:

$$P_{tvj} = P_t Q_{tvj} \tag{E.2}$$

where P_{tvj} is the specific price of model j, of vintage v, at time t. P_t is the average price per unit of quality, and Q_{tvj} is a measure of quality which is still embodied in the model at time t. In addition, he uses a depreciation factor which he assumes to be independent of the vintage and calendar year (t), but not independent of the model (j) and the age ($h = t\text{-}v$). In other words:

$$Q_{(t+1)vj} = d_{hj} Q_{tvj} \tag{E.3}$$

where d_{hj} denotes the depreciation factor, equivalent to one minus the rate of depreciation. Furthermore, for any given vintage of a prior year, v minus 1, the quality of a newer vintage of the same model one year later, v, can be expressed as:

$$Q_{tvj} = T_v Q_{t-1,v-1} \exp(u_{vj}) \; . \tag{E.4}$$

That is, the quality change in a new model can be regarded as a function of two separable components: an average component attributable to all goods of the same vintage, T_v; and a random component attributable to the vintage and the specific model, $\exp(u_{vj})$.

With regard to Equation E.4, Griliches (1971b, p. 9) remarks,

'This is a strong assumption about the character of technical or quality change, stating that any new version of model j can be expressed as so many units more or less than the old version of model j, this premium once established being fixed and independent of everything else.' However, the average improvement factor, T_v, need not be a function of other factors, that is, one could argue that other factors could be accounted for, which would reduce the error term, $\exp(u_{vj})$.

Griliches (1971b, p. 10) suggests that, from the above equations, one can estimate a log-linear equation for the change in price that occurs with each new vintage:

$$\ln P_{tvj} - \ln P_{t(v-1)j} \;=\; \ln T_v + \ln d_{hj} + u_{vj} - u_{v-1,j} \;. \qquad \text{(E.5)}$$

This price change would be attributable to technical changes in the quality of the goods. Unfortunately, as Griliches notes, there is an empirical problem of separating out the effects of quality improvement from the effects of depreciation.

A unique feature of the Cagan approach is that it does not involve specified characteristics. He assumes that characteristics do change from one vintage to another, and that they are different across models. In other words, his study makes use of the idea that one need not measure changes in characteristics in order to know that they occur. One can, alternatively, measure the effect of their occurrence without having to calculate the specific contribution made by each. As Griliches (1971b, p. 10) remarks, 'The major advantage of using secondhand market prices to measure quality change lies in freeing us from the necessity of choosing and specifying a limited list of commodity characteristics and estimating their relative contributions. Such lists are never complete and such estimates are never perfect.' In this respect, Cagan's model could be classified a price-linking approach.

In the above-mentioned empirical approaches, the current prices of goods are either: decomposed in terms of values attributable to specified characteristics, or compared to the current prices of used goods with the same characteristics. The first case could be regarded as an 'explicit analysis' of characteristics; the second as 'implicit analysis'. In an implicit analysis, of course, instruments other than characteristics, such as depreciation, must be utilized in order to isolate, and remove, a pure price effect.

Robert Hall (1971) performs an experiment that is similar to

Cagan's, but in addition to using depreciation as an anchor against a pure price effect, he also compares the prices of vintages that have the same levels of characteristics. He argues that with depreciation as the only anchor, there is an 'arbitrary normalization' due to a priori assumptions about the depreciation rate. With the additional information obtained from vintages having the same characteristics, those assumptions would not be necessary. Hall remarks:

> If all the characteristics are the same for two different vintages, then the existence of the functional relation requires that the quality index be the same for those two vintages. . . . The hedonic information that two vintages have the same efficiency embodied in them is exactly a normalization of the kind needed to estimate an index of embodied technical change or quality for all vintages. (Hall 1971, p. 259)

Hall conducted his study on half-ton pick-up trucks, in which he compared two makes, Ford and Chevrolet, from 1955 to 1966. Based on seven characteristics of these vehicles, as observed in the *Used Car Guide*, he estimated the pairs of vintages that were the same for each make. He then performed two types of regression experiments, in which he used this information as restrictions. One of the experiments was analogous to Cagan's, and the other analogous to Court's in which prices were regressed onto characteristics.

Following the early recognition received by the hedonic price studies in the 1960s and 1970s, numerous other studies have been conducted.[20] While nearly all of the earlier studies were on durable goods, many of the more recent studies have been on other types of goods and services.[21]

Conjoint Analysis

Conjoint analysis is a technique used by market analysts and economists to assess consumers' preferences towards goods or services. It involves the examination of a specific good or service, and the identification of varieties, or 'items', with different characteristics. Consumer preferences are then evaluated as a function of these characteristics. While conjoint studies have appeared extensively in the literature on marketing and applied statistics, the economic concepts underlying their use follow directly from microeconomic theory. In this sense, conjoint analysis is analogous to hedonic pricing methods of quality measurement: both employ regression procedures,[22] where coefficients reflect the influence of characteristics on quality.

The main difference between the two methods is that conjoint analysis does not use prices as a direct indicator of quality. Rather, it requires a survey of consumers' willingness to pay for hypothetical items, or 'choice sets', on the basis of rankings or rating scales. When the price of a good does appear in a conjoint survey, it serves only as an additional attribute of the good in question, that is, as an additional consideration in the participant's ranking of choices. Another difference between the two methods is that conjoint analysis often examines large numbers of categorical variables (or 'dummy variables' in a regression analysis), and not many continuous variables.

In both hedonic and conjoint theory, consumer utility is the concept that underlies revealed preferences, and therefore, estimates are made of the 'part-worth utilities', or marginal rates of substitution, for characteristics.[23] However, because conjoint analysis treats price as an attribute of the good, the relation between part-worth utility and revealed preference is not as clear as it is in hedonic analysis.

To expand on the conjoint framework, one could consider Lancaster's (1977) model for measuring changes in quality. A necessary condition for this model is that utility be separable between the good in question and the 'composite good' that represents all other goods. One could write:

$$U = U[u(c), v(s)] \tag{C.1}$$

where c is a vector of characteristics of the good, and s is a scalar representing the composite of all other goods.

In conjoint analysis, as in Lancaster's model, the consumer is required to make judgments based on the purchase of one, and only one, unit of the good. Thus, if s is measured in dollar units, y is the consumer's income, and p is the price of the good, we have $s = y$ minus p, which implies:

$$U = U[u(c), v(y-p)] \; . \tag{C.2}$$

As shown in the Lancaster model (Lancaster 1991, pp. 88-9), a change in utility can be evaluated as a function of changes in the characteristics *and* price of the good in question:

$$dU = U_1 \sum u_i dc_i - U_2 v' dp \,.$$ (C.3)

Hence, this equation can be used to approximate part-worth utilities in a conjoint analysis.

Let r be the rating scale that reveals a consumer's preferences, which is obtained during the survey. Under the simplifying assumption that U_2 and v' are constant, there is a linear relationship between utility and price, all else being equal.[24] Let r be normalized, from the design of the conjoint experiment, to have the value of 0 for the least-desired choice and 100 for the most-desired choice. It follows that r could be expressed as:

$$r = 100 \frac{U - U^0}{U^* - U^0}$$ (C.4)

where U^0 is the utility of the least-preferred choice and U^* of the most-preferred choice. This implies:

$$dr = \frac{100}{U^* - U^0} (U_1 \sum u_i dc_i - U_2 v' dp)$$

(C.5)

$$= \frac{100}{U^* - U^0} \sum U_1 u_i dc_i + \gamma dp$$

where γ is a negative constant. However, U_1 and u_i remain as functions of $u(c)$ and c, respectively.

The validity of a linear regression analysis would require constant marginal utilities of characteristics, i.e., constant values of U_1 and u_i. Under this assumption, and the fact that r is normalized to equal 0 for the least-preferred choice (r^0), one has the following regression equation for the jth choice set of attributes:

$$r_j = k dr_j + \mu_j \quad \{+ r^0 = 0\}$$

(C.6)

$$= (1 \; C_j. \; p_j) \begin{pmatrix} \alpha \\ \beta \\ \gamma \end{pmatrix} + \mu_j$$

where r_j is the rating for the jth choice set, k and a are constants, μ_j is the error term, ß is the vector of coefficients on characteristics, and $(1 \ C_{j,} \ p_j)$ is the row of exogenous variables. Finally, if r is the vector of all ratings in the conjoint data set, one can write:

$$r = (1 \ C \ p) \begin{pmatrix} a \\ \beta \\ \gamma \end{pmatrix} + \mu \qquad \text{(C.7)}$$

where 1 is the vector of 1s, C the matrix of characteristics across all choice sets, p the vector of prices, and u the vector of error terms.

To estimate changes in the quality of the jth choice set, one could rewrite Equation C.5 as:

$$dr_j = \sum_i \beta_i dC_{ij} + \gamma dp_j . \qquad \text{(C.8)}$$

This equation can now be used to answer the following question: if the characteristics of the jth item change, then by how much would its price have to change to leave the consumer indifferent between the current situation and the prior one? As discussed in Chapter 1, the answer to this question is the change in quality that has occurred as a result of the change in characteristics.

In the context of Equation C.8, dp_j now becomes the dependent variable and dr_j is set to zero. It follows that a proportional change in quality, q, could be defined as:

$$q \equiv \frac{dp_j}{p_j} = \frac{- \sum_i \beta_i dC_{ji}}{\gamma p_j} . \qquad \text{(C.9)}$$

With ß and γ estimated through the regression analysis of Equation C.7, the index of quality change in Equation C.9 can be approximated by substitution of these parameters. Hence, conjoint analysis provides a direct method for the measurement of a relative quality index.

The experimental, factorial design of conjoint analyses is often based on a full profile approach, where survey participants rank choice sets containing values (or 'levels') for all of the attributes considered.   In addition, for purposes of feasibility, the factorial design is usually fractional, i.e., it does not include all possible combinations of attribute values.   This design is often orthogonal, which requires that 'each level of one factor occurs with each level of another factor with proportional frequencies' (Green, 1974, p. 63).   The advantage of orthogonal designs is that the main effects of any two factors are uncorrelated, which allows for the efficient utilization of a small number of choice sets.   Finally, for ease in the administration of the survey, a bridging technique is sometimes employed, in which participants first rank a subset of possible choice sets, and then receive additional choice sets to rank among the original ones.[25]

IMPLICIT VERSUS EXPLICIT MEASUREMENT OF QUALITY CHANGE

As mentioned above, an implicit method of quality measurement would be based on the 'before' and 'after' price of a good, as in the study by Cagan, while an explicit approach would assign particular values to specified characteristics.   In most cases, an explicit approach is a 'hedonic' approach, while an implicit approach is associated with general price indexing, or price linking. A symmetric distinction between implicit and explicit methods would also apply to the measurement of changes in production costs: in the implicit case, a comparison is made of 'before' and 'after' production costs, while in the explicit case calculations are made regarding the observed costs of factor inputs.

An implicit analysis of characteristics, because it does not require a particular functional relation between specific characteristics and their associated values, is much more inclusive with regard to the types of quality changes that could be observed. As Cagan remarks with regard to his study on cars and depreciation:

> The method captures elusive changes in style and workmanship as well as obvious engineering improvements, and captures in addition all the minor but collectively important changes affecting quality, which a specified list cannot hope to cover in full.   In short, any difference (real or fancied) in the characteristics of two secondhand cars (aside from age) that leads the average buyer to pay more for one is recorded as a difference in quality. This is far more inclusive than measures like the hedonic index can possibly be. (Cagan 1965, p. 218)

It could also be argued that, whatever functional form one estimates for the relationship between characteristics and quality, over the long run that functional form is bound to change, and new characteristics of goods will arise. Hence, all functions relating characteristics to quality would be more accurate *ex post*, whereby they could attribute a '0 weight' to all characteristics that have not yet come into being. However, such *ex post* functions, by definition, would have no predictive ability.

As an example of this limitation in the use of an explicit analysis, one could consider the findings obtained in this study on the quality of sofas. The sofas examined were those listed in the *Sears Catalog* from 1928 to 1993. In examining these items, one observes that the weight of a sofa constitutes a characteristic that is reflective of its quality. In 1928, for example, a typical sofa could easily weigh over 200 pounds. In that year its weight was probably proportional to its quality, all else being equal, because the sofa that weighed more tended to contain more springs and/or wood, and consequently, tended to be more durable. Thus, a typical household in 1928, when given a choice of purchasing one of two apparently equal sofas of the same price, but with different weights, would be inclined to choose the heavier sofa. Because both of these sofas would have weights in the neighborhood of 200 pounds, and would require at least two strong people to carry it, the additional weight of the heavier sofa would not represent an extra burden to the household.

Yet, while weight may be *positively* related to quality with regard to sofas in 1928, it is definitely *negatively* related to quality over the time span 1928-1993. This observation is supported by the dramatic decline in the average weight of sofas, coupled with data on relative prices suggesting that heavier sofas are not, in fact, preferred (see Chapter 4). Furthermore, it appears rather logical that, all else being equal, a *substantial* reduction in the weight of a sofa *would* represent a quality improvement. This is especially the case in more recent times, in which households are much more mobile, and the costs of hiring movers are probably higher in relation to average income levels.[26]

This example of the weight of sofas illustrates how the explicit approach to quality measurement could render questionable findings. If the hedonic approach were first used in 1928 to evaluate the quality of sofas on the basis of their weight, then by 1993 the conclusion of such an analysis would be that the quality of sofas has gone down dramatically over the 60-year interval. However, that conclusion would contradict the fact that consumers have, somewhere along the line, preferred sofas of lighter weight and expressed that preference in their purchasing behaviour. In fact, one could be more specific: the introduction of polyurethane foam to sofas provided the same support as springs, but with much less weight, thereby offering the convenience of lighter weight without any loss in comfort.

Nevertheless, a clear advantage does lie with the explicit approach, if one needs to estimate the quality of an item for which accurate prices do not already exist, or for which prices are not established within a competitive market in equilibrium. In such cases, one would need to impute the quality of that item on the basis of its measurable characteristics. This imputation could be achieved based on the part-worth utilities, or shadow prices, of the same characteristics found for other items that do have competitive market prices in equilibrium. Moreover, the relationship between specific, measurable characteristics and observed prices could represent an important discovery in itself, especially if this information is used by firms in their analysis of strategies involving the development of new products.

For the measurement of productivity, implicit and explicit methods exist as well. Productivity improvements in an implicit sense could be referred to as cost reduction, while those in an explicit sense could be referred to as process innovation. As an implicit approach, the measurement of cost reduction examines the effects of *all* sources of change in a firm's production costs, while the measurement of process innovation would tend to identify, and find patterns in, new capital equipment and operating procedures. Just as the implicit measurement of quality improvement allows for changes in aspects of a good or service that are not considered in product innovation, such as the artistic appeal of a good, the measurement of cost reduction allows for changes in the productive process that would not normally be considered in the study of process innovation. For example, any change in the work place that reduces the disutility of labour could be a form of cost reduction, because it could substitute for the higher real wages that might otherwise be needed to compensate a given level of productive labour. Hence, in a broad sense, process innovation represents a proper subset of cost reduction, and therefore, is more limited in accounting for relevant sources of change in production processes. On the other hand, as mentioned in reference to quality improvement, an explicit approach could be more useful to firms in enabling them to arrive at strategies for future development.

NOTES

1. In the discussion of resource-based measurement in Chapter I, the X axis of Figure 1.6 (computer computations) was referred to by Triplett (1983) as an 'output' characteristic. However, as argued in that chapter, the applicability, usefulness and intuitive appeal of this characteristic follows from the fact that it can also be interpreted as an 'input' characteristic.
2. If one finds this assumption disturbing, one could always think of the food item as a vitamin C tablet.
3. Note that these definitions of quality change are *distinctly different* from the hypothetical definitions discussed in Chapter I in relation to Figure 1.6. That is, Q_1 and Q_2 in Figure 1.6 do not correspond to Q_1 and Q_2 in Figure 3.1, even though both sets of definitions can be found in the same source, Triplett (1983).
4. See, for example, Triplett (1983), pp. 288-304.
5. Such wants and desires are not restricted to consumer goods. For instance, a producer could desire certain features in the capital equipment that he purchases.
6. See Louviere (1988), p. 36.
7. See Triplett (1983), for example.
8. Throughout this text, vectors will be represented by bold typeface, e.g., z will represent the vector $(z_1, z_2)'$.
9. See Pollak (1989), p. 6.
10. Fisher and Shell, p. 31. In this quotation, and throughout Fisher and Shell's book, an 'x' is used instead of a 'z'. The letter 'z' is used here for consistency with the notation used for other models in this chapter.
11. Actually, the underlying dilemma may be seen as deriving from the unequal distribution of income. That is, there is a trade-off between (1) the pleasure received by higher-income households and (2) the nutritional requirements received by lower-income households.
12. For more detailed discussion of the issues associated with current methods of quality measurement for price indices, see: Gordon (1990), Lichtenberg and Griliches (1989), Triplett (1971) and Young (1989). For a brief, but interesting, history of some of the economic ideas on the adjustment of prices to account for quality change, see Diewert (1990).
13. The assumption of characteristics not being shared among different groups of goods may not be as strong an assumption as might first appear. The reason is that characteristics can often be specified in terms of the goods to which they apply. For instance, cars and food often have the same characteristics with regard to colour, but the colour of cars is quite a different concept than the colour of food: the person who prefers the appearance of a red car over a brown car may also prefer the appearance of brown (well-done) meat over red (rare) meat. In this sense, 'red' and 'brown' are *not* characteristics that are shared between food and cars.
14. There were actually two conditions that have been combined here into one, in view of their similarity.
15. For an detailed discussion of Lancaster's model and its relation to hedonic price functions, see Lucas (1975).
16. For consistency with the rest of this text, the notation '$P(z)$' is used here in place of Rosen's notation '$p(z)$'.

17. For additional discussion of the Rosen model, see also Bartik (1987) and Brown and Rosen (1982).
18. 'Model' is used here to mean a product model, like the 'Model-T Ford', as opposed to an 'economic model'.
19. According to Griliches (1971b, pp. 8-9), this approach first appeared in a paper by Burstein (1961), but Cagan (1965) had the first actual estimates based on this approach.
20. Examples of early studies are Adelman and Griliches (1961); Dhrymes (1971); Griliches (1964); Kravis and Lipsey (1974); and Triplett (1969).
21. More recent studies on durable goods would include: Blomquist and Worley (1981); Cropper, Deck and McConnel (1988); Gordon (1990); Griliches (1990); Triplett (1986); Triplett (1989); and Triplett (1990). Those on other goods and services would include: Ethridge and Davis (1982) on cotton; McMillan, Reid and Gillen (1980) on 'the value of quiet'; Messonier and Luzar (1990) on private hunting land; Palmquist and Danielson (1989) on erosion control; and Wilson (1984) on barley.
22. Conjoint analysis could use analysis of variance as an alternative to regression analysis, but the two techniques are equivalent for all practical purposes. See Louviere (1988), p. 45, and Winer, Brown and Michels (1991), pp. 291-333.
23. See Louviere (1988), p. 25.
24. This assumption may not be needed, because any utility function can be adjusted by a monotonic transformation. Hence, the original utility function could have been normalized to have this property, provided U_2 and v' are monotonic functions in $v(s)$ and s, respectively.
25. See Green and Srinivasan (1990), p. 9. For recent examples of conjoint analysis, see Mackenzie (1990); Halbrendt, Wirth and Vaughn (1991); and Anderson and Bettencourt (1991).
26. Alternatively, the lower moving costs due to lighter sofas could, just as well, be interpreted as a cost reduction for the household.

4. A new approach toward measuring quality change

The chairmen, porters, and coal-heavers in London, and those unfortunate women who live by prostitution, the strongest men and the most beautiful women perhaps in the British dominions, are . . . from . . . Ireland, who are generally fed with this root [potatoes]. No food can afford a more decisive proof of its nourishing quality . . .

Adam Smith (1776)

INTRODUCTION

Many studies have measured how quality has changed over time for various goods and services. However, few studies have measured these changes for time periods of more than fifty years. Some goods simply do not remain on the market for fifty years without being replaced by uniquely different goods (e.g., high-fidelity record players were replaced by compact disk players). Those that do stay on the market often become much less important than they once were (e.g., electric typewriters). Still others undergo so many changes (e.g., cars) that any systematic assessment of their improvements for more than two or three decades is extremely difficult. Thus, in spite of the historical importance of long-run quality change, one can easy understand why quality change, as measured in economics, has remained a short-run phenomenon.

This chapter will present the alternative view that quality change can be studied in a historical or evolutionary context, across several decades, and perhaps even centuries. This alternative view rests upon two central ideas. First, categories of goods based on their function can be established, so that quality improvement can be interpreted as broad changes within a given category. Two categories of this kind used in the present study are first, window fans and air conditioners, and second, cameras, movie cameras and camcorders. That is, an air conditioner is interpreted as a quality improvement over a fan, and a camcorder a quality improvement over a household movie camera. Secondly, at any point in time, the quality of a category of goods can be approximated by the quality of a specific good within that category, designated as the 'representative good'.

This representative-good approach (RGA) is not meant to be more rigorous than currently established methods of quality estimation. On the contrary, it is a less rigorous method by design. However, unlike many linking and hedonic methods of quality measurement, the RGA has less of a tendency to drift, or deviate, from an accurate measure of quality as more years are examined. The reason is that in each new year the measurement of quality change is based on the identification of a representative good for that specific year. In other words, the process of identifying a representative good for a given year is entirely independent of any results obtained for previous years. Consequently, by starting from scratch in each year, there is no accumulation of bias from one year to the next, as could often be the case in conventional and hedonic methods of quality measurement (see the previous chapter).

In addition, the RGA may be able to account for the introduction of new consumer goods before those goods undergo substantial cost reduction in their manufacturing processes. In this sense, the RGA can be used to identify and interpret sudden changes in living standards arising from sudden quality improvements.

Finally, the RGA may make quality estimation feasible on the basis of data found in historical documents such as the *Sears Catalog* (in existence from 1893 to 1993), *Consumer Reports* (since 1936) and the *New York Times* (since 1851). What is required for the RGA is a consistent and logical means of designating a representative good (and its price) in each period, and an ability to find that same representative good (and its price) in an earlier period. The period itself need not be a year, and could be much longer (e.g., ten years) depending on the rate of quality change for the good in question. A longer period may reduce the amount of data that would need to be collected and manipulated. On the other hand, if quality change occurs quickly then a long period could make it impossible to link representative goods in consecutive periods. Nevertheless, in view of the wealth of information contained in historical documents, the RGA could lead to useful findings on evolutionary change in the quality of goods.

THE REPRESENTATIVE GOOD APPROACH

With the definitions of goods based on broad interpretations of their purposes, hedonic methods for assessing quality change could be rather limited. For example, a standard hedonic analysis of the quality change in vacuum cleaners over the last forty years is feasible. However, a hedonic analysis of 'household cleaning devices' over the last hundred years, which would include both vacuum cleaners and brooms, would be burdened with finding an explanation of how to account for the uniquely-different characteristics of brooms and vacuum cleaners in the assessment of quality. In such cases, a price matching approach, such as the RGA, might be more feasible.

Let us define a 'good' at time t as actually being a set of items, in which there is at least one item that best reflects the average of the set in terms of quality. For instance, consider the product — gas ranges. Let good A_{1983} denote the set of all gas ranges in 1983, and let the representative item be the gas range that has the median price, denoted by p_{1983}. Using five-year intervals of time, in 1988 another representative item exists, with price p_{1988}. In this case a comparison of p_{1983} and p_{1988} would have little meaning in itself, because several factors besides quality change could have had an influence on them, by virtue of the fact that the two representative items exist at different points in time. On the other hand, one could ask the following question: was the representative gas range of 1988 on the list of items available in 1983, and if so, what was its price in 1983? Assuming the 1988 median item was available in 1983, one could call that item the '1983 future median item', because the item itself will become the median item in the future, but its price is in reference to 1983. To draw a clear distinction, one could call the median item of 1983, based on 1983 prices, the '1983 present median item' (see Figure 4.1).

There are two main differences between the 1983 present median item and the 1983 future median item: their characteristics and their prices. Because both items exist at precisely the same time, a cost reduction effect, a pure price effect, and an income effect cannot account for any of the difference in their prices. Their prices vary only because of their characteristics, and thus, the difference in price reflects the quality improvement in gas ranges from 1983 to 1988.

Now consider the difference between the 1983 future median item and the 1988 present median item. Both items are identical in

*Figure 4.1 Example of the separation of quality improvement
from other effects*

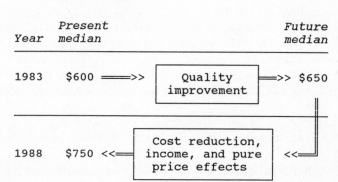

their characteristics; thus, quality change could not have had any
effect. Their price differences could have only resulted from a cost
reduction effect, an income effect, a pure price effect, or some
combination thereof.

In essence, the RGA is very similar to the price-linking method
utilized in the CPI calculation. Its only unique feature, as suggested
by its name, is in its identification and utilization of the
'representative good' for each period.

As another example, consider Figure 4.2, which provides an
illustration of quality changes among items in two periods. Period
0, or the 'base period', contains five models, A-E, with
corresponding prices $a_0 = 1$, $b_0 = 2$, etc. In the next period, Period 1,
Model A has dropped out; Model F has been added; and the prices
of Models B-E have been reduced by one unit. (If the good in
question is a computer, one could think of prices as being in
thousands.) The prices in Period 1 are $b_1 = 1$, $c_1 = 2$, etc.

For simplicity, assume that the quantity of items sold are equally
divided among the five models in each period, so that no weighting
of models by frequency is necessary. Assume, also, that the
number of items sold in Period 0 is the same as in Period 1. Let Q_0
and Q_1 be scalars that serve as index numbers of the quality of all
items in Periods 0 and 1.

Under these conditions, quality, as measured under the
conventional price-linking (CPL) approach, would be proportional to
the value of items at their base-period prices. The only item that

*Figure 4.2 Illustration of quality change among items in two
periods*

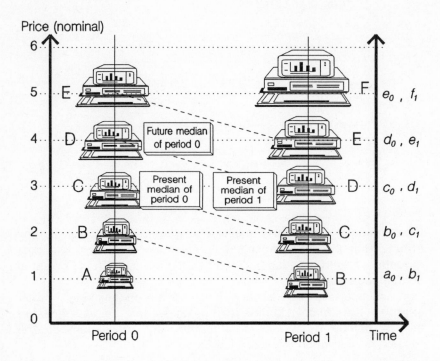

does not exist in the base period is Model F. However, under a
price-linking approach, the hypothetical value of F in Period 0 could
be estimated as:

$$\tilde{f}_0 = f_1 \frac{e_0}{e_1} \ . \tag{4.1}$$

Thus, one has:

$$Q_0 = a_0 + b_0 + c_0 + d_0 + e_0$$

$$Q_1 = b_0 + c_0 + d_0 + e_0 + f_1 \frac{e_0}{e_1} \ . \tag{4.2}$$

The proportional change in quality, $(Q_1-Q_0)/Q_0$, is then given by:

$$\left(\frac{Q_1-Q_0}{Q_0}\right)_{CPL} = \frac{f_1\dfrac{e_0}{e_1} - a_0}{a_0+b_0+c_0+d_0+e_0} . \qquad (4.3)$$

Under the RGA, the proportional change in quality would be based solely on the proportional change in the value of the representative good. Because Model C is the present median good and Model D is the future median good, one has:

$$\left(\frac{Q_1-Q_0}{Q_0}\right)_{RGA} \equiv \frac{d_0-c_0}{c_0} . \qquad (4.4)$$

With the numbers provided in Figure 4.2, one then has:

$$\left(\frac{Q_1-Q_0}{Q_0}\right)_{CPL} = \frac{21}{60}$$

$$(4.5)$$

$$\left(\frac{Q_1-Q_0}{Q_0}\right)_{RGA} = \frac{20}{60} .$$

In this hypothetical example, the RGA serves as a close approximation to the conventional price-linking approach.

Nevertheless, it is quite possible that the uniqueness of Model F may not be discovered and/or accounted for in Period 1. Suppose, for example, that Model F is treated as equivalent to Model E, even though it is priced higher in Period 1. This could occur if the higher price of F is simply attributed to a pure price effect. Also, the features of F that distinguish it from E may be different from the features of E that distinguish it from the other, lower-quality, models, which could lower the chances of F being recognized as a higher-quality item.

If F is not recognized as being distinct from E, then its estimated base-period price, $\tilde{f}_0$, could be taken as e_0 in Figure 4.2. One would then have:

$$\left(\frac{Q_1 - Q_0}{Q_0}\right)_{CPL} = \frac{e_0 - a_0}{a_0 + b_0 + c_0 + d_0 + e_0} \ . \tag{4.6}$$

In this case, given the numbers provided in Figure 4.2, the estimated proportional change in quality would be 26.67 per cent, in comparison to 35 per cent if F were recognized as a distinct model. Yet, such an error would not alter the estimated proportional change under the RGA, 33.33 per cent, because Model D would still be regarded as the representative good in Period 1.

One could hypothesize that, the more subtle the changes in quality are between periods, the greater will be the tendency of the conventional price-linking approach to underestimate quality change. Of course, over long periods of time, any small but systematic underestimation of quality change between consecutive periods could lead to a dramatic underestimation of quality change for the entire time span. For instance, suppose the true quality change were, in fact, 35.00 per cent in every five-year interval. Suppose the RGA consistently measured 33.33 per cent instead, while the CPL approach went back and forth between an underestimation of 26.67 percent and a correct estimation of 35.00 per cent. Let the initial quality index at time 0 be 100. After 100 years (or 20 five-year periods), the true quality index would be 29,946; the RGA quality index would be 23,650 (79 per cent of the true index); and the CPL quality index would be 15,835 (53 per cent of the true index).

One could argue that the mix-up that occurred between Model F and Model E in the above example would not create a problem for the RGA in Period 1, but would lead to its underestimation of quality change in Periods 2 or 3, when E and F are being considered as potential representative goods. However, at this time such a mix-up between E and F is much less likely to occur, because under the RGA, all of the focus and attention is placed on the analysis of representative goods. Consequently, the characteristics of potential representative items would be studied much more thoroughly than they would be in a conventional approach. This additional attention would be feasible, in view of the fact that much less attention would be paid to items that are not candidates for representative goods.

Under certain conditions the RGA could result in erroneous estimates if the prices examined reflect cyclical changes in the styles of various forms of merchandise. For example, suppose there are three types of men's shoes, A, B and C, as shown in Figure 4.3.

Figure 4.3 Example of cyclical change in styles, misinterpreted as quality improvement

Note: A, B and C reflect shoe types that never change in physical characteristics, but do vary in popularity through time.

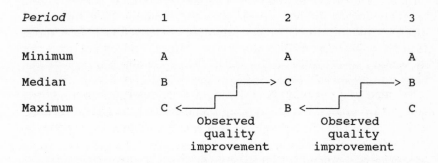

Period	1	2	3
Minimum	A	A	A
Median	B	C	B
Maximum	C	B	C

In Period 1, the minimum priced, least-popular shoe is type A, the median B, and the maximum priced, most popular shoe is type C. However, suppose that in Period 2 none of the shoes changes in terms of physical characteristics, but the median and maximum shoes switch positions, i.e., shoe B becomes more popular than C. Shoe C would then be the 'future median' for Period 1, and because it had the maximum price in Period 1, the RGA methodology would result in an observed quality improvement between Period 1 and Period 2. Taking this example further, suppose that in Period 3 the order is again A,B,C, exactly as it was in Period 1. The median shoe for Period 2 is C, and the future median shoe for Period 2 is B. But B was the maximum shoe in Period 2, and thus there would be another observed quality improvement recorded between Period 2 and Period 3. In this example, the situation in Period 3 is identical to that of in Period 1, but the methodology would find there to be continual quality improvement across the time span. This type of cyclical effect was not found, however, in the particular goods examined in this study.

    In summary, depending on the specific good being investigated, the time span being considered, and the rigour with which comparisons are made, the RGA could have certain advantages and certain disadvantages in comparison to conventional methods. An apparent disadvantage is that the conventional, price-linking method accounts for more sources of quality change, and attempts to place accurate weights on those sources of change. On the other hand, the RGA could be more appropriate in a long-run, or historical, context. With the RGA, the representative item is moved up or down in the ordered list of items (which can be weighted by revenue) whenever a new item is added somewhere in the list. In contrast, in the calculation of the CPI, goods which are actually different are often treated as the same. In addition, when a good that is unique first appears on the market, it is often not incorporated into the CPI calculation until much later. For example, Gordon (1990, p. 426) finds that the room air conditioner had appeared in the *Sears Catalog* and in *Consumer Reports* for 11 years before it became incorporated into the CPI.

As suggested above, in conventional and hedonic methods the accounting of all price and quantity changes can be costly in terms of the amount of information needed for collection and analysis. In efforts to contain those costs, certain quality improvements could easily go unreported. That is, conventional and hedonic methods often have a bias toward the under-reporting of minor and subtle quality improvements. In contrast, the RGA may not have this bias, although it is likely to be a less efficient estimator across any given pair of consecutive years, due to inaccuracies in the identification of the representative good.

One could argue, nonetheless, that over long time spans, e.g., 100 years, the higher year-to-year random fluctuations that would occur in the RGA due to inefficiencies in the identification of the representative good would be of minor importance. In contrast, a continual and cumulative drift away from accurate quality assessment (due to a bias in measurement) in a conventional or hedonic method could be an important source of error. In this sense the choice between a conventional or hedonic approach, on the one hand, and a representative good approach, on the other hand, could reflect a choice between efficiency and non-bias, respectively. Again, as demonstrated above, the longer the time span is, the more important the non-bias feature will be, and the less important the efficiency feature will be.

Finally, one should note that the concept of a 'representative good' being used as a summary indicator of a large group of goods has considerable precedence in economic theory. The consumer price index itself is based on a bundle of representative goods, which are occasionally changed to reflect quality improvements over generations.   Hence, the representative good approach, when applied to several different goods at the same time, can be looked upon as simply a more accurate, and more rigorous, attempt to identify the 'representative bundle' for a price index in each period.

METHODOLOGY

Source of Data

In the present study, five groups of household goods are examined: men's shoes; sofas and love seats; gas ranges; window fans and air conditioners; and cameras, movie cameras and camcorders.   The prices and the descriptions (in terms of characteristics) of individual items are obtained from Spring/Summer editions of the *Sears Catalog*, from 1928 to 1993, for every 5 years (1928, 1933, . . . , 1993).   For each group, every item appearing in the catalog was weighted equally, rather than by expenditure level, for which there is no publicly available information.   The equal weighting of each item could be a potential source of bias in the data.   On the other hand, even if expenditures are skewed to one side of the distribution of entries (e.g., expenditures on less expensive items being greater than on more expensive items) the findings, based on the differences among periods, could still be accurate provided this effect is consistent from period to period.

One of the issues addressed is how representative the data are with respect to general price movements of personal consumption expenditures in the United States.   On the one hand, the fact that the data come from a single source, the *Sears Catalog*, is desirable, because it reflects a well-defined and fairly consistent sample.   On the other hand, these data are subject to changes in the marketing strategy, and/or marketing circumstances, associated with the single firm — Sears Roebuck and Company.

Gordon examines price shifts in the *Sears Catalog*, and addresses the issue of whether they reflect price shifts in retail markets overall. He remarks, 'The most serious problem in the use of catalog prices is the possibility of a systematic difference in the secular growth rates of the same product sold by catalog and noncatalog outlets, due, for instance, to differential growth in the efficiency of catalog operations or changes in pricing policies' (Gordon 1990, p. 428). Gordon suggests, however, that whatever technologies are developed in catalogue operations, similar technologies are also likely to apply to non-catalogue competitors.

Gordon (1990) does observe that Sears underwent a shift in its pricing policies from the early post-war period to the late 1960s and early 1970s. Nevertheless, the present study begins in 1928, 19 years before Gordon's, and ends in 1993, ten years after Gordon's. Thus, the extensiveness of the present study would tend to diminish the relative effect of any such shifts. One must conclude that, in the long-run, the survival and success of Sears Roebuck and Company for well over a century implies that that the company has, for the most part, been quite competitive in terms of the quality and pricing of its products.

Ironically, in January 1993, Sears Roebuck and Company decided to discontinue the *Sears Catalog*, with the Spring/Summer 1993 edition being the last issue. Having existed for 98 years, the Catalog was an American icon, that had been 'next to the Bible, . . . the most popular home literature in America' (Schellhardt, 1993, p. B1). Nevertheless, the economic principles that were applied to data from the *Sears Catalog* could be applied equally well to data from similar sources (like *Consumer Reports*). Moreover, in future years linkages could be made between data from the *Sears Catalog* and data from more recent catalogs such as *Land's End*, *J. Crew* and *L.L. Bean*.[1]

Identification of the Representative Item

The representative item for each period was designated as the median of the sample of items appearing in the *Sears Catalog*. If there were an even number of items, the median price was taken as the average of the prices of the two middle items. In this particular case, a judgment was made as to which of the two middle items best represented a typical item of the period. That item was then identified as the present median item.

In some instances the median price was a price shared by more than one item. Thus, there was occasionally a choice of more than one median item, even when there was an odd number of items in total. In such cases, the potential candidates for the median item were eliminated if there were no corresponding future median item, in the previous period, with identical or very similar characteristics. In all cases, judgments were made on the basis of the best fits between future median and present median items, and on the basis of which items appeared to be most typical for the period.

Although some variation did exist with regard to the possibilities for arriving at the future median prices within the constraints of the methodological procedure, that variation was quite minor relative to variation in the prices of all items within a given year. Furthermore, the average variation of possible prices of present and future median items for a pair of consecutive periods was quite small relative to the variation of such variables across the 1928-1993 time span.

EMPIRICAL FINDINGS

Table 4.1 presents a summary of the data obtained for the study. (The raw data are presented in the Appendix (see pp. 212-27). Gas ranges were not available through the *Sears Catalog* in 1943 and 1948, and window fans and air conditioners were not available either, because of metal shortages during World War II. To compensate for this absence of information, the simplifying assumption was made that the gas ranges which had been available in 1938 were still applicable to 1943 and 1948, and the window fans which had been available in 1938 were still applicable to 1943. This assumption amounts to the idea that quality has not changed in periods in which the items were not available, since there is no evidence of any change, positive or negative.

Among the fans appearing in the 1928 Spring/Summer issue, none were window fans. In this case all of the fans in that year were regarded as 'potential' window fans in the sense that they could be placed inside or near a window. The top-of-the-line fan in that year was regarded as comparable to a window fan of the next period in terms of cooling effectiveness, and was therefore chosen as the future median. Beginning in 1938, however, only window fans (and later window air conditioners) were counted.

As the numbers in Table 4.1 suggest, men's shoes provided the most thorough set of data. For this group identical matches could always be found between future median items and their corresponding present median items in subsequent periods. This success at finding identical items for men's shoes was due to: the large sample size in each period, the slow rate of technological change in shoes relative to other goods, and the fact that the median price was often shared by several different shoes, allowing one to select only future median items with corresponding identical present median items in the next period.

For the other four goods, identical counterparts could not be

Table 4.1 Data summary of the five types of goods

| | Year | | | | | | |
	1928	1933	1938	1943	1948	1953	1958
Men's shoes							
Observations	66	71	92	117	104	114	123
Minimum	1.98	1.00	1.17	1.77	3.29	2.69	2.83
Maximum	5.95	4.00	4.69	6.45	11.95	11.95	19.00
Mean	4.17	2.39	2.97	3.91	7.92	7.89	9.10
Present Median	4.48	2.00	2.95	3.98	7.65	7.90	8.97
Future Median	3.79	3.98	2.98	5.00	7.95	8.85	9.90
Sofas and love seats							
Observations	19	15	27	10	14	4	4
Minimum	24.85	22.50	16.00	25.75	64.95	109.50	62.95
Maximum	117.95	46.85	81.00	77.85	215.00	164.50	189.95
Mean	73.46	32.85	48.02	44.66	127.46	127.00	129.45
Present Median	79.50	32.95	47.95	38.90	126.98	117.00	132.45
Future Median	86.85	30.95	47.95	69.75	129.95	164.50	169.95
Gas ranges							
Observations	9	3	7	0	0	9	18
Minimum	23.50	11.95	8.35	8.35	8.35	62.88	64.95
Maximum	80.50	49.50	69.95	69.95	69.95	239.95	269.95
Mean	49.17	29.10	38.71	38.71	38.71	138.61	155.78
Present Median	48.50	25.85	39.95	39.95	39.95	134.95	154.95
Future Median	48.50	25.85	39.95	39.95	69.95	169.95	209.95
Window fans and air conditioners							
Observations	10	3	3	0	2	13	19
Minimum	2.75	4.75	4.98	4.98	18.95	24.50	19.50
Maximum	26.45	17.50	14.75	14.75	47.50	394.50	379.95
Mean	10.20	10.03	8.69	8.69	33.23	137.56	181.36
Present Median	7.40	7.85	6.35	6.35	33.23	59.95	194.95
Future Median	26.45	6.35	6.35	14.75	47.50	314.50	249.95
Cameras, movie cameras and camcorders							
Observations	42	18	57	4	20	33	45
Minimum	0.89	0.79	1.55	2.97	7.75	2.79	4.47
Maximum	89.00	28.45	169.50	69.50	171.70	158.50	239.00
Mean	13.44	9.93	23.86	32.70	78.46	50.86	78.69
Present Median	8.95	9.90	17.65	29.17	76.11	29.50	67.80
Future Median	8.25	14.95	17.65	69.50	87.54	150.95	58.20

Table 4.1   Data summary of the five types of goods (concluded)

	Year						
	1963	1968	1973	1978	1983	1988	1993
Men's shoes							
Observations	109	84	73	79	81	60	42
Minimum	4.77	6.97	7.97	10.97	19.88	24.99	36.00
Maximum	17.70	20.97	32.97	43.00	69.99	84.99	88.99
Mean	10.97	13.93	18.18	26.48	43.21	53.07	61.93
Present Median	9.97	13.43	17.99	26.99	44.99	44.99	63.00
Future Median	10.97	13.97	25.70	31.99	34.99	69.99	NA
Sofas and love seats							
Observations	10	11	10	10	7	4	14
Minimum	41.95	59.95	149.95	129.95	299.99	149.98	349.00
Maximum	265.00	189.95	249.95	399.85	499.99	399.99	599.00
Mean	147.68	120.50	201.86	229.93	377.13	272.48	451.86
Present Median	162.48	119.95	202.45	179.95	359.99	269.98	449.00
Future Median	69.95	179.95	209.95	279.95	299.99	399.00	NA
Gas ranges							
Observations	13	15	13	19	12	22	27
Minimum	79.95	89.95	143.95	164.95	309.99	259.99	229.99
Maximum	329.95	479.95	460.95	974.95	859.99	889.99	1,069.99
Mean	175.33	205.77	280.65	405.21	500.82	542.72	619.99
Present Median	169.95	199.00	274.95	399.95	434.99	529.99	599.99
Future Median	189.95	189.95	316.95	419.95	549.99	399.99	NA
Window fans and air conditioners							
Observations	14	16	10	22	38	47	46
Minimum	18.88	10.95	134.95	114.00	34.99	39.99	24.99
Maximum	349.95	429.95	459.95	599.95	839.95	879.99	999.99
Mean	205.30	238.83	270.45	313.23	396.01	393.82	489.97
Present Median	229.95	239.95	256.95	294.48	384.95	399.99	499.99
Future Median	299.95	269.95	256.95	309.95	339.95	399.99	NA
Cameras, movie cameras and camcorders							
Observations	22	30	12	10	14	9	38
Minimum	1.79	4.19	10.75	13.50	99.99	39.99	39.99
Maximum	148.88	197.00	246.00	369.50	1,499.95	1,489.99	1,199.99
Mean	70.85	86.40	110.10	107.70	397.84	614.43	447.31
Present Median	67.06	78.50	106.75	59.50	264.99	429.99	339.99
Future Median	127.50	179.00	68.25	189.50	319.99	339.9	NA

found as easily, and in several cases pairs of items that were very similar, but not identical, had to be used. In finding similar pairs, when identical pairs could not be found, the characteristics that were regarded as most important were physical attributes, such as size, construction and advertised features. Other aspects of goods such as the brand name received less consideration. As one would expect, the difficulty in finding identical pairs was inversely related to the number of observations. (For a more detailed explanation of the selection of representative items, see the appendix to this chapter, p. 123)

Perhaps the most important aspect of the data is that there is strong evidence that the median item is, in fact, representative of the set of items in each period. In particular, the following observations were made for these four goods:

1. The mean (with equal weight per item) and median prices are very close throughout the time span.
2. The ratios of minimum/median and median/maximum are fairly constant across the time span.[2] Furthermore, for shoes, sofas and gas ranges, the median tends to be midway between the minimum and maximum on a logarithmic scale. For cameras and fans, the median is closer to the maximum, but is still reasonably distant from it.
3. Except for fans, the minimum/maximum ratio remains fairly constant throughout the time span, suggesting that the diversity of items does not increase over time, contrary to what some researchers might expect. That is, new high-quality items appear to enter the market no more or less rapidly than old low-quality items leave the market. For fans, on the other hand, old models do appear to linger on while new models are introduced.
4. The minimum, mean, median, and maximum prices appear to grow at roughly the same rate.

These observations can be seen directly in Figures 4.4 to 4.8. Taken together, they provide substantial evidence that the basic structure and distribution of these goods, at least as they appear in the *Sears Catalog*, remain fairly constant over the time span. This implies that, in each category, quality improvement in the representative item reflects overall quality improvement across all of the items.

Furthermore, as suggested earlier, the representative item in a

Figure 4.4 Price movements in men's shoes

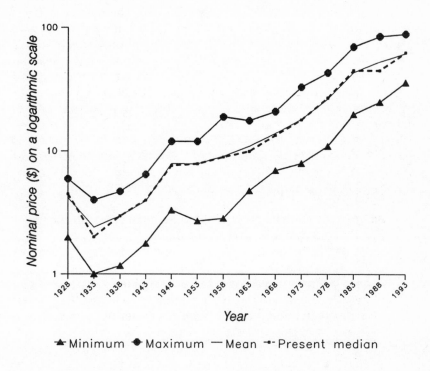

particular period could be higher in quality or lower in quality than the average item, if one could hypothetically find the average item weighted by revenue. Nevertheless, the consistency of the above-mentioned indicators across time provides evidence that the *rate of change* in the quality of the representative item is likely to be quite similar to the rate of change for that hypothetical average item.

Of course, certain perturbations exist in the time trends of these indicators. For example, for sofas (Figure 4.5) the year 1963 is exceptional in terms of the large dispersion about the mean and median. The maximum increases substantially from the previous period while the minimum declines substantially, and in the following year both minimum and maximum move back toward the mean. The low minimum for 1963, due to the presence of certain inexpensive sofas, might be attributable to the emergence of the 'recreation room' in US homes during that time.

Figure 4.5 Price movements in sofas and love seats

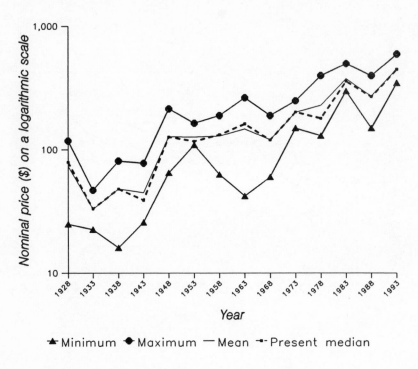

▲Minimum ●Maximum —Mean ‑‑‑Present median

THE ANALYSIS OF QUALITY IMPROVEMENT

An index was established for each good with the value of 100 in the year 1928, which would increase or decrease in proportion to changes in the quality of the representative item. The derivation of that index is presented in Table 4.2. Figure 4.9 presents the quality indices derived in Table 4.2 for the five types of goods. The rates of quality improvement for window fans and air conditioners, and for cameras, movie cameras and camcorders, dramatically exceed the rates for the other three goods. These findings provide overwhelming evidence that certain types of goods improve in quality faster than others. Furthermore, the magnitude of the estimated rate of quality improvement for cameras is so remarkable, *14,000 per cent over 65 years*, that this finding, in itself, is a notable discovery.

By performing an ordinary least-squares regression of the log of

Figure 4.6 Price movements in gas ranges

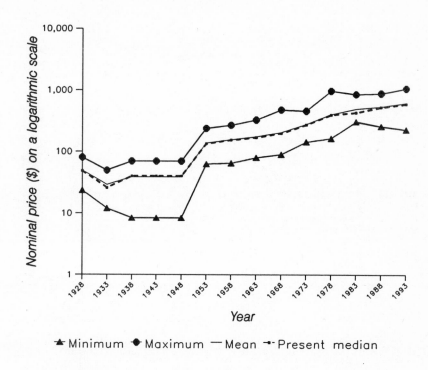

the quality index for each good against time, estimates were made of the rates of quality improvement.   These results of these regression analyses are summarized in Table 4.3.   As the table indicates, the estimates of quality improvement rates are all highly significant. In increasing order, these rates are: 2.07 per cent (per year) for sofas and love seats, 2.72 per cent for men's shoes, 2.80 per cent for gas ranges, 7.46 per cent for window fans and air conditioners, and 9.25 per cent for cameras, movie cameras and camcorders. For the small sample sizes of 14 observations, the Durbin-Watson statistics are not significant, although there is some suggestion that autocorrelation could be present for gas ranges and for fans and air conditioners.

Figure 4.7 Price movements in window fans and air conditioners

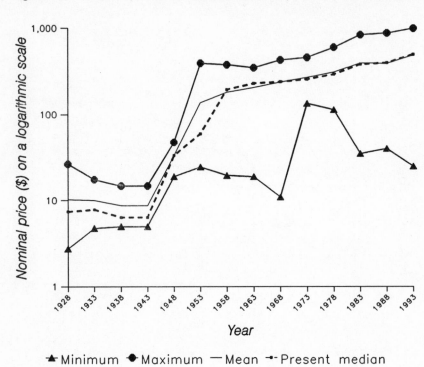

Year

▲ Minimum ● Maximum — Mean ▪▪ Present median

COMPARISON WITH THE GNP IMPLICIT PRICE DEFLATOR

Of the five types of goods considered in this study, men's shoes is the only one for which there exists comparable price indices for the GNP Implicit Price Deflator, which is derived from the Consumer Price Index (CPI) and Producer Price Index (PPI). In the case of the other four goods, there are discontinuities in the definition of categories from 1929 to 1993, making it impossible to identify a single, continuous trend. It is possible to compare the RGA price trend for one of the goods with the GNP implicit price deflator for a much broader category, like household appliances, but such a comparison would have little meaning.

For men's shoes, the comparable index for 1929-1993 is the GNP Implicit Price Deflator for 'shoes and other footwear' which includes

Figure 4.8 Price movements in cameras, movie cameras and camcorders

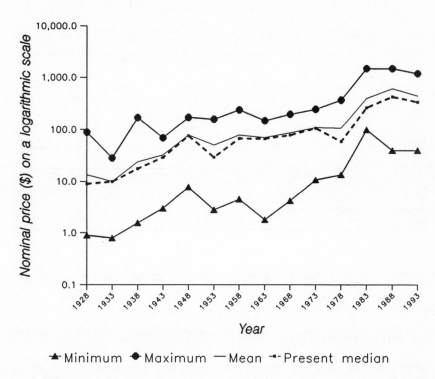

▲ Minimum ● Maximum — Mean ⚊·Present median

both men's and women's footwear. A disaggregation into shoes only or men's footwear only was not possible because of discontinuities in the CPI data.

Figure 4.10 provides a comparison of the derived price deflator for footwear, and the median cost per quality unit of men's shoes in the *Sears Catalog*.[3] To facilitate the comparison, the measures were normalized to equal 100 in 1958, which is the year near the centre of the time span. As the figure demonstrates, the two indicators are very similar across the time interval 1938 to 1988. Even though the measures are different in the first ten years of the time span, and in the last five years, the graph does provide evidence that, in certain cases, the RGA index could be a valid substitute for the GNP implicit price deflator.

The differences between the two measures could be due to a variety of factors. For instance, the CPI measure includes men's

Table 4.2   Derivation of a quality index based on the prices of representative goods

	Year						
	1928	1933	1938	1943	1948	1953	1958
Men's shoes							
Present median	4.48	2.00	2.95	3.98	7.65	7.90	8.97
Future median	3.79	3.98	2.98	5.00	7.95	8.85	9.90
Quality index	100.00	84.60	168.35	170.06	213.65	222.02	248.72
Sofas and love seats							
Present median	79.50	32.95	47.95	38.90	126.98	117.00	132.45
Future median	86.85	30.95	47.95	69.75	129.95	164.50	169.95
Quality index	100.00	109.25	102.61	102.61	183.99	188.30	264.75
Gas ranges							
Present median	48.50	25.85	39.95	39.95	39.95	134.95	154.95
Future median	48.50	25.85	39.95	39.95	69.95	169.95	209.95
Quality index	100.00	100.00	100.00	100.00	100.00	175.09	220.51
Window fans and air conditioners							
Present median	7.40	7.85	6.35	6.35	33.23	59.95	194.95
Future median	26.45	6.35	6.35	14.75	47.50	314.50	249.95
Quality index	100.00	357.43	289.13	289.13	671.61	960.16	5,037.1
Cameras, movie cameras and camcorders							
Present median	8.95	9.90	17.65	29.17	76.11	29.50	67.80
Future median	8.25	14.95	17.65	69.50	87.54	150.95	58.20
Quality index	100.00	92.18	139.20	139.20	331.71	381.55	1,952.4

Table 4.2   *Derivation of a quality index based on the prices of representative goods (concluded)*

| | Year | | | | | | |
	1963	1968	1973	1978	1983	1988	1993
Men's shoes							
Present median	9.97	13.43	17.99	26.99	44.99	44.99	63.00
Future median	10.97	13.97	25.70	31.99	34.99	69.99	NA
Quality index	274.51	302.04	314.31	449.01	532.19	413.90	643.89
Sofas and love seats							
Present median	162.48	119.95	202.45	179.95	359.99	269.98	449.00
Future median	69.95	179.95	209.95	279.95	299.99	399.00	NA
Quality index	339.71	146.26	219.41	227.54	353.99	294.99	435.96
Gas ranges							
Present median	169.95	199.00	274.95	399.95	434.99	529.99	599.99
Future median	189.95	189.95	316.95	419.95	549.99	399.99	NA
Quality index	298.77	333.93	318.75	367.44	385.81	487.81	368.16
Window fans and air conditioners							
Present median	229.95	239.95	256.95	294.48	384.95	399.99	499.99
Future median	299.95	269.95	256.95	309.95	339.95	399.99	NA
Quality index	6,458.1	8,424.1	9,477.3	9,477.3	9,975.3	8,809.2	8,809.2
Cameras, movie cameras and camcorders							
Present median	67.06	78.50	106.75	59.50	264.99	429.99	339.99
Future median	127.50	179.00	68.25	189.50	319.99	339.95	NA
Quality index	1,675.9	3,186.4	7,265.9	4,645.4	14,795.0	17,865.8	14,124.7

Figure 4.9 Quality improvement in the five goods

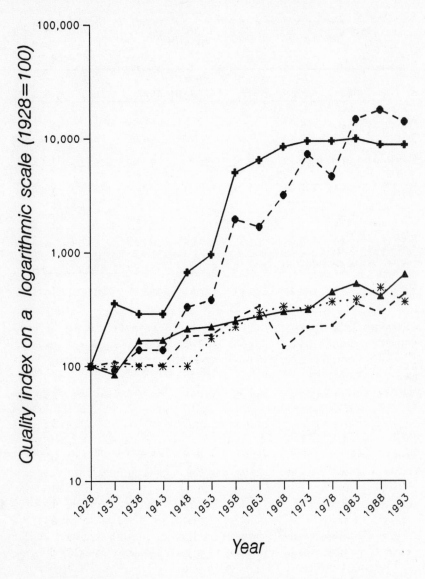

Men's shoes
Gas ranges
Cameras, etc.
Sofas and love seats
Air conditioners and fans

Table 4.3   Summary of regression results

Type of good	Quality-improvement coefficient		Durbin-Watson statistic	Adjusted R^2
	Annual increase in quality (%)	t-statistic of coefficient		
Men's shoes	2.716	12.57	2.31	0.924
Sofas and love seats	2.073	5.83	1.88	0.717
Gas ranges	2.799	9.82	0.94	0.880
Window fans and air conditioners	7.462	8.28	0.70	0.839
Cameras, movie cameras, & camcorders	9.252	15.84	1.96	0.951

and women's footwear, from all retail establishments. Also, footwear would include boots, trainers, slippers, etc. Thus, the difference could simply be due to the fact that each measure refers to a different group of items.

Another consideration is the dramatic fall in the prices of men's shoes in the *Sears Catalog* in 1928-33, followed by a small rise in prices combined with a much larger quality improvement in 1933-38 (see Table 4.1 and Figure 4.3). The cost per unit of quality for men's shoes at Sears therefore declines again in 1933-38, in spite of the rise in the median price. In the CPI, however, the cost per unit of quality rises in 1933-38. Perhaps the 1928-33 drop in prices at Sears was greater than the drop in other retail establishments, because at that time Sears was largely a mail-order company for rural areas, which may have been facing greater declines in the demand for shoes. In addition, it is possible that the CPI did not capture all of the quality improvements in shoes in 1933-38, which could explain why the CPI rises slightly during this period while the RGA index declines.

Similarly, the recent recession of the early 1990s could have caused a decline in the quality of shoes, as a result of declines in the income levels of various groups. If the CPI does not fully capture

Figure 4.10   Representative good index for men's shoes versus GNP implicit price deflator for footwear

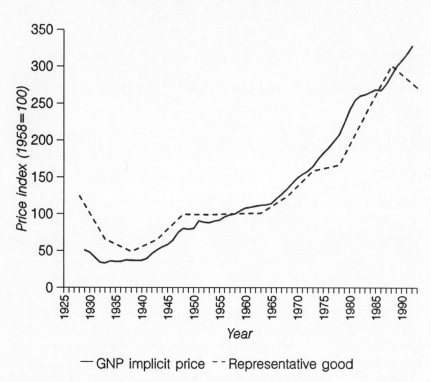

— GNP implicit price - - Representative good

the decline, then this effect could be one explanation for the difference in the two measures in 1993.   Of course, more information would be necessary for any of these hypotheses to be substantiated.

PLACING THE CPI IN PROPER PERSPECTIVE

Although the comparison between the CPI and RGA could be interesting for a variety of reasons, it should be obvious that such a comparison is limited in terms of usefulness. In constructing the RGA, for example, one could consider an air conditioner as a quality improvement over a fan, or a camcorder as a quality improvement over a camera. This interpretation of quality improvement is much broader than the interpretation used in the construction of the CPI.

Hence, a comparison between the results of the two methods would often be inappropriate in view of the large difference in their corresponding perspectives.

Moreover, as argued above, the RGA must be recognized as being relatively accurate only over long periods of time, while having the potential to be *inaccurate* on a year-to-year basis. In contrast, the CPI is accurate between consecutive years, but could be inaccurate in the long run, due to a systematic drift resulting from a small but consistent bias from year to year.

Furthermore, the key purpose of the CPI is not to measure long-run changes in quality, but to enable cost-of-living adjustments in wages, benefits, rents, etc., as discussed in Chapter 3. In this regard, the economic impact of the CPI is enormous. For instance, Juran (1992, p. 468) notes that for every 1.0 per cent increase in the CPI in 1986, Federal outlays, in nominal terms, were increased by $2.8 billion. In addition, for the same 1.0 per cent increase, personal income tax receipts were reduced by 1.8 billion (from what they would be otherwise) due to a redefinition of tax brackets. Consequently, it would be quite absurd for the *Sears Catalog*, or any other single document or journal, to be used as the basis for the CPI.

Finally, because of the economic and political importance of the CPI, the methodology for measuring it must be simple, clear and rigorous in each year, at the cost of underestimating the subtle, and often philosophical, changes in quality. Like the cartoon character Popeye, the CPI is what it is and that is all that it is. Therefore, economists interested in measuring long-run effects must look elsewhere to find an appropriate measure. In this sense, those who use the RGA should acknowledge that the RGA is not, and can never be, a *replacement* for the CPI. Conversely, those who construct and/or advocate the CPI methodology should not be opposed to other measurement techniques that are designed to answer an entirely different set of questions.

CONCLUSION

The basic concept of the representative good approach is analogous to the concept of the 'centre of gravity' in physics. That is, the motion of an object in space can be described by first observing the motions of various parts of that object, and then finding some aggregate measure that averages out those motions. Alternatively, one could find the one point located in that object's centre of gravity, and the motion of that point would best characterize the motion of the entire object as a whole.

With the RGA, there may be little guarantee that the designated representative good is, in fact, the item that best characterizes the group. Moreover, it is quite possible that no such item exists, because there is a dichotomy among the items in the group, or because there is a grey area in terms of whether certain items belong to the group. For example, if there is no 'medium' item, but only below-average and above-average items, then any item designated as the representative item would be either an overestimate or an underestimate. In the above analogy, this situation would correspond to a hollow body moving in space, in which the centre of gravity is located in a region where no actual part of the object exists.

Consequently, *the RGA is only useful in certain well-defined and well-behaved contexts.* As one would expect, its usefulness depends on how well the representative item captures the quality changes experienced by the group as a whole. This 'representativeness' of the representative item would need to be tested before any conclusions could be drawn from an RGA experiment.

Nevertheless, under certain circumstances the RGA can provide adequate estimations of quality change over long periods of time, as demonstrated in the present study using catalogue data. Furthermore, as shown in the case of men's shoes, the RGA price index can obtain results that are similar to those obtained by conventional methods. In this sense, it can also be used as a check against the other methods, just as the conventional and hedonic methods currently serve as checks against each other.

For long-run, or historical, studies of quality change, the RGA could be advantageous for a variety of reasons. As mentioned earlier, it could make the study of certain goods feasible, which would otherwise not be feasible using conventional or hedonic methods. Secondly, it tends to avoid sources of long-run bias, or drift, because the representative item is found 'from scratch' in each period. In addition, it could exploit a wealth of information currently available in historical documents such as the *Sears Catalog, Consumer Reports* and the *New York Times*. Finally, it could be used in conjunction with studies on product innovation, whereby the relative economic value of different technological improvements could be assessed.

There is one other advantage of the RGA that is probably the most subtle of its advantages, but may also be the most beneficial. That advantage lies in the fact that the RGA will always force one to have a concrete, and fairly specific, understanding of the particular good or service under consideration at any given period of time. Hence, when quality does change, those changes could be observed and clearly understood. Neither conventional nor hedonic methods may present this kind of snapshot picture of quality at each point in time.

With the RGA, for instance, one might envision the quality of personal computers changing from an IBM 'XT' in 1986, to an IBM 'AT' in 1989, a '386' in 1992, and a '486' in 1994. A hedonic function with coefficients on the variables associated with these computers (e.g., the speed of calculation, the disk storage space, and the amount of random access memory) would certainly be valid[4], but may not convey the same sense of quality improvement. In the conventional method, the perception of one type of computer replacing another would also be less clear, because all three types would still be in existence in 1992. In contrast, the representative good approach could be more helpful in its tendency to simplify, to clarify and to pinpoint what is actually meant by 'quality improvement' and what has actually happened over time to the good in question.

APPENDIX: RULES EMPLOYED IN OBTAINING DATA FROM THE *SEARS CATALOG*

The Choice of Goods

The five types of goods used in this study — men's shoes; gas ranges; sofas and love seats; window fans and air conditioners; and cameras, movie cameras and camcorders — were chosen for the following reasons:

1. They existed in significant quantities throughout the time span 1928 to 1993.[5]
2. Over that period, a wide variety of different kinds were sold.
3. Their descriptions in the catalogue were extensive, and allowed for the identification of characteristics.
4. They are very common in the economy, and common among households throughout the United States.
5. They tended to be sold as single items.[6]

6.   The five goods differed substantially among themselves in terms of their use and the materials used to construct them.
7.   In general, whether a household would, or would not, purchase one of the five goods, does not fluctuate greatly on the basis of shifts in tastes over the period, or on the basis of substitutes replacing the five goods.[7]

Men's Shoes

The data on men's shoes were quite extensive; the smallest number of observations in a given year was 42, in 1993, and the largest number was 123 in 1958. Men's shoes were chosen for the study instead of women's shoes for four reasons:

1.   It was observed that men's shoes were less subject to cyclical changes in style, which could distort the findings on quality changes (see pages 102-3).
2.   Women's shoes underwent many more 'small changes', in terms of appearance, than men's shoes, and thus, finding identical shoes between consecutive years was easier for men's shoes than for women's.
3.   The descriptions of men's shoes tended to be lengthier and contain more information than those of women's shoes.
4.   A much larger proportion of men's shoes were 'work shoes', which had undergone a great number of interesting quality changes between 1928 and 1993.

Shoes only, and not boots, trainers, or slippers were examined. The distinction between shoes and these other types of footwear was not a simple matter. What were often called 'shoes' in 1928 could be called 'boots' in more recent times. In fact, a 'shoe' in 1928 generally meant footwear that would cover the ankle, while the term 'oxford' at that time was used to describe what is now commonly called a 'shoe'. To ensure that the measurement of quality change was a true measure of physical, rather than semantic, changes, a rule was made that all footwear items taller than six inches from the bottom of the foot would be a 'boot', and not counted. 'Walking shoes' or other shoes made of cloth or synthetic material instead of leather, were counted as shoes, provided they did not resemble any sort of athletic shoe. Leather moccasins were regarded as shoes, but some other types of leather 'slippers', which had less coverage and support at the top of the foot, were not.

As with all of the five types of goods considered in this study, decision rules had to be made with regard to counting variations of the same item as one item or more than one item. Two shoes that were different in colour, but identical in every other respect, were counted as a single item, even if each had a separate picture and/or description in the catalog. An exception was made to this rule however, when the same shoes, but with different colours, had different prices.

Sofas and Love Seats

The data on sofas and love seats were much more limited in terms of the number of observations per period, which ranged from a minimum of only four, in 1953, 1958 and 1988, to a maximum of 27 in 1938. This limitation contributed to the difficulty of finding matching pairs of items between consecutive periods. Such pairs, therefore, were based on items with the most in common in terms of characteristics, rather than items with identical characteristics. The characteristics that were regarded as most important for determining comparable pairs were size (e.g., sofa versus love seat) and physical construction (e.g., foam versus coils in the cushions). The specific style of the sofa (e.g., 'Early American' versus 'French Provincial') was given secondary importance in finding comparable pairs.

One of the reasons for the small sample sizes for each period was that sofa beds, which existed as early as 1928, were not included. The reason for this exclusion was to establish a well-defined concept of a sofa as a single unit designed solely for the purpose of providing seating.

Large units that comprise in effect, two or more sofas, were not included, because it would then be ambiguous as to whether one should consider them as single units or as 'multiple sofas' whose prices should be divided by two or three depending on their size. Furthermore, the following three rules were established in cases where the price of a sofa was ambiguous:

1. *Different prices for the same unit due to different choices of upholstery.* In certain cases, especially in the earlier periods, a single sofa would have more than one price depending on the buyer's choice of upholstery. For example, one of the 'Davenport' sofas in 1928 was priced at $62.50 if the consumer chooses 'Jacquard Velour', $86.75 for 'Plain Mohair'

and $86.85 for 'Figured Mohair'. In such cases in which the difference between the minimum and maximum cost is not insignificant, the sofa was counted as *two* distinct items, i.e., as two observations regardless of how many choices of upholstery there are—one item being the sofa with the lowest-priced upholstery and the other the one with the highest-priced upholstery.

2. *Sofas sold only in combination with one or more lounge chairs.* Occasionally a sofa was not offered for sale as a single item, but was offered in a combination of one sofa and one lounge chair, or one sofa and two lounge chairs. In such cases an effective price was imputed for the sofa by subtracting from the combined price the separate price of the lounge chair. The price of the lounge chair alone, if not directly available, was often imputed from the difference in price between the combination of a sofa and lounge chair and the combination of a sofa and two lounge chairs.

3. *Modular units.* Especially in the most recent periods, modular units could be purchased, thereby rendering the sofa indeterminate in size and price. However, the vast majority of other types of sofas throughout the time span were approximately the size of one modular sofa consisting of two corner units and one central unit. Therefore, the price of a modular sofa was taken to be the sum of the prices of these three components.

The characteristics of sofas and love seats change dramatically from 1928 to 1993. They evolve from being rather bulky, partially metallic, single objects, to being much more mobile objects with removable cushions and light frames. Their fabrics also become more practical, being made of synthetic materials that are resistent to stains and easier to clean.

Gas Ranges

The technical changes that have occurred in gas ranges and stoves from 1928 to 1993 are quite dramatic. Unfortunately, the data on gas ranges are limited by the existence of only three items in 1933 (most likely due to the Great Depression) and their absence in 1943 and 1948 (due to World War II). The number of items starts to become substantial in 1958, in which there are 18 in contrast to only nine in 1953. The periods after 1958 vary in the number of items from 12 (in 1983) to 27 (in 1993).

Of the five types of goods examined in this study, gas ranges were the most accurately described by the *Sears Catalog* in terms of their features and physical characteristics. After 1948, identical pairs could generally be found between consecutive periods. For the earlier periods, pairs with the most in common were identified, based primarily on the size of the oven and the particular features that it offered. Because of the absence of identical pairs in those earlier periods, there may be some underestimation of the true extent of quality improvement between 1928 and 1953. Ranges that could run on both gas and coal, which existed from 1928 to 1948, were not included, nor were ovens that were 'built-in' (to the wall) because they did not have burners.

Window Fans and Air Conditioners

As mentioned earlier, there is a definite quality versus quantity problem in the data on fans and air conditioners. A large air conditioner, for example, which would cost, say, five times as much as a small air conditioner, may simply be able to cool five times as many cubic feet of space, all else being equal. In this case a change in the present median item from the small air conditioner to the large one would not reflect a true quality improvement, nor a true cost increase, since nothing would change on a 'per cubic foot' basis, except for the conveniences and/or inconveniences of the household having one instead of five air conditioners. Consequently, any trends in the median capacity of air conditioners, all else being equal, could be misinterpreted.

On the other hand, one could argue that a large air conditioner *could* reflect a quality improvement over a small air conditioner, if the owner of the small air conditioner does not possess enough small air conditioners to cool his home (or some portion of it) as extensively as he could with a single, large window air conditioner. In other words, the larger unit could be interpreted as improving the 'overall quality' of the entire home (or portion). Of course, one cannot tell from the available data how many small air conditioners would actually be substituted by a larger model. Hence, this interpretation of the change in quality would be difficult to estimate.

Cameras, Movie Cameras and Camcorders

The history of technological transitions in cameras from 1928 to

1993 is quite remarkable. One should bear in mind however, that the quality of cameras, movie cameras and camcorders is also a function of the film used and the equipment needed to process and present (or project) the developed film. With regard to the movie camera, for example, a more precise concept than its quality would be the quality of the combination of movie camera, film, film development (and related goods and services), projector and movie screen.

In recent times, camcorders have tended to cost considerably more than VCRs, while movie cameras have tended to cost less than movie projectors, and for camcorders there is no cost (or at least no explicit cost) for film development. In this respect, an argument could be made that the movie camera/camcorder unit has tended to increase in its relative importance as an integral component of photographic reproduction.[8]   Therefore, the rate of quality improvement that is estimated in this study for cameras, movie cameras and camcorders could be seen as lower than the rate that would apply to the combination of all related goods, in the sense that it does not account for the reduced relative costs of film, film processing and projection. As for picture cameras, on the other hand, the cost of film and development could have increased relative to the cost of the camera itself. However, such a change would be difficult to measure, because it would require, among other things, data on the average number of pictures per camera.

One problem that begins to occur in the 1950s, and worsens in more recent years, is the problem of accounting for camera components that are sold separately. If a camera could be purchased either with or without a particular component, such as a flash or camera case, then the price of the camera without the component was used. If the camera could only be purchased *with* a particular component, then the total price of the combined product was used as data, provided the additional component was minor in cost relative to the main unit. For example, a movie camera/movie projector combination would not be used as data, while a movie camera/carrying case combination would be used if the movie camera could not be purchased separately. Beginning in the 1980s some expensive cameras were sold without lenses, i.e., the lens would need to be purchased separately. In this particular case, the price of the camera was increased by the price of a common lens that would be used for that camera, because prior to the 1980s all cameras came with their own lenses.

The median camera in 1943 was unlike any of the cameras in

1938, perhaps because of a shortage of materials during World War II, and thus, the future median in 1938 was not available. Consequently, the future median was defined as the present median (as shown in Table 4.1), causing the quality improvement index to remain unchanged between 1938 and 1943 (as shown in Table 4.2).

No camera in 1973 could be found that was equivalent to the present median for 1978. However, a 1973 future median price was imputed by combining the price of a camera and a flash in 1973, where the combination of both was equivalent to the present median item for 1978, which was a non-separable camera and flash combination.

NOTES

1. Pisik (1993, p. A10) suggests that these three catalogues may be the most successful in the United States today, although she remarks that none of them would compare to the *Sears Catalog* in terms of the historical role that it played in American life.
2. The only exception would be the minimum/median ratio for window fans and air conditioners, due to the large fluctuations in the minimum.
3. The median price shown for 1929 is based on the linear interpolation between the 1928 and 1933 prices, i.e., it is the 1928 price, plus 0.2 x (1933 price minus 1928 price).
4. See Triplett (1986).
5. However, gas ranges did not actually take-off until after World War II. Also, gas ranges, fans, and certain types of cameras were not sold during the war years because of the shortage of strategic materials.
6. One exception was sofas, which were often sold as a package with lounge chairs. (See the Appendix to this chapter.)
7. There were some exceptions, however. For example, at various times during the period men's shoes were substituted by boots or by 'athletic shoes', sofas were substituted by sofa-beds (which were not counted as sofas in the study), and gas ranges were substituted by other types of ovens. On the other hand, for being personal consumption goods, these goods have continued to be in relatively high demand over the time span in question. In this respect they are quite different from goods such as horses, typewriters, or hula hoops, whose expansion or contraction could be associated with specific historical circumstances.
8. A television is also needed, but it is unlikely that a household would purchase one simply for the purpose of seeing the films produced with a camcorder. On the other hand, the household could be inclined to purchase a larger television than it would otherwise.

5. Estimation of cost reduction and income response effects

Some authors assume that if all the factors of production are doubled, the product will also double. This may be approximately true in certain cases, but not rigorously or in general . . . If, for example, one were to engage in the transportation business in Paris, it would be necessary to assume another business and another Paris.

Pareto (1879)

INTRODUCTION

Quality is 'relative' in the sense that one cannot actually measure the 'quality of good A', merely the 'quality of good A *relative* to good B'. On the other hand, one could consider an 'absolute' quality change when the quality of the same good, or type of good, is compared at different points in time. For example, let 'A_t' be a symbol denoting good *A* at time *t*, 'B_{t-1}' good *B* at time *t* minus 1, etc. *According to the perspective adopted in this study, if the consumer at time* t *is indifferent between 100 units of* A_t *and 115 units of* A_{t-1} *(where, hypothetically,* A_{t-1} *could also be purchased at time* t*), then the absolute quality change in good* A *from time* t-1 *to* t *is 15 per cent.* However, if different goods, *A* and *B*, increase in absolute quality in the same proportion between *t*-1 and *t*, then their *relative* quality, and relative prices (all else being equal) would not change.

The above notion of 'absolute quality change' has a unique feature: it requires *a decision by the consumer that is made at a single point in time, with regard to goods that exist at different points in time*. The concept itself seems paradoxical, but it is not. In Chapter 4 the apparent paradox was resolved through the interpretation of a good at time *t* as a *set of items* in which there is at least one that best reflects the average of the set in quality. As argued, if good A_{t-1} denotes the set of all men's shoes at time *t* minus 1, then the representative item might be the pair of shoes that has the median price. Let p_{t-1} denote the price of this representative item. At time t, another representative item exists, with price p_t. One finds that a comparison between p_{t-1} and p_t would have little meaning, because several factors besides quality change could have come into play, by virtue of the fact that the two representative items exist at different points in time. Nevertheless, a certain pair of shoes is found at time t-1 that is physically identical to the representative pair at time t. Let p_{t-1}^f denote the price of this specific pair of shoes at time t minus 1, where f indicates that the item will become the representative item in the future. It follows that the absolute quality change could be estimated through the comparison of p_{t-1} with p_{t-1}^f. If, for example, $p_{t-1}^f/p_{t-1} = 1.20$, then a 20 per cent increase in the absolute quality of men's shoes, between t-1 and t, could be estimated.

A symmetric, backward-looking approach could also be utilized in which the representative item at time t is compared to the item that used to be the representative item at time t minus 1. One could argue that the results are not generally the same, because the price of the former item could be reduced substantially by the next period due to supply-side changes. Nevertheless, the measurement of long-run effects should yield similar results between forward-looking and backward-looking methods.

In addition to quality change, another factor considered in this analysis is cost reduction, i.e., a reduction in the price of a good or service arising from increased productive capability. Negative cost reduction, as well as negative quality improvement, are not ruled out. The simultaneous consideration of quality improvement and cost reduction follows from the idea that some types of goods may be more inclined to experience one effect than the other. (See Chapter 7.) Of course, in drawing a distinction between quality improvement and cost reduction, one must automatically rule out the resource-cost interpretation of quality change.

In industries that undergo rapid quality improvement, firms often dramatically reduce the prices of items that have recently become obsolete (or out of style), in order to clear their inventories. One might then question if the methodology employed in this study, when applied to these 'inventory-clearing' prices, would overestimate actual cost reduction, in the sense that the firm is implicitly paying the consumer for the service of removing an item from its shelves. On the other hand, one could argue that the economic rents and economic losses that firms experience as a result of under- and over-stocking merchandise would tend to cancel each other out in the long-run.

A third factor examined is real income, under the assumption that it causes shifts in demand curves, and, as a consequence, shifts in relative prices. The distinction between the income effect and quality improvement effect could be quite subtle. Consider, for example, an exogenous increase in income due to the discovery and exploitation of a natural resource that is only exported and not consumed by the domestic economy (see Chapter 3). This increase in income would lead to an overall rise in the quality of goods and services because consumers, on average, would simply be able to afford higher quality items (including imports). In this case, however, the extent to which the income change leads to a quality change is not an aspect of the income effect on prices. Rather, it would be an effect that would lie 'underneath' the quality improvement effect. The reason is that the income effect in this analysis is defined as the effect of income on prices *above and beyond* any actual effect on quality.

Another distinction that must be drawn is between the income effect and the cost reduction effect. Under the assumption of perfect competition, the price of any good will equal its marginal cost. Nevertheless, a shift in demand due to a change in income would lead to a movement *along* the supply curve, while cost reduction would be associated with technological change, i.e., a movement *of* the supply curve.

One could begin with the following formulation:

$$\ln p_i(t) \;=\; \alpha_i + \beta_i[\ln I(t)] + \phi_i t - \delta_i t \qquad\qquad (5.1)$$

where:

p_i $\equiv$ the price of good i;

t $\equiv$ time;

α_i $\equiv$ a constant for the initial conditions for good i;

I $\equiv$ real income;

β_i $\equiv$ the response of the price of good i to changes in real income (as an elasticity);

ϕ_i $\equiv$ the rate of *relative* quality improvement; and

δ_i $\equiv$ the rate of cost reduction.

The parameters β_i, ϕ_i and δ_i are constant, for simplicity. Although this formulation is *ad hoc*, it could be derived fairly easily in a formal model, which is precisely what is done in the next chapter.

Equation 5.1 is not an equation suited for regression analysis, because the separate effects of quality improvement and cost reduction are not identifiable. The solution to this problem, discussed below, is for one to measure quality improvement separately, and then subtract the effect from both sides of the equation. One then has 'price per constant unit of quality' on the left side of the equation, which leaves cost reduction as the only coefficient of time.

Perhaps the greatest concern in the use of this approach is that, in order for the income effect to exist, long-run supply curves cannot be flat. This concern is addressed in the next section. Additional concerns, which are also addressed, are:

1. In Equation 5.1, relative prices are direct functions of *relative* quality improvement, rather than *absolute* quality improvement, but then how does absolute quality improvement come into play?
2. It has yet to be resolved how 'real income' could be measured in a framework that allows for continual changes in quality.
3. Equation 5.1 leaves out the possibility of a pure price effect, which might limit its usefulness for applied work.

LONG-RUN SUPPLY CURVES

Although the model examines long-run effects, supply curves are not assumed to be perfectly elastic at the minimum average cost, for four reasons:

1. The empirical findings of this study (shown below) imply that long-run supply curves are not, in fact, perfectly elastic for the goods examined.
2. The model is based on the idea of a continual flow of new and improved goods, and thus, a continual flow of economic rents from innovation. The Keynesian cliche that 'in the long run we are all dead' is analogous here — *in the long run, all the specific goods and services, that we know of today, no longer exist*! When demand for a specific good increases, industry analysts may decide not to expand productive capacity, because they may estimate that, by the time this new capacity is in place, a

new substitute of higher quality could have been developed that
requires a different type of capacity. In effect, there is always
an opportunity cost to firms expanding the production of the
same item in industries that undergo continual product
innovation. It follows from this concept of opportunity cost
that the long-run supply curve is upward sloping.

3. Due to the scarcity of certain natural resources associated with
some types of goods and services, supply curves per unit of
population could rise as populations increase.

4. In a model of a single good, shortages of the factors of
production, especially labour, need not come into play.
However, the framework adopted here is that a large proportion
of all goods and services are improving in quality, and the
majority of them are being demanded more as incomes rise.
Hence, with increased demand across-the-board as incomes
rise, and increased wages to accommodate the increased skills
needed to produce higher-quality goods, long-run supply curves
could be upward sloping.

It is worth noting that in some cases, e.g., under increasing returns
to scale, one would expect *downward-sloping* supply curves. This
would not be inconsistent with the presence of an income effect on
demand, but would merely reverse its direction. Only a perfectly
horizontal supply curve would negate the existence of an income
effect.

An Initial Perspective on the Effect of Changes in Income

For simplicity, assume that there is zero population growth, or
equivalently, that the economic model under consideration is on a
per capita basis. One could start by examining a single good, in
which there are evolutionary changes in the price per constant unit
of quality. In this context, a quality improvement in the good, all
else being equal (including the price per common unit), could be
interpreted as a reduction in the price *per constant unit of quality*.

Now consider demand and supply curves in price and constant-
quality-units space, as shown in Figure 5.1. One could begin at time
0, with the demand and supply curves D_0 and S_0, in which there is
equilibrium at Point A. In general, quality improvements in the good
would cause shifts in both supply and demand. However, these
shifts would be peripheral to the discussion at hand. For simplicity,
assume there is only one type of technological change: cost

Figure 5.1   The perfectly elastic, long-run supply curve

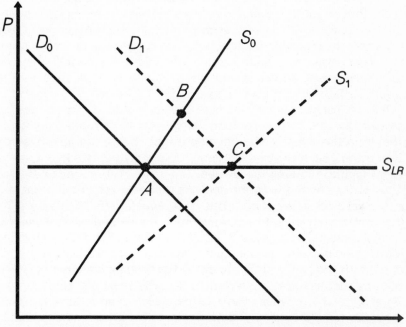

Quantity (in terms of constant units of quality)

reduction, while the quality per unit does not change. It will become apparent that the effects examined below would not be different by the relaxation of this assumption.

Cost reduction in the industry in question would be straightforward; there would simply be a downward shift in the supply curve, and a corresponding drop in the price per constant quality unit, plus a secondary income effect on demand due to the effective increase in real purchasing power. However, for the moment, one could hold off on considering a cost-reduction of this kind (in the industry in question), and instead begin by considering the effect of an initial change in real income. Specifically, assume that real income increases due to an average, or overall, cost reduction in all of the other industries.[1] Furthermore, assuming the income elasticity of demand for the good in question is positive, one has an upward rise in the demand curve to D_1, as shown in Figure 5.1. There is, then, a tendency for the equilibrium point to move from *A* to *B*.

The shift from D_0 to D_1 would be gradual. As the price rises in the movement from Points *A* to *B*, higher profits would be realized in the industry in question, and thus firms would be encouraged to expand operations. Consequently, the number of firms in the industry would rise, and supply will shift outward to S_1, at the same time that demand is shifting upward. The market for the good, therefore, never arrives at Point *B*, but relocates at Point *C*, the result of both an increased demand due to increased real income, and an expanded supply to meet that demand. It could then be argued that the long-run supply curve, S_{LR}, is perfectly elastic, as shown in the figure. The 'income effect' discussed in this study would then be zero, because long-run supply adjusts to meet the exact increase in long-run demand.

One could now add to the analysis the effect of a cost reduction in the industry in question. This cost reduction is reflected by the downward shift in S_0 to S_0' in Figure 5.2. Instead of beginning at Point *A*, one might begin at Point *A'*, and end at Point *C'*. The same result would occur if the cost reduction happens at any time *between* periods 1 and 2. Actually, the best perspective could be the one that assumes a gradual shift in the short-run supply curve from S_0 to S_1' between the two periods. In any case, the cost reduction would lead to a downward shift in the long-run supply curve, and the extent of that downward shift would be equivalent to the cost reduction effect.

As shown in Figure 5.2, the same shift in the long-run supply curve would occur in the industry with or without the shift in demand.[2] *Without* the increase in demand, the price would shift from P_0 to P_0'; *with* that increase, it would shift from P_1 to P_1'. In either case, the cost reduction effect would be the same, and the changes in demand would have no effect on prices in the long run. However, this framework is challenged in the next section.

The Existence of an Upward Sloping Long-run Supply Curve

As suggested in the beginning of this discussion, perfectly elastic long-run supply curves, in the face of upward shifts in demand, may not be consistent with a general equilibrium framework. If, on the average, demand is increasing in most industries per constant unit of population, and supply is expanding in most industries as well, then the total demand for labour in the economy would exceed the supply, until the labour market adjusts. The price of labour would

Figure 5.2 The effect of cost reduction in all industries

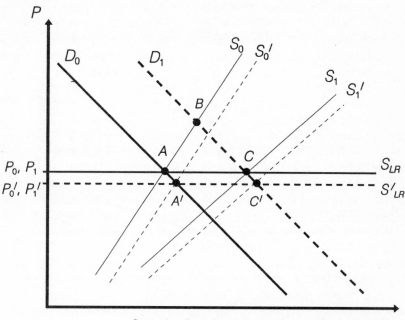

Quantity (in terms of constant units of quality)

therefore rise as production expands, which, in turn, would impair the ability of most industries to expand as much as they would like.[3]

Higher wages, of course, would be consistent with the increases in income that give rise to the upward shifts in demand. In fact, the only way that wages could *not* rise, while income increases, is if the wage share of total income in the economy were to constantly decrease, which may not be politically feasible in the long run.

Furthermore, many of the cost reductions that would occur would actually be quality improvements, and would only be cost reductions 'per constant unit of quality'. Therefore, many of the increases in real income would be quite subtle. These increases would not, for example, be picked up entirely by the Consumer Price Index. (See Chapters 3 and 4.) Thus, real wages would increase without that increase being fully recognized in the national accounts. The less detection there is of these cost reduction and quality improvement effects, the more unwilling labour would be to accept employment at wages that appear to be lower according to the CPI and other indicators.

Consequently, long-run supply curves would not be flat in the face of overall increases in income, because of supply constraints. Figure 5.3 illustrates this point by repeating the same effects as those in

Figure 5.3 An upward-sloping, long-run supply curve

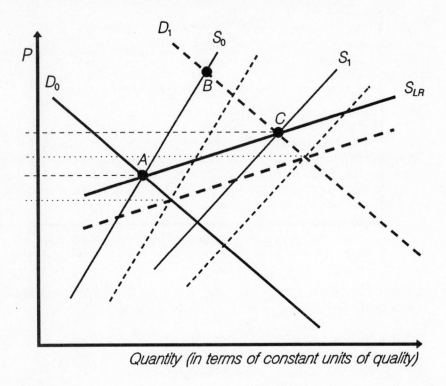

Quantity (in terms of constant units of quality)

Figure 5.2, only with the supply curve in period 1, S_1, not shifting as far to the right. The solid lines display the effect of an overall increase in real income, and consequent increase in demand for the particular good in question, without a specific cost reduction in that particular industry. The dashed lines display the same effect, only with a cost reduction. In either case, the same, positive, income effect occurs, due to an *upward sloping long-run supply curve*.

In some industries, of course, suppliers would be severely constrained in their ability to shift the supply curve outward to meet increases in demand. Examples are real estate, precious metals, and other industries closely associated with natural scarcity. In these cases, S_1 in Figure 5.3 could be quite close to S_0, and thus, Point C could be close to Point B. The income effect would then be more pronounced. In conclusion, the income effect would be expected to vary considerably across industries, from being negligible in some to substantial in others.

Finally, as argued above, in an innovative environment firms that expand the production of an existing good incur an opportunity cost of not devoting more resources to the production of a newer model. Therefore, one could envision upward-sloping supply curves that are consistent with a steady-state framework, where specific goods associated with any given supply curve will eventually become obsolete. Segerstrom adopts a similar perspective, and develops a 'dynamic general equilibrium model of economic growth', in which, 'Firms devote resources to discovering new superior products . . . Other firms devote resources to imitating new superior products, and successful innovators cannot count on earning dominant firm profits forever. Because of product innovation, individual products eventually become obsolete' (Segerstrom 1991, p. 826). However, he assumes constant returns to scale in the model, where 'firms . . . face no capacity constraints' (p. 812). This CRS condition is not consistent with the usual requirements for *static* equilibrium. Rather, a model of innovation that would be consistent with both long-run and static equilibrium would have upward-sloping supply curves in the static case. As suggested, short-run curves would 'begin' to flatten out in the long-run, but would 'vanish' before they become completely flat, as new products come on line.[4]

SIMULTANEOUS ESTIMATION OF QUALITY AND A PURE PRICE EFFECT

Given the previous definition of ϕ_i as the 'relative' rate of quality improvement, one can break down ϕ_i into two components: ϕ_i^A for the rate of absolute quality improvement for good i, and ϕ^m for the mean (weighted by expenditures) rate of quality improvement across all goods. Goods not yet in existence would have zero weight, which is not inconsistent with weights based on expenditure levels. One then has:

$$\phi_i = \phi_i^A - \phi^m .$$
(5.2)

Another interpretation of ϕ^m is that it is a 'deflationary effect' due to the combined influences of 1) quality improvement (or decline) occurring in all goods, and 2) competition among goods for the consumer's budget, which is fixed in the static case. For example, suppose there is zero absolute quality improvement in good i, but positive quality improvement in good j. The quality improvement in good j would tend to lower the price of good i per constant unit of quality, because the consumer's willingness to spend more on good j implies that he would have less to spend on good i. Thus, the price of good i per constant unit of quality would decline, all else being equal. For these reasons, this effect, and the parameter ϕ^m, will be called 'the deflationary effect of the budget constraint'.

Making use of ϕ_i^A, one finds that the log of the price of good i, per constant unit of quality, is given by:

$$\text{In } (price\ per\ constant\ unit\ of\ quality) = \text{In } p_i(t) - \phi_i^A t . \quad (5.3)$$

If one now adds another component that is independent of all real effects, and is simply a pure price effect, $\Omega(t)$, then by Equations 5.1 and 5.2:

$$\text{In } p_i(t) - \phi_i^A t = \alpha_i + \beta_i[\text{In } I(t)] - \delta_i t - \phi^m t + \Omega(t) . \quad (5.4)$$

For convenience, the terms in Equation 5.4 are explained again in Table 5.1, and heuristic examples are provided to explain each of the separate terms.

Thus far in this analysis the concepts of 'price' and 'price per constant unit of quality' have had limited meaning, in light of the large variety of factors that could influence them. A much more useful concept than the price in monetary units would be the exchange value of a good. Thus, with a particular good as the numeraire, the log of the 'real' price of good i, per constant unit of quality, would be given by:

$$\text{In } \left(\frac{Quality\ Units\ of\ Numeraire}{Quality\ Units\ of\ Good\ i} \right) = \quad (5.5)$$

$$\text{In } \left(\frac{Price\ per\ Constant\ Unit\ of\ Quality\ for\ Good\ i}{Price\ per\ Constant\ Unit\ of\ Quality\ for\ Numeraire} \right)$$

Table 5.1   Explanation of the terms appearing in Equation 4

Term	Description	Example of how a change could occur in the price per constant unit of quality
$\ln p_i(t)$ minus $\phi_i^A t$	Log of price per constant unit of quality	
a_i	Constant term	(fixed)
$\beta_i [ln I(t)]$	Income effect	Neither the quality of hamburgers nor the quality of sushi goes up, but after a rise in income sushi becomes relatively more desirable, and rises in price relative to hamburgers.
$-\delta_i t$	Cost reduction effect	The quality of a calculator does not change, but its price is reduced due to increased productivity by the manufacturer.
$-\phi^m t$	Deflationary effect of the budget constraint	The quality of sugar does not change, but sugar becomes relatively less desirable as the quality of other products, especially sugar-substitutes, goes up.
$\Omega(t)$	Pure price effect	Nothing real changes in terms of quality, production, income, or tastes, between the beginning of a particular period and the end of the same period. However, in the interim a monetary expansion leads to an inflation, which raises all prices and income levels proportionally.

$$= (\ln p_i(t) - \phi_i^A t) - (\ln p_n(t) - \phi_n^A t) \qquad (5.6)$$

$$= (a_i - a_n) + (\beta_i - \beta_n) \ln I(t) - (\delta_i - \delta_n) t . \qquad (5.7)$$

by Equation 5.4, where n denotes the numeraire. Note that the pure price effect and the deflationary effect of the budget constraint both drop out. Furthermore, once prices are measured in terms of a numeraire, the parameters a, ß and δ for good i are meaningful only to the extent that they differ from the values of the same parameters that would exist for the numeraire in Equation 4. Hence, without loss of generality, one can attribute values of zero to a_n, ß$_n$ and δ_n. One then has:

$$(\ln p_i(t) - \phi_i^A t) - (\ln p_n(t) - \phi_n^A t) = a_i + \beta_i \ln I(t) - \delta_i t . \qquad (5.8)$$

For the numeraire, Equation 5.4 reduces to:

$$\ln p_n(t) - \phi_n^A t = \Omega(t) - \phi^m t . \qquad (5.9)$$

For ease of notation, let the left-hand side of Equations 5.5 to 5.8, the log of the 'real' relative price of a quality unit of good i in quality units of the numeraire, be denoted by $\hat{p}_i$. Equation 5.8 then simplifies to:

$$\hat{p}_i = a_i + \beta_i \ln I(t) - \delta_i t . \qquad (5.10)$$

For consistency, the income at time t should also be based on constant quantity units of the numeraire. The term I in Equation 10 and in earlier equations has denoted real income. Thus, if I° is observed income, in unadjusted nominal terms, one has:

$$\ln I(t) = \ln I^\circ(t) - (\ln p_n(t) - \phi_n^A t) \qquad (5.11)$$

where the second term on the right is the log of the price per constant quality unit of the numeraire. Therefore, given data on I°, and data on the price per quality unit of the numeraire, estimates of

In $I(t)$ can be derived based on Equation 5.11, which could then serve as input for Equation 5.10. Once data on the $\hat{p}_i$s are derived, these would also serve as input for Equation 5.10, from which estimates of a, β and δ could be obtained through regression analysis. Table 5.2 provides a summary of the necessary steps in the analysis.

Table 5.2   Summary of methodology

Step	Variables	Procedure
1	$p_i(t)$ $p_n(t)$	From data on the historical prices and characteristics of goods, identify the (present) median good for each period. Note the specific characteristics of these median goods, and record their nominal prices. Among the different goods to be examined, identify the good that will serve as the numeraire.
2	$\phi_i^A(t)$ $\phi_n^A(t)$ $\bar{\phi}_i^A$	For each period except the last, find the 'future median' good in that period which is identical in terms of characteristics (or as similar as possible) to the median good of the next period. Then estimate the percent change in Absolute Quality = (Future Median minus Present Median) / Present Median, = $\phi_i(t+1)$, the growth rate between t and $t+1$. (See Table 4.2.) From these percentages, generate a *cumulative quality index* for each good. Regression analyses of the log of this cumulative quality index against time will generate estimates, for each good, of the average rate of absolute quality improvement, $\bar{\phi}_i^A$.
3	$\hat{p}_i(t)$	Calculate, for all t except the first and for all goods except the numeraire: $\hat{p}_i(t) = [ln\, p_i(t) - \phi_i^A(t)t] - [ln\, p_n(t) - \phi_n^A(t)t]$, which is the log of the real price of good i (in the first period) relative to the numeraire.
4	$ln\, I(t)$	Obtain data on nominal income levels $I°(t)$ and deflate them by the price per constant quality of the numeraire: $ln\, I(t) = ln\, I°(t) - [ln\, p_n(t) - \phi_n^A(t)t]$.
5	a_i, β_i, δ_i	Given $\hat{p}_i(t)$ and $ln\, I(t)$ from Steps 3 and 4, for all goods except the numeraire, perform regression analyses on the equation: $\hat{p}_i = a_i + \beta_i\, ln\, I(t) - \delta_i t$. (See Table 5.1.)

MEASUREMENT OF COST REDUCTION AND INCOME RESPONSE EFFECTS

As discussed above, a regression of the log of the relative price index against time and the log of 'real income' renders estimates of the cost reduction rate and income effect. The cost reduction rate, or 'δ_i', would be estimated as the coefficient of time, and the income effect, 'β_i', as the coefficient of the log of income. The constant would be irrelevant in this case, as it would be a function of the units of measure.

In the present study, men's shoes were chosen as the numeraire. The reasons for this choice were: data on men's shoes were available for all periods, and the identical representative items could be found between periods. In addition, it was expected that a large proportion of households, at all income levels, would purchase men's shoes in any given year, and men's shoes could be less subject to disturbances during the time span than any of the other four goods.

Table 5.3 first derives a 'Relative Price Index' for the five types of goods, which is the price of a good, *per constant unit of quality*, *relative* to the price of the numeraire, men's shoes, per constant unit of quality. These relative price indices are displayed in Figure 5.4 on a logarithmic scale. They are also used as input for the regression analyses presented below. The other variable considered in the analysis, income, was estimated as personal consumption expenditures (PCE), which was believed to be a relevant indicator of income, with regard to purchases of the goods in question.[5] Logs of the real PCE per capita were also used as input for the regression analyses, based on the derived prices per quality unit of men's shoes. Table 5.4 provides the raw data used in the analysis. As explained in the table, constraints in data availability required a change in the time span from 1928-1993 to 1929-1992.

OLS regressions of the form indicated in Equation 5.10 were conducted, and the results are shown in Table 5.5. Men's shoes were not considered, since the *relative* price index per constant unit of quality for men's shoes is 100 at every point in time, by definition.

The Durbin-Watson test for autocorrelation is not significant in any of the tests, although the low value of 0.98 for window fans and air conditioners is suggestive of autocorrelation. A cost-reduction trend is significant (at $p < 0.05$) for three of the four goods, while for fans it was nearly significant, at $p = 0.058$. The

Table 5.3 Derivation of a relative price index

Price per constant unit of quality = Price x 100 ÷ Quality Index

Year	1928	1933	1938	1943	1948	1953	1958
Men's shoes	4.48	2.36	1.75	2.34	3.58	3.56	3.61
Sofas	79.50	30.16	46.73	37.91	69.01	62.13	50.03
Gas ranges	48.50	25.85	39.95	39.95	39.95	77.07	70.27
Fans and ACs	7.40	2.20	2.20	2.20	4.95	6.24	3.87
Cameras	8.95	10.74	12.68	20.95	22.94	7.73	3.47

Year	1963	1968	1973	1978	1983	1988	1993
Men's shoes	3.63	4.44	5.72	6.01	8.45	10.87	9.78
Sofas	47.83	82.01	92.27	79.08	101.70	91.52	102.99
Gas ranges	56.88	59.59	86.26	108.85	112.75	108.65	162.97
Fans and ACs	3.56	2.85	2.71	3.11	3.86	4.54	5.68
Cameras	4.00	2.46	1.47	1.28	1.79	2.41	2.41

Relative price = Price per quality unit ÷ price per quality unit of numeraire

Year	1928	1933	1938	1943	1948	1953	1958
Men's shoes	1.00	1.00	1.00	1.00	1.00	1.00	1.00
Sofas	17.75	12.76	26.67	16.20	19.27	17.46	13.87
Gas ranges	10.83	10.93	22.80	17.07	11.16	21.66	19.48
Fans and ACs	1.65	0.93	1.25	0.94	1.38	1.75	1.07
Cameras	2.00	4.54	7.24	8.95	6.41	2.17	0.96

Year	1963	1968	1973	1978	1983	1988	1993
Men's shoes	1.00	1.00	1.00	1.00	1.00	1.00	1.00
Sofas	13.17	18.45	16.12	13.16	12.03	8.42	10.53
Gas ranges	15.66	13.41	15.07	18.11	13.34	10.00	16.66
Fans and ACs	0.98	0.64	0.47	0.52	0.46	0.42	0.58
Cameras	1.10	0.55	0.26	0.21	0.21	0.22	0.25

Relative price index = Relative price x 100 ÷ relative price in 1928

Year	1928	1933	1938	1943	1948	1953	1958
Men's shoes	100	100	100	100	100	100	100
Sofas	100.00	71.89	150.27	91.28	108.61	98.40	78.17
Gas ranges	100.00	101.00	210.59	157.68	103.06	200.08	179.98
Fans and ACs	100.00	56.24	75.88	56.81	83.64	106.23	64.97
Cameras	100.00	227.40	362.21	448.13	320.73	108.77	48.20

Year	1963	1968	1973	1978	1983	1988	1993
Men's shoes	100	100	100	100	100	100	100
Sofas	74.21	103.98	90.84	74.14	67.79	47.45	59.32
Gas ranges	144.67	123.85	139.21	167.27	123.19	92.33	153.86
Fans and ACs	59.35	38.80	28.68	31.29	27.64	25.29	35.12
Cameras	55.15	27.74	12.85	10.67	10.61	11.08	12.31

Figure 5.4 Relative price index

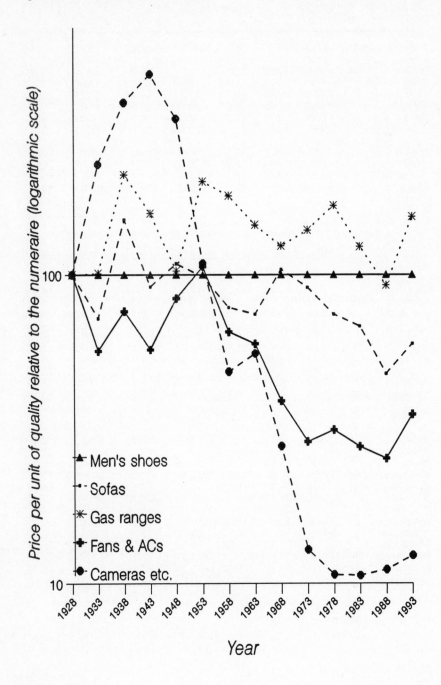

Table 5.4   Derivation of relative price indices and real personal consumption expenditures, to be used in the regression analysis

---

Relative Price Index (1928 = 100)

Year	1929	1933	1938	1943	1948	1953	1958
Sofas	94.38	71.89	150.27	91.28	108.61	98.40	78.17
Gas ranges	100.20	101.00	210.59	157.68	103.06	200.08	179.98
Fans and ACs	91.25	56.24	75.88	56.81	83.64	106.23	64.97
Cameras	125.48	227.40	362.21	448.13	320.73	108.77	48.20

Year	1963	1968	1973	1978	1983	1988	1993
Sofas	74.21	103.98	90.84	74.14	67.79	47.45	56.94
Gas ranges	144.67	123.85	139.21	167.27	123.19	92.33	141.55
Fans and ACs	59.35	38.80	28.68	31.29	27.64	25.29	33.15
Cameras	55.15	27.74	12.85	10.67	10.61	11.08	12.07

---

income-response effect was highly significant for gas ranges ($p = 0.006$), and approaching significance for sofas and cameras (p = 0.067 & 0.084, respectively).   When taken together, these results strongly support the existence of cost-reduction and income-response effects.

An explanation can be offered for the relatively low significance of the income effects for fans and cameras: These goods have undergone rapid quality improvement and cost reduction throughout the time span.   Consequently, the observed income effect could exist, but could be masked by the larger swings in prices attributable to these other effects.   Perhaps, with the addition of data from sources other than the *Sears Catalog*, these income effects would be more pronounced.

It is somewhat surprising that gas ranges had a higher income response rate than sofas, because one would tend to think of sofas as being more of a luxury item.   One would explanation is that, as incomes have increased, and homes have increased in size, households have tended to replace their stoves by larger, more elaborate ones.   In contrast, they could have also tended to purchase less expensive sofas for secondary purposes, such as for a recreation room, basement, or porch.

The relatively low income effect on window fans and air conditioners could be strongly related to the substitution of window

Table 5.4 Derivation of relative price indices and real personal consumption expenditures, to be used in the regression analysis (concluded)

Estimated real Personal Consumption Expenditures (PCE)

Year	1929	1933	1938	1943	1948	1953	1958
A = Cost per constant quality of numeraire	0.91	0.53	0.39	0.52	0.80	0.79	0.81
B = per capita PCE	636	366	495	729	1,196	1,458	1,694
Per capita PCE in 1928 $ (B/A)	703	693	1,264	1,396	1,497	1,835	2,105

Year	1963	1968	1973	1978	1983	1988	1993
A = Cost per constant quality of numeraire	0.81	0.99	1.28	1.34	1.89	2.43	2.23
B = per capita PCE	2,030	2,786	4,002	6,385	9,635	13,452	16,028
Per capita PCE in 1928 $ (B/A)	2,504	2,808	3,133	4,759	5,106	5,544	7,180

Sources: Relative cost indices from Table 5.3. Personal consumption expenditures per capita based on: Personal consumption expenditures from US Dept of Commerce, Bureau of Economic Analysis, 1993; and population estimates from US Dept of Labor, Bureau of the Census, 1993.

Note: The years 1929 and 1992 were used instead of 1928 and 1993, because comparable population and PCE data were not available for 1928, and no data were available for 1993 because this table was prepared in March 1993. The relative cost indices for 1929 and 1993 were estimated through interpolation. That is, the 1929 value was calculated as the sum of the 1928 value and 20 per cent of the difference between the 1933 value and the 1928 value. Similarly, the 1992 value was the sum of the 1993 value minus 20 per cent of the difference between the 1993 and 1988 values.

air conditioners by central air conditioning systems (which were not included in the data), especially in higher-income homes.

The incredibly high values of the estimated cost-reduction and income-response coefficients for cameras, movie cameras and camcorders, should not be surprising to people who are familiar with the industry. Indeed, the relatively recent emergence of 'disposable cameras' in neighbourhood chemist shops where film is sold, serves as further evidence for the remarkable rate of cost reduction in the

Table 5.5   *Regression results on the cost-reduction and*
           income-response effects

Type of good	Sofas and love seats	Gas ranges	Window fans and ACs	Cameras etc.
Cost-reduction effect				
Estimated coefficient (per cent)	4.607	6.182	5.289	16.134
t-statistic	2.51	3.37	2.12	3.09
Income-response effect				
Estimated coefficient (Elasticity)	1.047	1.737	0.947	2.779
t-statistic	2.03	3.38	1.35	1.90
Durbin-Watson statistic	1.83	1.73	0.98	1.28
Adjusted R-squared	0.51	0.42	0.68	0.84

industry as a whole.

Figure 5.5 summarizes the estimated rates of quality improvement, cost reduction and income response for the five goods examined in this study. The figure indicates that each of the three forces do have a certain degree of independence for each good. On the other hand, the highest rates all coincide at the same good: cameras, movie cameras and camcorders. This finding for cameras implies that the three forces are not entirely independent, and that in certain cases they may act to facilitate each other.

The positive correlation between observed quality-improvement rates and cost-reduction rates implies that some goods and services could be more inclined to undergo *both* types of technical change than others. Of course, when both forces occur simultaneously, they nullify each other in terms of their overall effect on prices. The underlying reasons for these observed magnitudes of quality improvement, cost reduction and income response are explored in Chapter 7.

Figure 5.5 Summary of estimated evolutionary forces acting on prices, 1928-1993

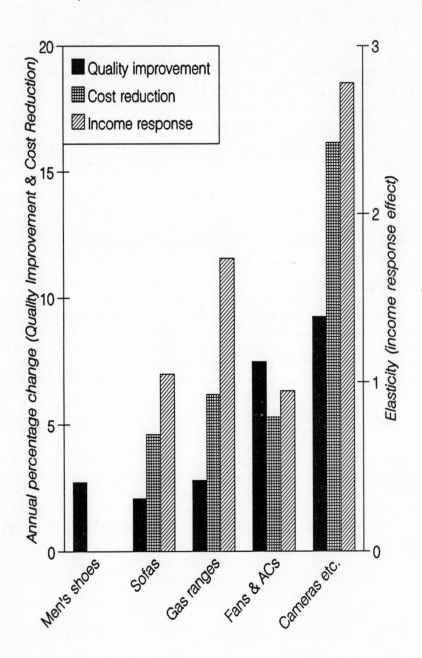

NOTES

1. One must also assume that there is no change in the prices of inputs to the industry in question — an issue that is addressed later.
2. Although the demand shift would, in reality, influence the production processes of the firms in the industry, it would be impossible to determine, off hand, what direction that influence would take. In light of the complexity of this issue, the simplest assumption, for an arbitrary industry in general, would be that the extent of cost reduction is independent of upward shifts in demand.
3. The same may be said of other inputs to production that tend to exist in limited amounts, especially land, fuel and rare minerals.
4. In many respects, this framework could be regarded as Schumpeterian — see Schumpeter (1934).
5. With income expressed in terms of personal consumption expenditures, as opposed to other measures, there are less distrubances attributable to cyclical trends in savings and in the purchases of homes.

6. A model on long-run evolutionary change

It is of course true that quality is much more difficult to 'handle' than quantity . . . Quantitative differences can be more easily grasped and certainly more easily defined than qualitative differences; their concreteness is beguiling and gives them the appearance of scientific precision, even when this precision has been purchased by the suppression of vital differences of quality. The great majority of economists is still pursuing the absurd ideal of making their 'science' as scientific and precise as physics, as if there were no qualitative difference between mindless atoms and men made in the image of God.

Schumacher (1973, pp. 48-9)

Equation 5.1 was an *ad hoc* expression based largely on intuition, but in this chapter that intuition is supported by a theoretical model. As is always the case with theoretical models, economists rely on simplifying assumptions in order to avoid an unmanageable degree of mathematics. Consequently, the prevailing logic among economists has been, 'All models are *wrong* — some are *useful*.' The model presented here is no exception, although the simplifying assumptions are not seen as overly restrictive.

To understand the need for simplifying assumptions, one could first assess the situation that would exist without them. For example, quality changes in goods over time could be seen as shifts in the g_i parameters of the utility function:

$$U = U[g_1(t)x_1, g_2(t)x_2, ..., g_n(t)x_n] \qquad (6a)$$

where g_i is a function of t, and x_i is the number of units of good i consumed. One then has the static maximization problem:

$$\max \ U = U[g_1(t)x_1, g_2(t)x_2, ..., g_n(t)x_n] - \lambda[\sum_{i=1}^{n} p_i x_i - I(t)] \qquad (6b)$$

where p_i is the price of good i, and $I(t)$ is real income at time t. One simplifying assumption that is implicit in this model is that all individuals (or households) are the same. Differentiation of Equation 6b renders:

$$p_i = \frac{u_i g_i(t)}{\lambda} \ ; \quad \lambda = \frac{\sum_{i=1}^{n} u_i g_i(t)}{I(t)} \qquad (6c)$$

which implies:

$$p_i(t) = \frac{g_i(t) u_i I(t)}{\sum_i x_i g_i(t) u_i} \ . \qquad (6d)$$

On the supply side, let $C_i(x_i, t)$ be the minimum cost of producing x_i at time t (for the representative firm). Increased productivity, or cost reduction, could be interpreted as the tendency for the marginal cost to decline over time, i.e.:

$$\frac{\partial}{\partial t} \frac{\partial C_i(x_i, t)}{\partial x} < 0 \ . \qquad (6e)$$

In perfect competition, with firms as price takers and profit maximizers, marginal cost will equal the price, i.e.:

$$p_i(t) = \frac{\partial C_i(x_i, t)}{\partial x} \ . \qquad (6f)$$

In this simple model, there are n quality-related functions to be estimated, $g_1, g_2, ..., g_n$, and n cost-related functions $\partial C_1(x_1, t)/\partial x_1$, $\partial C_2(x_2, t)/\partial x_2$, ..., $\partial C_n(x_n, t)/\partial x_n$. Thus, with data on prices and quantities at various points in time, there are $2n$ equations for estimating the parameters of these $2n$ functions: n equations of the form of Equation 6d and n of the form of Equation 6f. However, the system is far from linear and would be very difficult to estimate, even if each function, $(g_i$ or $\partial C_i(x_i, t)/\partial x_i)$ contains a single parameter, e.g. $g_i(t) = q_i^t$ or $\partial C_i(x_i, t)/\partial x_i = k_i^{-t}$.

One assumption that would make the model feasible for analysis is that the income level, alone, determines the budget share spent on a good. In other words, good i is a set of items that vary in price. If the relative prices of all of these items decline, for example, then the individual would purchase a higher quality item than he purchased before, so that his budget share for that good will remain unchanged (and vice versa for a rise in relative prices). In short, at a given level of real income, I_0, an individual will spend z_i per cent of his income on good i, regardless of p_i. Of course, this assumption relies on the idea that, in the static case, p_i does not fluctuate greatly. For instance, suppose that an individual is accustomed to spending 40 per cent of his or her disposable income on food, and the prices of all food items decline while other prices rise, leaving real income unchanged. By the above assumption, the individual would still be inclined to spend 40 per cent on food, but would purchase food of higher quality. However, if his real income changes, then this 40 per cent could also change.

The above assumption is equivalent to the simplifying assumption that the price elasticity of demand is equal to 1.0 for all goods. In a static analysis of consumer behaviour, this assumption could be quite restrictive. However, the model presented here is a dynamic model, in which elasticities of demand in the static case are peripheral to the issues at hand. Hence, the assumption is appropriate because of the simplicity that it offers to the analysis, without sacrificing applicability.

The main benefit of this assumption is that a Cobb-Douglas utility function can be used to approximate the utility function of consumers. This does not mean that a single Cobb-Douglas utility function is assumed — rather, a unique one is assumed *only at each fixed level of real income*.

In addition, each good is assumed to represent only a small portion of the total budget. Consequently, the simplifying assumption is made that only relative prices change within a period (i.e., in the static case), without significantly affecting real income. On the other hand, income is assumed to change significantly between periods, and thus, distinctly different parameters of the Cobb-Douglas (C-D) utility function would apply to different periods.

The model begins with the utility function:

$$U = \prod_{i=1}^{N} c_i^{g_i} \qquad (6.1)$$

where c_i represents the quantity of good i consumed by a particular individual. Maximization of the log of utility, subject to a budget constraint, is given by:

$$Max \ln U = \sum g_i \ln(c_i) + h(I - \sum p_i c_i) \qquad (6.2)$$

where I is income and p_i is the price of good i. This renders:

$$g_i = \frac{c_i p_i G}{I} \qquad (6.3)$$

where

$$G = \sum_{i=1}^{N} g_i . \qquad (6.4)$$

By Equation 6.1, one finds:

$$u_i = \frac{g_i U}{c_i} . \qquad (6.5)$$

Consequently, Lancaster's expenditure equivalent index of quality change, $\mathscr{L}$, would be given by:

$$\mathscr{L} = \sum_{j=1}^{J} \frac{g_j}{G} \frac{dc_j}{c_j} \qquad (6.6)$$

for any group of goods $j = 1,..., J$; $J < N$, in the economy. (See Equation L.9 in Chapter 3.)

Equation 6.6 provides a simple, yet revealing, interpretation of quality change as a function of changes in the consumption of goods within a group. The parameter g_i/G represents a relative measure of the utility derived from good i, per proportional unit of consumption.

Let us now consider the evolution of goods and services, in which the g_is change across periods in accordance with changes in the quality (physical characteristics) of goods. In this case G, the sum of the g_is, would change as well. Changes in the g_is would reflect changes in absolute quality, while changes in the g_i/G parameter would reflect changes in relative quality. (See the discussion of absolute and relative quality in Chapter 5.) On the one hand, g_i/G, or relative quality, should be the variable of interest, because it is consistent with the movement of observed prices across time. On the other hand, g_i, or absolute quality, allows for an assessment of *real* income. That is, because the g_is increase as absolute quality improves, the level of real income, I, also changes over time as a function of the g_is:

$$I_t = I_t(g_1, \ldots, g_N) .$$ (6.7)

For ease of notation, let:

$$g_i^* = \frac{g_i}{G} .$$ (6.8)

In the discussion that follows the i subscript is left out for simplicity.

At present, g^* represents two important concepts: the budget share for a particular good, and a relative quality index. The notion of it being a quality index, however, is clouded by the fact that other factors could have an influence on it besides changes in the characteristics of a good. Specifically, as a parameter of the utility function that is subject to evolutionary change, the parameter g^* can also reflect changes in tastes.

As mentioned earlier, *distinctly different Cobb-Douglas approximations to the utility function would be applicable to distinctly different levels of income.* In other words, in the static case in which income is fixed, utility maximization is approximated in terms of a specific C-D utility function. After a substantial change in the level of income, however, a *new* C-D utility function, with different values for the g_is, would then be applicable. Therefore, in the context of an a priori Cobb-Douglas approximation, the g_i parameters, or budget shares, could be reinterpreted as implicit functions of real income.[1]

Given this perspective, g_i^* could be expressed as a function of both an income component and a physical-characteristics component:

$$g_i^* = g_i^* (Q, I) \qquad (6.9)$$

where Q represents the matrix of characteristics for all goods. That is, $Q = (q_{ij})$, in which q_{ij} is the magnitude of the jth characteristic for the ith good. (See Chapter 2.) Because g_i^* is a function of G, it must be a function of the characteristics of all goods, which is consistent with the existence of substitutes and complements.

One could assume, for simplicity, that there is separability between income and physical characteristics in the g_i^* function, i.e.:

$$g_i^* = g_{iQ}(Q) \, g_{iI}(I) \qquad (6.10)$$

where g_{iQ} and g_{iI} represent distinct functions with regard to good i.

It is important to note, once again, that the function $g_{iI}(I)$ does not have any bearing on the consumer's maximization of utility subject to a budget constraint, which is, in contrast, a static problem in which real income, I, is fixed. The only relevance of $g_{iI}(I)$ in relation to the static maximization problem is through its fixed value, which is a function of the fixed value of I.

The usefulness of the function $g_{iQ}(Q)$ for empirical research could be limited. In itself, it suggests that hedonic pricing methods could be used, but accounting for all of the relevant characteristics of goods could be difficult, depending on the particular goods in question.

An alternative, evolutionary approach could make use of the notion that Q is a function of time, i.e., $Q = Q(t)$. Therefore, over long periods of time, and under the assumption of *systematic* evolutionary change in the quality of goods and services, one could write:

$$q_i(t) = g_{iQ}(Q) \qquad (6.11)$$

where $q_i(t)$ represents a quality variable that accounts for physical changes, but the actual magnitudes of those changes lie underneath

the function itself. In essence, Equation 6.11 captures the very meaning of evolutionary change in goods.
   These results imply:

$$g_i^* = q_i(t) \, g_{ii}(l) \ .$$

(6.12)

As mentioned above, c_i denotes the quantity of good i consumed by each individual, where all individuals are identical. One could then write:

$$c_i = \frac{x_i}{L}$$

(6.13)

where x_i is the total quantity of good i, and L is the population. By Equations 6.3, 6.8 and 6.13, the total demand for good i could be expressed as:

$$x_i = \frac{g_i^* \, lL}{p_i} \ .$$

(6.14)

Because cost reduction occurs on the supply side, the production processes of firms would need to be considered. For simplicity, assume that a firm produces only a single good, and firms producing the same good are identical. Let M_i be the number of firms producing good i, which, like the quantity of good i produced and the total number of different goods, may change over time. One then has:

$$y_i = \frac{x_i}{M_i}$$

(6.15)

where y_i is the output of each firm producing good i.
   When considering the production processes of firms, one would have difficulty in analysing capital accumulation and cost reduction as two separate phenomena, because both are, in large part, alternative interpretations of the same process. That is, if both effects were considered in the same model, it would be impossible for one to distinguish clearly between the two, and thus, impossible

to measure the separate effect of each. The simplest solution to this problem is to have labour as the only scarce factor of production, and have the productivity of labour enhanced over time.[2]

A simple production function that would allow for long-run changes in labour productivity would be given by:

$$y_i = a_i s_i^{b_i} \tag{6.16}$$

where s_i is the employment level of a firm producing good i, and a_i and b_i are parameters ($a_i > 0$; $0 < b_i < 1$).

For the remainder of this discussion, the i subscript will be left out for simplicity, though one should bear in mind that production is different for different goods, i.e., the a and b parameters, as well as the employment level, vary among goods.

Firms maximize profits given an exogenous wage rate, w, which is the same for all firms producing all goods. Thus:

$$Max\ \pi\ =\ py - ws \tag{6.17}$$

$$\Rightarrow\quad p = \frac{ws}{by} \tag{6.18}$$

One can now solve for labour, s:

$$ws = bpy \tag{6.19}$$

$$= bpas^b \tag{6.20}$$

$$\Rightarrow\quad s = \left(\frac{bap}{w}\right)^{\frac{1}{1-b}}. \tag{6.21}$$

This result, in turn, enables the derivation of a supply curve, since:

$$x = Mas^b \quad \Rightarrow \tag{6.22}$$

$$x = Ma^{\frac{1}{1-b}} \left(\frac{b}{w}\right)^{\frac{b}{1-b}} p^{\frac{b}{1-b}} . \tag{6.23}$$

With Equation 6.14 as the demand curve and Equation 6.23 as the supply curve, one can now solve for x and p simultaneously.

By Equation 6.14:

$$p = \frac{g^* IL}{x} \quad \Rightarrow \tag{6.24}$$

$$p = g^* ILM^{-1} a^{\frac{-1}{1-b}} \left(\frac{bp}{w}\right)^{\frac{-b}{1-b}} . \tag{6.25}$$

Let $m = M/L$, which is the number of firms (producing good i) per unit of population. Equation 6.25 can be simplified to:

$$(ap)^{\frac{1}{1-b}} = g^* I m^{-1} \left(\frac{w}{b}\right)^{\frac{b}{1-b}} . \tag{6.26}$$

Looking back at the original production function (Equation 6.16), cost reduction can be seen as resulting from an increase in either a_i or b_i. However, of these two parameters, b_i is more likely to stay constant over time. This is because b_i could reflect among other things, the bureaucratic or organizational difficulties that occur in any productive effort. Even as technologies advance, in fact, one could still envision the same kind of constraints on the growth of the b_i parameter. Furthermore, by the principle of decreasing marginal returns, b_i would normally be expected to remain less than one, regardless of the time period. In view of these considerations, the a_i parameter is a much better candidate, in the framework of this model, for reflecting most types of productivity increases.

Consequently, in terms of evolutionary change across periods, one could write:

$$a_i = a_i(t) . \tag{6.27}$$

In the present model, the number of firms in industry i, per unit of population, is exogenous. Of course, one could regard this variable as endogenous in a more detailed general equilibrium model. For instance, an assumption could be made that firms enter the market until profits are zero. On the other hand, the perspective of the present study is that there is a continual flow of innovative discoveries in both quality improvement and cost reduction. The returns, or Schumpeterian rents, arising from these innovative discoveries would be inconsistent with a zero-profit assumption.[3] The only exception would be if firms are assumed to counterbalance completely those returns on innovation with their prior expenditures on R & D. This exception, however, would require perfect foresight on the part of the firm, which is not an appropriate concept in the study of innovation and invention. (If it were all things would be invented at time zero!) Equivalently, one could interpret the exogeneity in the number of firms as being due to barriers to entry, in which firms hold patents or copyrights on the particular items that they market or on the capital equipment that they use. In the context of a continual flow of new patents and copyrights over long periods of time, this framework would be consistent with dynamic equilibrium.

At this point, the stage has been set for the derivation of the final equation of the model. One finds:

$$\frac{\ln a + \ln p}{1-b} = \ln g^* + \ln l - \ln m + \frac{b \ln\left(\frac{w}{b}\right)}{1-b} \tag{6.28}$$

by Equation 6.26, and

$$\ln g^* = \ln q(t) + \ln g_i(l) \tag{6.29}$$

by Equation 6.12,

$$\Rightarrow \quad \ln p(t) = b \ln (w/b) \quad \textit{Initial conditions}$$
$$+ (1-b) \ln q(t) \quad \textit{Quality change}$$
$$+ (1-b) \ln l + \ln g_i(l) \quad \textit{Income effect} \tag{6.30}$$
$$- \ln a(t) - (1-b) \ln m(t) \quad \textit{Cost reduction.}$$

In the end, the model reiterates the idea that there are three evolutionary influences on the price of a good over time: *(1)* quality improvements in the good itself, *(2)* changes in demand due to changes in income, and *(3)* cost reduction (or productivity improvement) in the good's production process. Note that the variable m, the number of firms (producing good i) per unit of population is, in this case, regarded as an aspect of cost reduction. That is, since there are decreasing returns to scale, the costs per unit are positively related to the size of the firm, and thus, inversely related to the number of firms per unit of population, all else being equal. In conclusion, Equation 6.30 reflects a formal interpretation of the *ad hoc* expression displayed in Equation 5.1 of Chapter 5.

One should recognize that the direction of changes in price need not be a simple matter. For instance, a rise in income could lead to a reduction in the quality of certain goods and services. As an example, under the assumption that fast food is lower in quality than home-cooked meals, the emergence of fast food in the United States could be interpreted as a quality *reduction* in food, that has arisen because of the increased demand for leisure as incomes rise. Alternatively, fast food might be interpreted as a quality reduction that is also associated with a cost reduction, where the time devoted to food preparation is considered a cost.

Finally, it should be noted that the derivation of Equation 6.30 involved the simplest of microeconomic modelling concepts, and therefore does not represent an important discovery in terms of microeconomic theory itself. In fact, one of the goals of this derivation was to demonstrate that the theory expressed in the form of Equation 5.1 in Chapter 5, does *not* require a sophisticated model to support it. Rather, it requires only a basic understanding of the various forms of technological change and the microeconomic interactions that normally exist among consumers and producers. In this sense, the model presented here is only one (though perhaps the simplest) of many possible models that could have been used to support that theory.

NOTES

1. Prices in this context must be seen as relative prices, so that their average (weighted by expenditures) remains constant, and real income can be measured in relation to a numeraire. Otherwise, the real income level itself would be a function of the price level, and the utility function could no longer be regarded as a reasonable approximation.

2. The use of labour as the only scarce factor in models involving technological innovation is not uncommon — see, for example, Segerstrom (1991).
3. See Schumpeter (1934).

7. Long-run determinants of quality and relative prices

> The transition from a paradigm in crisis to a new one from which a new tradition of normal science can emerge is far from a cumulative process, one achieved by an articulation or extension of the old paradigm. Rather it is a reconstruction of the field from new fundamentals, a reconstruction that changes some of the field's most elementary theoretical generalizations as well as many of its paradigm methods and applications.
>
> *Thomas Kuhn (1970, pp. 84-5)*

A DEEPER LOOK INTO QUALITY MEASUREMENT

Introduction

As with many other aspects of modern economics, quality measurement has become standardized in accordance with specific methodological practices, such as those mentioned in Chapter 3. As a result, much of the research has been about methodology, and not about the evolution of goods or services. This aspect of quality measurement is quite unfortunate, because potentially useful areas of thought remain unexplored. Before engaging in the methodological practice of price indexing, economists should study the details and nuances of quality change.

Tables 7.1 to 7.5 are constructed on the basis of this philosophy. They provide several examples of quality improvement in the five goods considered in this study. In addition, Figures 7.1 to 7.5 illustrate the remarkable degree of quality improvement in these goods by presenting examples of the descriptions and pictures that appeared in the *Sears Catalog*. When looking at the pictures for 1928, one notices that only the shoes and sofas seem to have characteristics that are similar to those of their 1993 counterparts. However, even for these two goods, the descriptions of their physical characteristics reveal dramatic differences.

*Table 7.1   Examples of quality improvements from 1928 to 1993,
as found in the* Sears Catalog: *men's shoes*

Year	Improvement
1933	Shoes with ventilating holes
1938	Shoes with 'no laces'
1943	Steel 'safety toe' in work shoes
1948	Shoes with a 'crepe rubber sole and heel'
1953	Shoes with a 'nylon mesh front', instead of leather
1958	Tan suede leather
1963	'Neoprene' oil-resistant crepe rubber soles for work shoes
1968	Dress shoes with 'Corfam' 'poromeric' uppers (man-made material)
1973	The 'hiking shoe' with sturdy leather construction outside and soft leather inside, steel supports, and very thick rubber soles and heel
1978	New line of 'lightweight' casual shoes with 'Searofoam' soles and heels
1983	Six-inch high work shoes with cushioned ankles and soft 'glove-leather' lining (a feature previously associated with hiking shoes only)
1988	Walking shoes with an upper portion made of fabric
1993	Leather walking shoes with a removable padded insole

Quality Change versus Product Innovation

One advantage of the representative good approach presented in Chapter 4 is that it facilitates the study of both quality improvement and product innovation simultaneously.   Product innovation is normally studied as a distinct field, in which patterns of technological change, or 'technological trajectories', are observed in the evolution of particular lines of products. Attention is paid to the nature of the innovative process, and to the factors that have acted to enhance or diminish that process.   However, the economic

*Table 7.2   Examples of quality improvements from 1928 to 1993,
as found in the* Sears Catalog: *sofas and love seats*

Year	Improvement
1933	Rayon tapestry available for some sofas
1938	'Louis XV' style, 'London Lounge', and 'Kidney' style sofas
1943	'Duncan Phyfe Sofa', with a solid wood frame of finished mahogany
1948	Sectional sofas
1953	Foam rubber cushions
1958	'Tubular Steel' construction
1963	'Refined French Provincial Design' with 'Serofoam' cushions
1968	Cushions with 'Scotchguard' fabric protector
1973	'Expanded-and-fabric-supported' vinyl covers in Spanish and English styles
1978	Small modular pieces in 'corner', 'wedge', 'armless', and 'ottoman' units
1983	Cushions with 'polyester fiberfill'
1988	Coordinating 'throw cushions' which can be added to the sofa's existing cushions
1993	InnerSoft™ cushions with 'a resilient set of springs . . . sandwiched between layers of dense polyurethane foam'

importance of specific product innovations is often not addressed. Rather, the importance of a good appears to be weighted subjectively by the researcher, partially on the basis of the scientific appeal of an innovation.[1] Thus, among the wide variety of physical changes that occur in goods and services, high tech innovations frequently receive the most attention, not necessarily because of their economic importance, but because of their scientific 'impressiveness'. In contrast, the measurement of quality change is usually independent of scientific appeal.

Along the same lines, the study of product innovation rarely

Table 7.3   Examples of quality improvements from 1928 to 1993,
as found in the Sears Catalog: *gas ranges*

Year	Improvement
1933	'Oven Racks pull out like shelves — sustain heaviest pans while extended'
1938	Thermostats that maintain the temperature of the oven at the desired level
1943	
1948	
1953	Ovens with windows
1958	'Built-in' ovens that fit into the wall
1963	Four-hour timer that sets oven to warm at end of cooking period
1968	Electronic ignition instead of pilot light
1973	'Continuous cleaning' (non-stick) coatings
1978	Self-cleaning ovens
1983	A temperature probe, which is inserted into the item to be cooked, and oven adjusts the temperature according to a pre-programmed schedule for the internal temperature of the item
1988	'Electronic digital thermostat with platinum-tipped sensor'
1993	Ranges with 'spill-proof burners'

examines artistic innovations, in spite of the their enormous economic importance in many industries. One reason for this may be an overall view, whether correct or not, that scientific innovations have a stronger connection to research effort (in terms of expenditures, the philosophy of the firm, etc.) than artistic innovations. According to this view scientific innovations may be more predictable than artistic ones.[2]

In essence, quality measurement reveals the overall economic importance of new goods, while product innovation focuses on the scientific aspects of how and why new goods are developed. The

Table 7.4 *Examples of quality improvements from 1928 to 1993, as found in the* Sears Catalog: *window fans and air conditioners*

Year	Improvement
1933	An adjustment on an oscillating fan that enables it to also be used as a non-oscillating fan
1938	Attic and window fans
1943	
1948	Fan with 'self-oiling bearings' and with 'vibrationless motor . . . heavily cushioned in rubber'
1953	AIR CONDITIONER
1958	Air conditioners with 'built-in thermostats'
1963	Larger capacity, 23,000 BTU air conditioner which can cool up to 1,500 square feet
1968	Central air conditioning systems
1973	Central air conditioning with '"Silent Sentinel" . . . fan control: electronic thermostat senses outdoor temperature and automatically determines the most efficient fan speed'
1978	New line of 'high efficiency' central air conditioning systems
1983	Programmable electronic timers for air conditioners
1988	Combination air conditioner/dehumidifier
1993	Portable, 'windowless' air conditioners

two areas of study are obviously interrelated, but a common ground between them could be difficult to find. Perhaps the representative good approach to quality measurement could, in fact, provide that common ground. That is, the RGA carries out quality measurement, but at the same time defines a specific pattern of change, or 'technological trajectory', that can be studied from the standpoint of process innovation. Hence, it can help to 'marry' the two branches of thought, and thereby contribute to each.

One consequence of the marriage between quality measurement

*Table 7.5 Examples of quality improvements from 1928 to 1993,
as found in the* Sears Catalog: *cameras, movie cameras
and camcorders*

Year	Improvement
1933	Indicator on movie camera that keeps track of the amount of unexposed film
1938	Movie cameras with different speeds and with interchangeable lenses
1943	Movie cameras with 'rotating turret head for 3 lenses'
1948	Flash cameras (i.e., cameras with flashes attached)
1953	'Parallax correction' in movie cameras
1958	Polaroid self-developing cameras
1963	Movie cameras with automatic 'zoom' lenses
1968	Cameras with 'electronic flashes' with rechargeable batteries (as opposed to disposable one-shot flash bulbs)
1973	'Pocket instamatic camera' which is only 2 1/2 x 5 x 1 inches in size
1978	Movie cameras that record SOUND
1983	Video cameras
1988	Video cameras with automatic focusing, and with built-in (as opposed to external) microphones
1993	'Twin lens' camcorder that can 'switch instantly from normal to 12x zoom'

and product innovation would be a clearer understanding of the economic importance of different innovations. In particular, it could help to remove the current bias among product innovation studies toward technological breakthroughs or scientifically-interesting discoveries.

As an example, consider the two categories of goods, sofas and gas ranges, and an innovation that occurred in each: for sofas, polyurethane foam in cushions replaced metal springs, and for gas ranges, an electrical self-ignition device replaced the pilot light in some models. In the study of product innovation, it is likely that the

Figure 7.1 Men's shoes in the Sears Catalog: *1928 and 1993*

1928: $5.50 Brown Kidskin 67L4462 D-E width; 67L4463 B-C width; Black Kidskin 67L4464 D-E width 67L4465 B-C width; Sizes, 5 to 11. Shipping wt., 2 1/2 lbs. . . .
[W]e have built-in special steel arch supports, ventilated insoles and have added rubber heels for more comfort. The soles are GENUINE GOODYEAR WELT, sewed clear around the heel seat to make the shoes hold their shape. (*Sears Catalog*, Spring/ Summer 1928, p. 250)

1993: A thru D. . . . Leather walking shoes . . . comfort feature genuine leather uppers . . . Removable one-piece contoured, cushioned insoles with heel pads. Roomy box toes and light-weight, man-made soles and heels absorb shock. Imported. C. 3-eyelet moc-toe oxford offers you natural comfort with every step. 67 W 77423F--Brown 67 W 77424F--Gray 67 W 77425F--Black Wt. 1.75 lbs...$49.99 (*Sears Catalog*, Spring/ Summer 1993, p. 370)

Figure 7.2 Sofas and love seats in the Sears Catalog: *1928 and 1993*

1928: This soft deeply cushioned set . . . Furnished with either bed davenport or stationary davenport. . . . deeply padded with downy layers of fine springy flax fiber and fluffy felted cotton. Back, seats and cushions are spring filled . . . birch frames, finished brown antique mahogany. Upholstered in Figured Jacquard Velour or Plain or Figured Mohair. . . . Outside of backs and ends

beneath the arms are upholstered in plain velour . . . Includes reversible cushions of . . . ratine tapestry. . . . Length, 82 in.; Seat, 64x23 inches; Shpg. Wt. 215 lbs.; . . . Velour $76.85; Plain Mohair $94.65; Figured Mohair $94.75. (*Sears Catalog*, Spring/ Summer 1928, p.717)

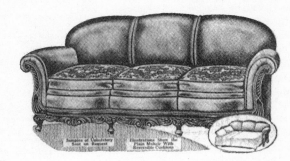

1993: A thru G. These leather-look pieces are fashioned from supple vinyl with Prefixx™ protective finish, so spills wipe up with mild soap and water.

Hardwood frames are reinforced with sinuous steel for extended wear. 18-inch seat height. Sectional with sleeper (A) and sleeper (G) have 4 1/2-inch innerspring mattress and open to 90 inches long. Dimensions are approximate. . . . More comfort in motion pieces on pages 754 thru 756. (D) Sofa measures 83Wx37Dx35H inches. F 1 R 5170 1NH--Wt 125...$449.00 (*Sears Catalog*, Spring/Summer 1993, p. 753)

Figure 7.3 Gas ranges in the Sears Catalog*: 1928 and 1993*

1928: A Four-Hole GAS RANGETTE
. . . of solid cast iron and finished in
French Gray Stainless and Acid
Proof Enamel. . . . Oven Door Panel
Is White Porcelain Enameled. The
Black Parts are finished in a durable,
glossy black enamel that protects
them from rust. . . . Slide Easy Cast
Iron Grates permit shifting of
utensils without lifting. The Reliable
Thermometer in oven doors tells the
heat of oven at all times . . . Burns
natural or manufactured gas only.
. . . Catalog No. 22L1367; Cash
Price $32.85; . . . Oven Measures,
Inches 18 x 17 x 11; Cooking Top,
in. 25x18; Height to Cooking Top,
in. 34; Floor Space Inches 25x19;
Shpg. Wt., Lbs. 170. (*Sears
Catalog*, Spring/Summer 1928, p.
765)

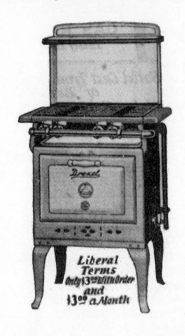

1993: A thru G. Ranges on
these two pages are pilot-
free with self-cleaning
automatic ovens. Include
two removable chrome-
plated oven racks and
porcelain enameled broiler
pan with grid. . . . imported
from Mexico. A. $18/$19
Monthly.** Deluxe
backguard with fluorescent
worklight. Electronic
thermostat. Dual time/temp.
No L.P conversion kit
required. Wt. 196 lbs. 22 R
73919N--Black-on-black
...849.99   22 R 73915N--
White-on white...899.99
(*Sears Catalog*, Spring/
Summer 1993, p. 1510)

Figure 7.4 Window fans and air conditioners in the Sears
Catalog: *1928 and 1993*

1928: Arctic Fans for Health Giving
Coolness; $7.85; 10-Inch
Oscillating; Our price for this fan is
lower than you will be able to find
elsewhere, quality considered. For
110-volt city current only. Shipping
wt., each, 8 pounds. 20L3593.
(*Sears Catalog*, Spring/Summer
1928, p. 573.)

1993: A thru C. Portable
windowless air conditioners . . .
lightweight . . . Units take up less
than 12 by 15 inches of floor space
. . . Unique cylindrical fan and ultra-
efficient cooling unit for whisper-
soft operation . . . Units feature programmable 6-hour timer and adjustable
thermostat. Built-in water tank collects water from dehumidified air and
features automatic shut-off when full and 'full tank' signal light. Units
discharge heat from the rear. Imported. C. 5500 Btuh model. $14/$15

Monthly. Unit weighs only 55
pounds, light enough to carry
up stairs or over door sills with
the recessed handles. 2
independent fan speeds and 3
cooling settings let you choose
the exact level of comfort you
need, from a gentle breeze to
full-powered air conditioning.
Oscillating vents. Almond-
color cabinet. 0.9-gallon tank.
Fan operates at 165 CFM.
115-volts, 6.3 amps, 695
watts, 60 Hz AC.
31½Hx10¼/Wx 14 3/8 D
inches. 32 R 72063--Wt.
69lbs. . . . . . $699.99 (*Sears
Catalog*,Spring/Summer 1993,
p. 968)

Figure 7.5 Cameras, movie cameras and camcorders in the Sears Catalog: *1928 and 1993*

1928: BROWNIE CAMERAS . . . Simple to operate. Has two shutter speeds--instantaneous and time, and has different diaphragm stops so that you can readily control light conditions. Shpg. wt., 2 1/2 lbs. 3L41050--No. 2 Box Brownie. Takes picture size 2 1/4 x 3 1/4 inches . . . . $2.29 (*Sears Catalog*, Spring /Summer 1928, p. 558)

1993: Panasonic PV-22 with 8x zoom A thru C. Panasonic camcorder feature digital auto shutter with light sensitivity as low as 1 lux (midnight). Edit features include flying erase head for clean transitions and audio/video dubbing (B and C also feature synchro edit, edit search, VHS index search and bookmark search). Color digital fade allows you to add black, white or random fade variations to

your recordings. All models include these accessories: 8-function wireless remote, 5 watt color enhancement light, Play Pak adaptor, 2-hour battery pack, battery recharger, AC adaptor, cables and shoulder strap. Imported. Warranted.** B. $19 Monthly.* 8x power zoom auto zoom focus lens. Remote conveniently stores in unit. Uses battery 52074, sold below. 45/8Hx33/4Wx85/8D inches. 57 R 53622--Wt. 5.31 lbs....$899.99 (*Sears Catalog*, Spring/Summer 1993, p. 1460) innovation in sofas would either be ignored entirely, or at best, receive little attention. The reason is that polyurethane foam would be seen as a product innovation in the chemical industry, but then not be given the credit it is due in the furniture industry. As a new chemical, polyurethane foam is 'scientifically more interesting' than it is as a physical substitute for coils in sofas. Furthermore, the idea of adding to a piece of furniture a material that someone else had invented in another industry does not convey quite the same intellectual worthiness that is normally associated with product innovation.

On the other hand, in a study on product innovation, an electrical self-ignition device in a gas range would probably be looked upon as an important invention. Rather than reflecting a simple substitution of one spring-like object for another, it involves electrical components, and the conversion of one form of energy to another, both of which convey a strong sense of scientific discovery. Furthermore, there is a solid connection between the invention of the device and its incorporation into the final product, while in the case of polyurethane foam in sofas the raw material and the final product are developed in distinctly different industries.

Thus, in studying product innovation one would be more likely to conclude that gas ranges underwent much more technological change than sofas. That conclusion, however, would reflect a bias against product innovations that are not scientifically interesting. Of the two innovations mentioned above, it is clear from examining sofas and ovens today that the polyurethane foam innovation was much more important. That is, the vast majority of sofas sold today do have this feature, or something similar to it. In contrast, most gas ranges continue to have a pilot light rather than an electrical ignition switch.

Non-separability of Product Quality

The cost reduction process can be seen as being both additive and separable with regard to the individual items that comprise a particular good, and analogously with regard to the individual goods within a sector, or the individual sectors within the economy as a whole. This separability results from the fact that there is a cost for each item produced, and that cost is incurred by the consumer regardless of the other items he or she happens to purchase. In contrast to cost reduction, the quality improvement process is by no means additive or separable. (See Chapter 2.)

One reason for the nonadditivity of quality is that goods often act together to provide more utility than the sum of the utilities that they each provide separately. The quality of raw meat would be impossible to assess if there were no device for cooking it. In essence, if one were to attempt to measure quality under such circumstances, one would be measuring the 'sound of one hand clapping'.[3] Because of nonseparability, quality improvement for the economy as a whole cannot be taken as the sum of quality improvements of individual goods, nor even as the sum of quality improvements of individual sectors.

Another aspect of nonseparability is that goods and services are linked in terms of time. If, theoretically, time and money were to remain interchangeable in the same proportion with regard to the consumption of all goods, then time could be treated as a component of the allowable budget, and one would simply have a more complicated budget constraint in the maximization problem (Lancaster, 1977, pp. 166-8). However, in reality there is no constant trade-off between expense and time — different goods have their own unique requirements of each.

As an example of the interlinkage of time, the VCR enables a person to record a television programme that he might otherwise see only when it is run. Consequently, the VCR has created a new control over time, causing its quality to be linked to the quality of all other activities that would otherwise be foregone. If a film that someone wanted to see on television were showing at the same time as a concert that he also wanted to attend, the VCR would allow him to see both. In this sense, the quality of the VCR is in part, a function of the quality of television programming.

Hence, because of nonseparability, the methodology of quality measurement employed in this and other studies can never be seen as an exact technique, but simply as a technique that can provide a first approximation for the measurement of a highly complex phenomenon. The notion that one good increases the utility generated from another good, even if both are in different sectors, need not be inconsistent with the model presented. It is often the 'relative' quality of goods that counts, in spite of our efforts to isolate an 'absolute' effect. For instance, better TV dinners would increase the quality of television, and better televisions would increase the quality of TV dinners, since each would enhance the utility obtained from consuming, or experiencing, the other. However, when their prices are compared at the same point in time, one would most likely find that the 'relative' price of the TV dinners goes up when the TV dinner tastes better, and the 'relative' price of televisions goes up when television reception improves.

STATEMENT OF HYPOTHESES

The following hypothesis may seem obvious to many observers, and is supported very strongly by the results presented in Chapters 4 and 5.

Hypothesis I

Over long periods of time, rates of cost reduction and quality improvement will be significantly different among different types of goods and services.

To many economists this hypothesis may be 'common knowledge'. However, if this is the case, then one might expect economists to take the next step and address the question: *Which* goods and services undergo more quality improvement and cost reduction than others?   The answer to this question could be useful for the strategic planning carried out by firms and by nations.   Moreover, the topic could have importance outside economics, in the areas of history and anthropology.

To some extent the question has already been addressed. It has been considered in economic development and international trade, especially with regard to the issue of the net barter terms of trade between primary commodities and manufactures. The question has also been addressed in the literature on industrial organization and technological change (Dosi, 1988).

Nevertheless, many of the studies that have addressed the question have been either inconclusive, or at best, not convincing. Furthermore, many may be described as passing fancies, that have received little attention in the economic community after they were first published. In short, while Hypothesis I may appear obvious to most economists, economists have failed to explain *why* some goods improve in quality more than others, or *why* productivity improves in some processes faster than it does in others.

This failure of economists to explain Hypothesis I occurs primarily because of the manner in which technological change is studied, and because of the way goods are classified. As mentioned in earlier discussions, technological change is studied in economics with a focus primarily on the firm. Instead of asking which goods undergo the most cost reduction and quality improvement, economists ask which *firms* have been best able to carry out product innovation and process innovation. The two questions could be very different for a variety of reasons, for example:

1. In studies of product innovation there is often a bias toward technological change that is scientifically interesting, which would leave out many sources of quality improvement, as well as sources of cost reduction.
2. Most of the firms that conduct a great deal of R & D are heavily diversified in a variety of products and services. Therefore, the connection, as observed empirically, between the growth of firms and the growth of their individual products could be quite weak.
3. Firms that undergo considerable cost reduction and/or quality improvement may not experience growth, because of comparable progress among their competitors.

With regard to the classification of goods and services, economists studying technological change have tended to group goods into large categories. One advantage of large categories, such as clothing, food and furniture, is that they can be used to arrive at conclusions for the entire economy as a whole. In addition, published information on prices, revenues, R & D expenditures, etc., are often only available at this level of aggregation, which makes life much easier for the researcher. However, Hypothesis I applies to much finer categories of goods. For instance, in the case of furniture, cushioned furniture, such as sofas, beds and chairs, have improved in quality much faster than non-cushioned furniture, such as tables, desks and bookshelves (which could have actually declined in quality).

Another aspect of current methods of characterization, which is also due to the emphasis on the firm, is that goods are often classified on the basis of production methods, or on the basis of incidental, but easily identifiable, characteristics. One example is the separation of goods into primary products and manufactures. In this case, a fresh tomato and a pound of iron ore belong to one type of good, while a can of tomatoes and a pound of stainless steel belong to another. Such a classification scheme does serve useful purposes, but not, necessarily, the purpose of investigating why goods vary in their rates of quality improvement and cost reduction.

Another classification scheme is the separation of goods into electrical and nonelectrical products (or equipment). There is a widely-held view that electrical goods undergo more quality improvement and cost reduction than nonelectrical goods. However, in a large number of cases, electrical equipment does not represent a unique type of good from the standpoint of consumption, but rather, the embodiment of quality improvement in a preexisting, mechanical good. Clocks, typewriters, screwdrivers, can openers, thermometers and adding machines (now calculators and computers) are all available in the form of electrical devices, which are quality improvements over their mechanical predecessors. Moreover, Abrams and Bernstein (1989) observe that, in the near future, many more nonelectrical goods and services will become electrical, such as books, cars and even birth control devices.

In view of the complications that arise from the emphasis on the firm, and from common practices in the classification of goods, the central idea that is conveyed in Hypothesis I needs to be expressed in more precise terms. Consequently, the following revision is proposed:

Hypothesis I'

Over long periods of time, rates of cost reduction and quality improvement will be significantly different among different sets of goods and services, where these sets are defined in terms of the purposes they serve.

Hypothesis I' is certainly more specific than Hypothesis I, though there will always be some ambiguity as to what is meant by the *purpose* of a good or service. (See Chapters I and 2.) The results obtained for the five goods examined in Chapters 4 and 5 provide strong support for this hypothesis.

Consider, as an example, two similar goods: inexpensive watches and luxury watches. Even though both goods are 'watches', they are quite different from each other: they are sold at very different prices and different establishments, and they are often purchased by different consumers. Yet, perhaps the most distinct difference between them is that they serve different purposes. The £5.00 watch that one buys from a vender on the street serves a single purpose — to measure the time. In contrast, the watch at a jewellery shop, priced at £500, is more an item of jewellery than it is a device for measuring time.

The manufacturer of an inexpensive watch will tend to make few improvements to the watch that increase its quality. His main interest is to produce it as cheaply as possible, provided it meets some minimum standard of accuracy. In fact, he *must* act in this manner if he is to remain in business. The manufacturer of luxury watches, in contrast, has many other considerations, such as the artistic appeal of the watch. Thus, in the long-run, watches will *evolve* according to a specific pattern: luxury watches will increase in quality, and inexpensive watches will become even more inexpensive, without changing in quality.

Another example is the car market, where a similar pattern can be observed. Inexpensive cars are designed to meet some minimal standards in terms of comfort and driving performance, while luxury cars are designed for comfort, prestige and exceptional driving performance. In cars, however, one observes that the minimum standard has improved over time. For example, automatic transmission and air conditioning are now frequently being demanded by those who purchase the lowest quality cars, which was not the case four decades ago.

These considerations suggest another hypothesis, which may also be obvious to some observers:

Hypothesis II

The amount of quality improvement and cost reduction that will occur over long periods of time is a function of the relative importance of quality improvement and cost reduction to the purposes served by those particular goods and services.

As discussed in Chapter 3, cost reduction in this case may be implicit, rather than explicit. For example, a faster computer may be a 'cost reduction' over a comparable slower computer, if one measures costs in terms of both price and time.

While Hypothesis I' is easy to test empirically, Hypothesis II is not, because there is no obvious way for one to measure the 'relative importance' of quality and cost in the minds of consumers. However, 'relative importance', or the desirability of alternative choices, is measurable, and in fact, is measured quite often in the social sciences and marketing research. In terms of historical data, proxies are used, such as the relative proportions of advertisements that appeal to quality improvement as opposed to cost reduction.

While it is not a popular subject in economics, the study of the desirability of alternative choices is firmly grounded in the other social sciences and in business studies. One example of such work in economics is Scitovsky's examination of behavioural aspects of human consumption.   For instance, he discusses the sensory perception of goods and services in the context of externalities:

> Most externalities . . . are sensory stimulants, and the good ones are always the by-products of those goods and services, or of those features of goods and services, which aim at providing entertainment, amusement, aesthetic pleasure, and other forms of stimulation.

He goes on to say:

> Sounds and sights, the main sources of sensory stimulation, are not easy to confine, and what is pleasing to one person's ears and eyes is often also pleasing to other people's. . . . By contrast, comforts and want satisfaction usually lack these spill-over effects. Since many comforts come from the substitution of mechanical power for man's muscular power, they often have unpleasant side effects, such as noise and air pollution. (Scitovsky 1976, p. 86)

This distinction between goods designed to appeal to the senses, and those designed for a specific physical purpose, suggests an explanation for why some goods have greater inclinations toward quality improvement than others.[4]

As an example of the applicability of these concepts to recent findings, consider the observations made by Grilli and Yang (1988) in their study of long-run international price movements, from 1900 to 1986. They find that beverages actually increase in price relative to all manufactured goods, while manufactured goods increase in price relative to other food products. Nonfood agricultural raw materials decline in price the most.

One notices that nonfood agricultural raw materials are designed to meet a minimum physical standard, and do not appeal to the human senses, except to the extent that they are handled by workers. In contrast, beverages do appeal to the senses. They tend to be consumed for pleasure more than for nutrition, with the possible exception of milk. That is, in the vast majority of cases people will drink a beverage, even when water is available, and even if the beverage itself does not offer much in terms of nutrition. With regard to juices, which are nutritious in terms of their vitamin content, consumption of a vitamin tablet and a glass of water would be more cost-effective, suggesting that, even in this case, appeal to the senses does play an important part in the consumption decision.

Most of the beverages examined by Grilli and Yang are in a form that is similar to the form they are in when consumed. The same is not true for other food products, however, and thus, quality improvement in their case would occur further along in the production chain. For instance, flour may not improve in quality while bread may. This idea coincides with the distinction between goods that meet a physical requirement and those that are designed to appeal to the senses. These findings suggest a third hypothesis, which is similar to Hypothesis II, but more restrictive.

Hypothesis III

The more goods and services are designed to appeal to the senses, as opposed to providing a specific physical function, the greater will be their tendency to improve in quality. However, if time-saving, labour-saving, or life-saving is an aspect of quality, rather than of cost, then in this sense quality improvement could also be substantial for goods performing a specific function.

This hypothesis is not an absolute rule, but simply the statement of a *tendency*. A good can only improve in quality if the quality improvement is desired by consumers. The more an improvement is desired, the greater will be consumer willingness to pay for the improvement, and the greater will be the impetus among suppliers to find ways to provide that improvement. The question then becomes, 'What makes some improvements more desirable than others?' As the hypothesis suggests, the desirability of improvements in goods and services is a function of sensory appeal (and pain alleviation), implicit cost savings, and positive health and safety requirements. In fact, virtually all R & D on new products could be categorized as serving at least one of these goals.

This hypothesis relies on the principle that consumers do not want goods or services, but instead want the function that those goods and services provide. To some extent, this concept is similar to the characteristics approach; for instance, the protein content of a food item is a characteristic and also is an aspect of the item's function of providing nutrients. However, unlike the notion of characteristics, the concept of a good's function does not restrict the number of relevant variables that characterize the good. Rather, for every good there is a function (or set of functions), and given that function, there is an open-ended set of possibilities with regard to three aspects of quality improvement: sensory appeal, implicit cost savings, and health and safety.[5] If at least one of these three aspects is important in relation to the good's function, then the good is likely to improve in quality.

As an example of the notion that quality improves in relation to the *function* of the good, Juran discusses the history of women's hair nets. Originally, women wore hair nets to hold their hair in place after visits to the hairdresser. Two companies competed in this market, and developed items that varied in terms of colour, the type of fibres, and the production process. However, 'both competitors became extinct when a chemist came up with a spray that could invisibly hold women's hair in place' (Juran 1992, pp. 73-4). Thus, hair spray became a quality improvement over hair nets, because it provided the same basic function, but had a greater appeal to the senses.

Often a good serves a function that is unrelated to sensory appeal, implicit cost reduction, or health and safety. Examples would include products used in construction (such as building materials), certain types of office supplies (such as plain white paper), and objects that one does not normally perceive (such as internal automotive parts). However, there is an obvious continuum in the extent to which goods and services can be associated with sensory appeal, implicit cost reduction, and health and safety. Consequently, what is required is some means of objectively measuring this association, and then seeing if there is a significant relationship between it and observed quality change. Surely, this is no simple matter, but perhaps proxies could be used based on advertising, labelling, surveys, or other similar information.

Among these proxies, one that is particularly useful is the number of new product innovations that are expected to occur in various types of goods and services. Rich sources of information in this area are Abrams and Bernstein's books, entitled *Future Stuff* and *More Future Stuff* (1989 and 1991 respectively), which describe a wide range of new consumer products that firms intend to supply in the near future.[6] The new products listed are among the most interesting and thought-provoking ones out of all the possible choices, which was clearly the authors' intention. Nevertheless, these selected innovations are likely to reflect trends that have existed for quite some time.

In order to demonstrate how the above-mentioned hypotheses could be tested, a simple analysis was conducted of the innovations reported in *Future Stuff*. The same type of analysis could have also been done with *More Future Stuff*. Comparable references on product innovation may exist as well, though these tend to specialize in particular lines of products, or require considerable research work in piecing together a useful data set.

As shown in Table 7.6, the 275 innovations appearing in *Future Stuff* were subdivided by: the function of the good or service (ten general categories were chosen); the type of quality improvement that it offers in terms of an appeal to the senses or cognitive appeal; and the type of cost reduction. To shed light on Hypotheses I-III, four types of quality improvement were used: audio/visual, taste/smell, touch/comfort and contemplative/issue oriented. Similarly, three types of cost reduction were identified: pecuniary (i.e., cost reduction in the simplest sense), time saving and space saving. In many cases judgment calls were required in the assignment of only one value to each parameter for each innovation. For example, '50 per cent leaner pork' was classified under the function 'health/hygiene/safety' because the innovation was specifically designed with health in mind, whereas 'buffalo meat' was classified under 'food/beverage' even though it is nutritionally preferable to beef. The product names in the table are those used in *Future Stuff*, which provides a complete explanation of what each product is, its probability of being marketed, and its likely date of arrival into the market.[7]

In theory, one might expect all of the innovations to be quality improvements, since they all involve new goods and services with unique characteristics. Cost reduction, in contrast, would only involve a productivity improvement on the part of the firm, with no change in the final product. However, a broader view of cost reduction was used here, in which a new product could be a cost reduction if it provides the same function as an older product but at a lower cost to the user. The 'anticavity pill', for instance, provides the function of tooth preservation at a much lower cost than dental visits. Furthermore, the concept of cost reduction is broadened to include the costs of time and space.

Table 7.7 presents a summary of this categorization scheme. Of the 275 innovations, the most prevalent function is health/hygiene/ safety, which scored very high in quality improvement and low in cost reduction. The opposite effect is seen in the second most prevalent function, household maintenance, which scores relatively low in quality improvement and high in cost reduction. By Hypothesis III, household maintenance would tend to display less quality improvement and more cost reduction since it is less related

Table 7.6   Innovations in Future Stuff *(Abrams and Bernstein, 1989), by function, type of quality improvement, and type of cost reduction*

First Column: Function (1 = Health/Hygiene/Safety, 2 = Household maintenance, 3 = Exercise/Participatory entertainment, 4 = Sedentary entertainment, 5 = Transportation, 6 = Information Processing, 7 = Food/Beverage, 8 = Communication, 9 = Clothing/Linens, 0 = Transactions/Shopping)

Second Column: Quality improvement (1 = Audio/Visual, 2 = Taste/Smell, 3 = Touch/Comfort, 4 = Contemplative/Issue oriented, 0 = None)

Third Column: Cost reduction (1 = Pecuniary, 2 = Time saving, 3 = Space saving, 0 = None)

50% Leaner Pork	1	2	0	Puddle Detector	1	3	0
Anticavity Pill	1	4	1	Rayon Extractor	1	4	0
Bear Repellent	1	4	0	Smart Pill Bottle	1	4	0
Bola-Snare	1	3	0	Smoke-Check Badge	1	2	0
Cholesterol-Free Eggs	1	2	0	Sonic Painkiller	1	3	0
Cholesterol-Reducing Pwdr	1	2	0	Sports Shock Meter	1	4	0
Computer Dental Crowns	1	4	1	Sting Buster	1	4	0
Digital Hearing Aid	1	1	0	Stress Gum	1	2	0
Elec. Shock Protector	1	4	0	Sunburn Protection Meter	1	4	0
Electrified Birth Control	1	4	0	Suntan in a Bottle	1	3	2
Elec. Bandage Dressing	1	3	0	Super Carrots	1	2	0
Electronic Deodorant	1	2	0	Super Pore Cleaner	1	3	0
Eye Braces	1	1	2	Telescopic Eyeglasses	1	1	0
Female Condom	1	3	0	Time-Release Birth Control	1	3	0
Fever Check	1	4	2	Time-Release Eye Drops	1	3	2
Fire Emergency Lifeline	1	4	0	Time-Release Fluoride	1	2	1
Fish-Eye Lens	1	1	0	Toddler Hair-Wash Board	1	3	0
Freezing Humans	1	4	0	TV Eyeglasses	1	1	0
High-fiber Cupcakes	1	2	0	Vilest Taste	1	2	0
Holographic Contact Lens	1	1	0	Vital Systems Monitor	1	4	0
Home Cholesterol Test	1	4	1	Ways to Quit Smoking	1	2	0
Home Glucose Test	1	4	2	Wrinkle-Reducing Pillow	1	3	0
Home Strep Test	1	4	1	X-Ray-Less Mammogram	1	4	0
Homing Device Implant	1	4	0	'Bark Stopper' Dog Collar	2	4	0
Impotency Pills	1	3	0	Biodegradable Plastic Bags	2	4	0
Infant Safe Seat	1	3	0	Bread Fresher	2	2	1
Kiss Moisturizer	1	3	0	Butler-in-a-Box	2	1	2
Le Funelle	1	3	0	Computer Alarmcard	2	1	0
Living Skin Equivalent	1	3	0	Computerized Decorator	2	4	0
Low-Calorie Beef	1	2	0	Digital Measuring Tape	2	1	0
Low-Proof Liquor	1	2	0	Dome Homes	2	4	1
Most Intelligent Toilet	1	4	1	Doorbutler	2	0	2
Noise Canceler	1	1	0	Edible Pet Spoon	2	3	0
Non-Fattening Fat	1	2	0	Embalmed House Plants	2	1	2
No-Calorie Sugar	1	2	0	Hand-Scanning Lock	2	0	2
Painless Dental Drill	1	3	0	Improved Christmas Tree	2	1	0
Panic-Alarm Wristwatch	1	1	0	Intelligent Toilet	2	3	0
Phone Shields	1	3	0	Letter Sledder	2	3	2
Poison Ivy Vaccine	1	4	0	Microwave Clothes Dryer	2	0	2
Pregaphone	1	1	0	More Intelligent Toilet	2	3	0

Table 7.6   Innovations in Future Stuff *(Abrams and Bernstein,*
1989), by function, type of quality improvement, and
type of cost reduction (continued)

Movable Phone Jack	2	1	2	Idea Salon	3	4	0
Nailless Horseshoe	2	4	0	Interact. Satellite Theater	3	1	0
Non-Choking Dog Collar	2	4	0	Mega Ball	3	1	0
Pet Grooming Device	2	3	2	Memory Card Camera	3	1	0
Plastic Nails	2	0	1	Night Golf	3	1	0
Polka-Dot Geraniums	2	1	0	Non-Contact Pen	3	3	0
Privacy Windows	2	1	2	No-Slip Racquetball Glove	3	3	0
Refrigerator Cold Saver	2	0	1	Oversized Golf	3	1	0
Refrigerator Kitty Bowl	2	4	0	Perfect Line Golf Ball	3	1	0
Robot Dog	2	1	2	Punch Meter	3	4	0
Robot Lawn Mower	2	0	2	Rent-a-Cat	3	3	0
Rotary Blade Paper Cutter	2	3	2	Retrieving Duck Decoy	3	1	1
Round Refrigerator	2	0	2	Rotat. Home Observatory	3	4	0
Tamper-Proof Packaging	2	4	0	Seat Bicycle Pump	3	0	3
Self-Cleaning House	2	0	2	Sexual Risk Game	3	4	0
Self-Stirring Saucepan	2	0	2	Simulated Golf	3	1	0
Self-Weeding Lawn	2	0	1	Ski Valet	3	3	3
Smart House	2	4	2	Sweet-Spot Tennis Rack.	3	3	0
Smart Shades	2	3	2	Swimming Propulsion Dev.	3	3	0
Solar Air Conditioner	2	4	0	Swingspeed Bat	3	1	0
Solar Lighting System	2	4	0	Table Tennis Server	3	1	0
Solar Roofing Material	2	4	1	Two-Way-Mirror Birdfeeder	3	1	0
Solar Windows	2	4	1	Umpire Tennis Balls	3	4	0
Solar-Powered Cooker	2	4	1	Uphill Skiing	3	1	0
Squeeze Screwdriver	2	3	0	Virtual World	3	1	0
Super Laundry Detergent	2	0	1	Walking Desk	3	3	0
Supercart	2	0	2	Water Walkers	3	3	0
Touchless Faucet	2	3	1	Wind Weapon	3	1	0
Voicekey	2	1	1	3-D Home Video	4	1	0
Water Battery	2	4	0	3-D Sound	4	1	0
Weed Kicker	2	3	0	Binocular Glasses	4	1	0
Window Shatter Protector	2	0	1	Concert Halls at Home	4	1	0
Archer's Laser Finder	3	1	0	Customized Music Casset.	4	1	2
Aquatic Exercise Machine	3	3	0	Dial 'M' for Movies	4	1	0
Automatic Pool Cover	3	0	3	Digital Audiotapes	4	1	0
Body Music	3	1	0	Digital Speakers	4	1	0
Camera Stabilization Lens	3	1	0	Dual Deck VCR	4	1	0
Compact Disk Recorder	3	1	0	Electric Train Attache'	4	1	0
Computer Songwriter	3	1	0	Flat TV	4	0	3
Diagrammatic Knitting	3	1	0	Hal: Phone-Activated VCR	4	1	2
Dry Sports Chair	3	3	0	Hand-held Sports Monitor	4	4	2
Electronic Book	3	4	2	High-Definition TV	4	1	0
Electronic Fishing Lure	3	1	0	Interactive Game Network	4	1	0
Elec. Still Photography	3	1	0	In-Flight Entertain. Sys.	4	1	0
Home Steam Room	3	3	0	Kids' TV Monitor	4	5	2
Five-Bladed Boomerang	3	1	0	Motion Simulator	4	3	0
Gyro Exercise Machine	3	3	0	Music Therapy	4	1	0
Home Body-Condit. Spa	3	3	0	Personal Betting Machine	4	4	2
Interactive Game Pavilion	3	1	0	Private Listening at Home	4	1	0

Table 7.6   Innovations in Future Stuff *(Abrams and Bernstein, 1989), by function, type of quality improvement, and type of cost reduction (concluded)*

Item				Item			
Robot Horse Racing	4	1	0	Arracacha	7	2	0
Self-Improv. Chamber	4	4	0	Buffalo Meat	7	2	0
Smart TV	4	1	0	Carbonated Milk	7	2	0
Smarts Chair	4	4	0	Freeze-Dried Compr. Food	7	0	3
Super Movies	4	1	0	Fresh-Fruit Wrap	7	2	1
Talking VCR Rem. Contl.	4	1	0	Frozen beverage mug	7	2	0
Video-on-the-go	4	1	3	Mamey	7	2	0
Walking TV	4	1	3	Meals for Kids	7	2	2
Anti-Noise Controls	5	1	0	Mini Portable Oven	7	0	3
Automatic Tire Chk. & Fill	5	4	0	Oca	7	2	0
Auto TV-Monitor System	5	1	0	Pickle Quick	7	2	0
Car Video Navigation Sys.	5	1	2	Potato Ice Cream	7	2	0
Collision-Avoidance Sys.	5	4	0	Resealable Can	7	0	1
Drive by Wire	5	0	1	Self-Cooling Can	7	2	0
Driver Personality Key	5	0	2	Super Spud	7	2	0
Electric Car	5	4	1	Vend. Mach. French Fries	7	2	2
Flying Car	5	1	0	Flat Satellite Antenna	8	1	3
Flying Saucer	5	4	0	Holograph phone	8	1	0
Four-Wheel Steering	5	4	0	Message Stopper	8	1	2
Heads Up Display	5	1	0	Picture Phone	8	1	0
Levitation Vehicle	5	1	0	Port. Voice-Act. Translator	8	4	2
Light-Sen. Car Win. & Mir.	5	1	0	Selection Telephone	8	1	2
Mini Rover	5	3	0	Sound Wedge	8	1	2
Multifuel Vehicles	5	0	1	Talking Glove	8	4	0
Night-Vision Display Scrn.	5	1	0	Telephone Smart Cards	8	0	1
No-Flat Spare Tire	5	0	1	Telephone Voice Changer	8	1	0
Plastic Engines	5	0	1	Two-receiver Phone	8	1	0
Remote-Control Car Starter	5	0	2	Video Telephone	8	1	0
Satellite Navigation	5	1	2	Watch Pager	8	1	3
Smart Suspension	5	3	0	Biodegradable Diapers	9	4	0
Turbine Engines	5	0	2	Cool Pillow	9	3	0
Two-Cycle Auto Engines	5	0	1	Deodorant Underwear	9	2	0
CD Rom	6	0	2	Hot/Cool Fabric	9	3	0
Comp. Meal Planning	6	4	2	Mood Suit	9	1	0
Desktop Video	6	1	0	Safe, No-Iron Cotton	9	4	0
Do-It-All Comp. NotePad	6	1	0	Snore-Reducing Pillow	9	1	2
Electronic Newspaper	6	4	2	Ultrasonic 3-D Clothes	9	3	0
Guerrilla Info. Network	6	4	0	Velcro Cloth Diapers	9	4	0
Large-Capac. Smart Cards	6	0	1	Xerographic Bedsheets	9	1	0
Noise Meter	6	1	0	Computer Shop-at-Home	0	0	2
Pocket Computer	6	4	3	Drive-Buy Advertisements	0	1	2
Pocket Printer	6	0	3	Electronic Promotions	0	0	2
Prayer Wristwatch	6	4	2	Electronic Supermarket	0	1	2
Solar-Powered Briefcase	6	4	2	Grocery Smart Card	0	0	2
Spy-Satellite Photos	6	1	0	Home Shopping for Kids	0	1	2
Voice-Activ. Typewriter	6	1	1	Smart Cards	0	0	2
Weather Cube	6	4	2	Supermrkt Self-Checkout	0	0	1
World's Sm. Weather Stat.	6	4	2	Visual Smart Cards	0	0	2
Write-Top Computer	6	3	2				

Table 7.7 Breakdown of innovations in Future Stuff by quality improvement and cost reduction categories

The function served by the innovation and the number of cases observed	Quality Improvement Category (%)					Cost Reduction Category (%)			
	Audio/ Visual	Taste/ Smell	Touch/ Comfort	Contem -plative	Total (Y)	Pecuniary	Time saving	Space saving	Total (X)
Health/Hygiene/Safety (63)	14.3	23.8	28.6	33.3	100.0	9.5	7.9	0.0	17.5
Household Maintenance (49)	20.4	2.0	20.4	30.6	73.5	24.5	36.7	0.0	61.2
Participatory entertnmt (45)	53.3	0.0	28.9	13.3	95.6	2.2	2.2	6.7	11.1
Sedentary entertainment (29)	75.9	0.0	3.4	13.8	93.1	0.0	17.2	10.3	27.6
Transportation (24)	37.5	0.0	8.3	20.8	66.7	25.0	20.8	0.0	45.8
Information Processing (17)	29.4	0.0	5.9	47.1	82.4	11.8	47.1	11.8	70.6
Food/Beverage (16)	0.0	81.3	0.0	0.0	81.3	12.5	12.5	12.5	37.5
Communication (13)	76.9	0.0	0.0	15.4	92.3	7.7	30.8	15.4	53.8
Clothing/Linens (10)	30.0	10.0	30.0	30.0	100.0	0.0	10.0	0.0	10.0
Transactions/Shopping (9)	33.3	0.0	0.0	0.0	33.3	11.1	88.9	0.0	100.0
All Functions (275)	34.5	10.9	17.5	23.3	86.2	11.3	20.7	4.4	36.4

Regression of the per cent total for quality improvement onto the per cent total for cost reduction: Observations = 10; Constant = 107.96; X coefficient = -0.601; t-Statistic of X coefficient = -4.58; R-Squared = 0.72

to sensory appeal or health. Hence, Hypothesis III is supported by these data.

Similarly, the lowest level of quality improvement is seen in transactions/shopping, which also has the highest level of cost reduction. The lowest levels of cost reduction are in clothing/linens and exercise/participatory entertainment, which are both closely associated with sensory stimulation. These additional comparisons of the functions in Table 7.7, as well as many other comparisons that could be made, provide strong evidence in support of Hypotheses I-III.

Finally, it is evident from Table 7.7 that there is, indeed, a dichotomy between quality improvement and cost reduction, such that the two are negatively related across different types of goods. A simple, preliminary method of testing this negative relation is through an ordinary least squares regression of the 'total' for quality improvement (labelled 'Y' in the table) against the total for cost reduction (labelled 'X').[8] This regression does provide preliminary support to the notion that there is some level of trade-off between quality improvement and cost reduction. Of course, more information would need to be analysed before any definitive conclusions could be made.

A fourth hypothesis is proposed, involving a supply-side issue:

Hypothesis IV

Cost reduction by firms can be severely constrained by natural scarcity. Therefore, depending on the material requirements of a particular good or service, cost reduction can be negative.

The basic notion of the cost reduction process is that, as man acquires more knowledge and control over his environment, he will be able to produce goods more efficiently. Thus, assuming that suppliers have an incentive to lower costs, there is an evolutionary tendency for increased productivity. This, indeed, was one of the basic ideas underlying the model presented in this study.

There are two important constraints, though, that man cannot overcome at present. These are the impracticality of producing chemical elements from other chemical elements, and the finiteness of the earth's surface. The first of these means that man simply cannot 'produce', in the basic sense of the word, chemical elements like aluminum, copper, lead, tin, zinc, manganese and nickel — but must find them ready-made. There is only a fixed sum of these materials on the earth's surface, and thus, a fixed supply in the long-term sense. Unless or until the technology is obtained to colonize space, the supply of these materials will remain fixed, regardless of how efficient the machinery is to mine it. Of course, the decreasing marginal returns from having to dig deeper will be experienced first, before the actual supply limits are reached, but such decreasing returns are simply another aspect of the same problem — the finiteness of the earth's surface.

It is easy to see that this same problem exits for fossil fuels. In theory, fossil fuels could, themselves, be produced by man from other materials. However, at present the process for doing so would simply be too expensive — more energy could be required to produce the fuel than the amount of energy it provides.

One could argue that plant and animal matter are also subject to the same constraints resulting from the finiteness of the earth's surface, e.g., the limited supply of adequate climates, water, fertilizer and sunlight. However, there is a fundamental difference between minerals and animal or plant matter: if the price of tobacco rises relative to the price of cotton, a field once used to grow cotton could be converted to grow tobacco. If the price of nickel rises relative to the price of aluminum, an aluminum mine cannot be converted to a nickel mine.

The idea that scarcity factors may give rise to an increase in the relative price of metals is hardly new, and evidence already exists for it. Grilli and Yang state, 'relative prices of metals in the 1900-86 period . . . show a clear primary tendency to fall, but a secondary tendency in the opposite direction. If one computes a parabolic . . . trend . . . the second term is found to be positive and statistically significant, whereas the first term is negative and statistically significant' (1988, p. 30). As Grilli and Yang suggest, the observed secondary price trend in metals supports the original theory held by classical economists, that primary goods will rise in price relative to manufactured goods due to decreasing marginal returns in the use of land.

On the other hand, technological change *can* result in lower mineral prices when demand is reduced due to substitution of the minerals by more plentiful materials. Copper wiring for telephone lines is being replaced by silicon fibres, for example, and metals are continually being replaced by plastics and fibreglass. As we know, in the long run fossil fuels could be substituted by other resources in the production of energy, as wood had been substituted by fossil fuels.

None the less, chemical elements are quite unique in that they will always have their specific chemical properties, which are likely to be called upon in the production of new goods as technology progresses. Thus, while copper wiring may be substituted by silicon fibres today, there is still a high probability that some other use of copper will come along tomorrow that silicon cannot substitute. In essence, *chemical elements have a 'lifetime membership' in the club of materials that will be used in the production of new products*. Hence, chemical elements that are not plentiful, or chemical elements that must be extracted from the earth, have an evolutionary tendency to rise in price, in spite of what short-term trends might indicate.

One would expect cost-reduction to occur more slowly for minerals and fossil fuels than for other goods, all else being equal, because of the depletion of natural supply as more materials are extracted. Whether such cost reduction is positive, negative, or zero, would depend on how one goes about deflating current price figures. The key issue, however, is how the rates of price change for minerals and fossil fuels compare with those for other goods. Meadows, Meadows and Randers (1992) argue that these *rates of change* will affect the economy long before any dramatic changes occur in the absolute quantities of minerals and fuels. They focus on the concept of 'throughput' which they define as 'the flow of energy and/or material from the original sources, through a system (where it may be transformed), and out the ultimate sinks' (p. 279). They argue:

> The limits, let us be clear, are to *throughput*. They are *speed limits*, not space limits, limits to flow rates, not limits to the number of people or the amount of capital (at least not directly). To be beyond them does not mean running into an absolute wall. It may even mean that material and energy throughputs can still grow for a while, before negative feedbacks from overstressed sources or sinks force them down. But down is the direction that throughputs will have to go, by human choice or by strong and unpleasant natural feedbacks. (Meadows, Meadows and Randers 1992, p. 99)

In conclusion, cost reduction is not a random process, but seems to occur at different rates for different types of goods. Goods that must be extracted from the earth's surface, and cannot be produced from simpler components, are more likely to undergo slower cost reduction, or even negative cost reduction.[9]

It is clear that Hypotheses I-IV could not be tested empirically without considerable difficulty. Nevertheless, with sufficient ingenuity on the part of economists interested in evolutionary change, the task would not be impossible. For example, the five goods examined in this study confirm Hypothesis I' quite strongly, and add a small element of support to Hypotheses II and III. Photographic equipment does involve a much greater appeal to the senses than gas ranges, and also had a much higher rate of quality improvement. However, many more goods would need to be examined before any broad-based conclusions could be drawn. Perhaps the most beneficial aspect of the above hypotheses is simply that they serve as a guide, and motivation, for the development of additional ideas on evolutionary change.

RE-EXAMINING THE CLASSICAL DEBATE ON THE NET BARTER TERMS OF TRADE

Over the past two centuries economists have argued that long-run trends in prices could vary among different types of goods. Several classical economists believed that primary commodities have an evolutionary tendency to increase in price relative to manufactured goods.[10] Their argument was straightforward: primary commodities would undergo price increases due to decreasing returns to scale and increases in population. In contrast, manufactures would decline in price, due to technical innovations in production and to increased specialization of labour.[11] It is likely that, in their time, these tendencies were readily apparent.

This basic argument remained long after the period of the classical economists. Keynes stated that manufactures exhibit constant returns to scale, while agricultural products exhibit decreasing returns. He argued that these tendencies, in combination with population growth, would lead to lower relative prices of manufactured goods, and thus, to lower terms of trade for European countries.[12]

Prebisch (1950) and Singer (1950), writing independently, postulated an alternative view, in which the supply curve for primary goods shifts to the right faster than the supply curve for manufactures. This tendency, plus the notion that primary goods, especially agricultural products, have a lower price elasticity of demand than manufactures, enabled them to conclude that the relative prices of primary goods would eventually decline. Of the two components of their argument, the one pertaining to price elasticity was not difficult to defend. The other component, that supplies of commodities increase faster than those of manufactures, needed a concrete explanation. Perhaps some of the technological changes occurring in their time would have been relevant to their argument, such as advances in the uses of machinery in agriculture. However, the explanation they offered was along different lines — primary products were being produced by competitive firms, while manufactures were produced by larger and/or better-organized oligopolies. Thus, productivity improvements in primary production would be passed on to consumers in the form of lower prices, while productivity improvements in manufacturing would result in higher returns to the factors of production. [13]

W. Arthur Lewis addressed the issue of evolutionary price changes by developing a North-South trade model, where labour is the only scarce factor of production (Findlay, 1984.) [14] The North produces only steel and food; the South only food and coffee. Each sector experiences labour-saving technical change, but, by assumption, technical change in the North occurs fastest in the food industry, and in the South fastest in the coffee industry. With food as the numeraire, the relative price of coffee and steel at each point in time is determined on the supply side, based on relative labour productivities. Under these conditions, coffee prices continually decline relative to steel prices, and the terms of trade continually deteriorate against the South. Lewis's solution, therefore, was for the South to upgrade food production at the expense of coffee production. This strategy would prevent the terms of trade from deteriorating, and would benefit the South by enhancing the relative abundance of food, and by making steel relatively cheaper to import.

One could argue that primary products do undergo more cost reduction than quality improvement, and vice versa for manufactured goods. Examples are not difficult to find. Primary products like salt, wheat, sugar, vanilla, coffee beans, timber, etc. have not changed much in quality, per unit weight, over the last hundred years. Manufactured goods like phonographs, vehicles, clocks and houses certainly have. The trends in the relative costs of producing both types of goods is less clear cut. For example, a pound of sugar has probably become much cheaper in relation to the price of the highest quality radios produced over the past fifty years. Yet, that same pound of sugar has probably become *more* expensive in relation to the lowest quality radios.

Spraos (1980) reviews several of the studies on this subject and provides some of their data. He finds that a trend does exist, but his most recent data are not as convincing. As he sees it, a basic problem is that there are too many sources of 'noise' and too many arbitrary decisions in the analysis that would be left to the econometrician. For example, World War II creates a large void in the data, and there is no established rule for how that void should be analysed in relation to the rest of the time series. Also, the decision to include or exclude petroleum products makes a substantial difference in the results. In the end, Spraos finds his results to be inconclusive, and remarks, 'while the deteriorating tendency [of the terms of trade] cannot be decisively refuted, it is open to doubt when . . . the record up to the 1970s is taken into account' (Spraos 1980, p. 126). In a more recent study Sapsford (1985) contends that Spraos's econometric techniques were responsible for his inconclusive findings, and that, with other techniques, more conclusive results are possible that support the hypothesis of deteriorating terms of trade.

Spraos suggests that the apparent deterioration of the terms of trade for primary commodities may be due to a *quality bias*, i.e., the occurrence of undetected quality change, causing a bias in the valuation of goods. Although the term quality bias is commonly used, it can lead to significant confusion about the evolution of goods and services. In general, 'bias' refers to the tendency for data to be misleading because they are influenced by an unknown, or unobserved, phenomenon. Therefore, the use of the term quality bias carries with it the implicit assumption that quality change cannot be observed, nor explained.

Spraos presents evidence against the presumption that manufactures undergo more quality improvements than primary products:

> It is sometimes thought that primary products do not lend themselves to quality improvements, . . . But the most cursory look at some facts will convince otherwise . . . In Kenya the proportion of coffee beans of highest quality (AA) harvested in 1957-8 was 0.20%; in 1964-65 it was 16.30% . . . In Greece 60.1% of cotton output in 1954 had a staple length of 25 mm or less and only 11.3% of 28 mm or more; in 1970 the respective proportions were 0.1% and 97.3% . . . The conclusion is not that the NBTT [net barter terms of trade] series are free of quality bias; only that the alleged direction of the bias is a matter which cannot merely be asserted; it needs to be demonstrated. (Spraos 1980, pp. 117-18)

Covering the period 1900-1986, Grilli and Yang (1988) find:

> [T]he relative prices of all primary commodities fell on trend by 0.5 percent

a year and those of nonfuel primary commodities by 0.6 percent a year. . . . confirm[ing] the sign, but not the magnitude, of the trend implicit in the work of Prebisch (p. 1).

They criticize the findings of earlier studies, stating:

> Long-term movements in the terms of trade of developing countries were either inferred from those of certain industrial countries or from the movements in the prices of primary commodities relative to those of manufactured products . . . without accounting for changes in the volume or composition of exports of the developing countries. . . . Yet instead of generating caution, the paucity of the available empirical evidence generated a tendency in the opposite direction: strong conclusions were derived from evidence that was weak in both accuracy and economic significance. (Grilli and Yang 1988, p. 2)

However, they themselves mention that there could be problems in interpreting their own results because of quality bias.

The terms of trade between primary commodities and manufactures continues to be a relevant concern, especially for countries that depend heavily on primary exports as a major source of revenue. Yet, the issue among economists appears to have remained primarily within the realm of econometrics, where there has been little interest in the subtle, though unquestionably important, problems of quality measurement.

In summary, the focus of studies on the net barter terms of trade has been on changes in the prices of the same goods. As a result, price changes would be attributed to factors such as decreasing returns to scale and labour specialization (in the case of the classical economists) and oligopolies and inelastic demand (in the case of Prebisch and Singer). That is, various evolutionary forces are believed to act on the production and/or marketing of goods, *while the goods themselves are seen as unchanging physical entities*.

Under the framework in which the qualities of goods do not change, a change in the terms of trade against the South would mean that the South would have to give up more to get less. But suppose the North manufactures a *new* good, whose price and quality are higher than the average price and quality of previous Northern goods. When the change in the terms of trade is observed, the result would, again, be *interpreted* as change in favour of the North and against the South. The economist making the observation would report a downward trend in the terms of trade, which would suggest that the South is having to give up more, in order to get less. Yet, in actuality, the South is getting a 'better' good in return for its unchanged exports. Consequently, within the context of the original framework, which assumed that goods do not change, there has been a quality bias in the terms of trade calculation, and the South is not as badly off as it appears. (Although the South may be worse off in the sense of having a slower rate of economic growth, due to the types of goods it produces.)

Indeed, instead of the assumption made in most terms of trade estimations that quality bias does not exist, an opposite assumption is equally plausible: *the purchasing power of commodities in relation to manufactures changes precisely because of quality change*. If this is, indeed, the case, then when such quality change is thrown out of the calculation of purchasing power, the calculation itself has limited meaning. Effectively, one is throwing out the baby with the bath water.

The view taken in this study is that any evolutionary trends in the relative prices of different types of goods cannot be understood without knowledge about the quality changes that also occur. Quite simply, when the quality of goods change, then the goods themselves are no longer the same, and there can be no real meaning in the changes in their prices. As one would expect, this view becomes more appropriate the longer the period of time being studied, because over time the physical differences among manufactured goods in the earliest and latest periods rise substantially.

Furthermore, little could be gained in terms of understanding from an examination of the *average trend* for the entire 'primary products' or 'manufactures' groups. Specific subdivisions of primary and manufactured goods have provided useful information on price movements and quality change, and therefore, follow-up studies should be performed to make full use of those subdivisions. Economists should find out why different subgroups experience their own price trends, instead of repeating, indefinitely, the same nostalgic experiment on primary and manufactured goods.

NOTES

1.   Scientific appeal, itself, may not be uniform across the natural sciences. For instance, innovations in applied physics and engineering may be more highly regarded among economists, at least subjectively, than innovations in biology. However, this is only the impression that one gets from examining the literature, and has not been tested empirically.

2.   The predictability of innovations, however, is a complex issue that is well beyond the scope of this study. See, for example, Nelson and Winter (1982).

3.   See Fisher & Shell (1972, pp. 27-8) for a thorough and interesting discussion on the nonseparability of refrigerators and ice cream.

4.   One should be careful to make a clear distinction between psychological factors that form the basis of long-run effects, and those that involve the marketing of goods and the associated short-run effects of firms drawing attention to their products. For a thorough discussion and literature review of marketing effects, see Streenkamp (1989).

5.   As suggested earlier, other features could include a good's intellectual appeal, ethical appeal, cultural (or 'counter-cultural') appeal, or spiritual appeal.

6.   *Future Stuff* was published in the UK in 1990 under the title, *Towards 200l: A Consumer's Guide to the 21st Century.*

7.   The vast majority of these products have a very high probability of being marketed sometime in the 1990s, and many of them have already arrived.

8.   Technically, a Tobit regression analysis would have been more appropriate because both variables are bounded by the values of 0 and 100.

9.   In the particular case of metals, however, the data are often quite difficult to interpret, because several metals are produced as by-products from the mining of other metals. That is, production processes are not separable. For instance, a rise in demand for metal X could lead to a fall in the price of metal Y, because the expansion of mining operations for metal X, to meet the increased demand, may create an oversupply of metal Y. A proper analysis of metal prices, therefore, would require a multi-dimensional production function.

10. See Mill (1848), Ricardo (1817) and Torrens (1821).

11. See Grilli and Yang (1988).

12. See Grilli and Yang (1988), Keynes (1912) and Keynes (1920).

13. See Grilli and Yang (1988), pp. 28-9.

14. For additional information on Lewis's development models, see Lewis (1978, 1982a, 1982b and 1983).

8. The quality of economic literature

> There was a serious weakness in the neo-classical synthesis to which most of the profession seems to have been oblivious. The theory of market equilibrium, . . . can accommodate accumulation and change only by making the assumption that buyers and sellers have 'correct foresight' of the future course of prices. A world of correct foresight is not a world in which human beings live. From this point, the argument takes off into an elaboration of mathematical structures which have no point of contact with empirical reality.
>
> *Joan Robinson (1980, p. 94)*

While economists measure the quality of virtually all products in the economy, they appear to have the most difficulty in assessing the quality of their own product — economic literature. Problems that exist in the characteristics of economic literature in general bear directly on the specific topic of quality measurement in the following ways:

1. Just as one cannot sharpen a physical object without the use of a harder one, or tune a musical instrument without hearing one that is in tune, economists cannot measure the quality of goods any better than they can measure the quality of their literature.

2. One might expect the obsession that so many industries have toward improving the quality of consumer goods to carry over to economics, where economists would have at least some interest in quality measurement beyond what has been traditionally required for the construction of price indices. However, the lack of interest in this area may be more a function of the characteristics of economic literature itself than a function of the actual economic importance of quality improvement.

3. Conversely, improvements in the methods that economists use to measure the quality of goods and services could lead to improvements in the way that they evaluate their own outputs.
4. The particular problems that exist in the economic literature on quality measurement serve as good examples of the problems that exist in economic literature in general.

Hence, quality measurement and the quality of economic literature are integrally related.

Criticism of economic literature has grown enormously over the past three decades, from both within and outside of the field. This chapter could not possibly do justice to that vast body of critical ideas, which, if they were grouped together as a single topic in economics, could easily constitute the largest one. The most common criticisms relate to the self-serving character of economic thought: 'empty formalism', theory for theory's sake, and measurement for measurement's sake. That is, observers have noted that little or no attention is paid in economics to the actual usefulness of ideas when it comes to resolving public issues or to understanding the true causal factors underlying actual economic phenomena. Such criticisms have been expressed in the full spectrum of communication styles, from rigorous philosophical arguments on the underpinnings of useful knowledge, to humorous anecdotes detailing the misadventures of the 'assuming economist'.[1]

The proposed solutions have been as diverse as the criticisms. Among the most talked about are:

1. Economic ideas must be testable, and consequently, economics, like natural science, can accumulate useful knowledge about the world as it actually exists.[2]
2. Economists should admit that their work is oriented toward rhetoric, and in so doing they will be more honest, if nothing else.[3]
3. Economics should simply become more applied and empirical, and less theoretical.[4]

As mentioned above, quality measurement serves as a useful example of one area of economic thought that could be associated with these problems and proposed solutions. Like many other important concepts in economics, the concept of quality measurement has fallen subject to the application of routine procedures, and to the influence of elaborate mathematical models that have found their way into well-defined niches of economic literature. Price-index economics, for example, lays claim to its own interpretation of cost-based quality. For various reasons unrelated to scientific methods of inquiry, economists involved in quality measurement can add to the multitude of publications that support previously documented ideas. Given this problem, the measurement of quality in economics will only be as useful as the quality of economics itself.

One of the greatest shortcomings in the literature, which could be attributed to the empty formalism associated with quality measurement, is the lack of attention paid to the meaning of what is being measured. In particular, quality change has no meaning if there is not a clear understanding of the distinction between one good and another. That is, to measure quality change, one must first ask how similar two items have to be in order to treat them as being within the same category of goods. To be at all useful, this must be a scientific question, not a semantic one. For example, air conditioners are, for most practical purposes, a quality improvement over fans, and camcorders a quality improvement over household movie cameras. Nevertheless, if fans and air conditioners, or movie cameras and camcorders, are treated as different goods in an accounting methodology, then quality improvements could, in effect, go undetected. In terms of the 'big picture', the quality improvements that would be left out in this manner could possibly represent the most important forms of quality improvement that have occurred throughout history.

One may still ask: what harm is being done? Why not have everyone interpret quality change in their own way? The harm lies in the loss of understanding and the deprivation of progress in our knowledge about economic evolution. Certainly, economists could be allowed to interpret quality change in their own way, and simply not pay much attention to the concept of quality change itself. But society would then be left with a need to establish a new concept to replace what quality change is primarily meant to represent — the actual economic importance, or value, of technological changes in goods and services. As argued in Chapter 1, this replacement of terms may have already happened to some extent, with the new concept being product innovation.

Perhaps one of the most important aspects of the concept of quality change is that it is one of the few economic phenomena that is truly *cumulative*. Looking at the improvements, for example, in photographic equipment between 1928 and 1993, one develops a clear sense of evolutionary change that has a life of its own. In recent decades, in fact, one might say that this form of human progress has overshadowed all other forms.

Yet, how can economics keep up with, or at least recognize, the progress of the material world it is supposed to measure? As mentioned above, the critics have rightly pointed out that the characteristics of economic thought itself must change. In short, most economists should think differently, and place greater importance on the usefulness of ideas.

However, few critics have addressed the issue of *why* economists should want to change in this way. If most economists had the inclination to change their perspectives on economics, then many would have done so from the beginning. That is, much of the critical literature, while correct, falls largely on deaf ears (Eichner 1983). This literature appeals primarily to the minority of economists for whom such criticism would not apply. In this sense, the critical literature is also self-serving, and is studied primarily by the small number of people who are most interested in contributing to it.

The problem, in a nutshell, is that critiques of economic ideas rely on the assumption that economists will change their ideas in order to meet intellectual (especially epistemological) objectives. This assumption is not realistic. Economists benefit financially from the ideas they present, i.e., there is a market for economic reasoning (Earl 1983 and Eichner 1983). In this sense, the economist cannot be expected to be any more benevolent about the ideas he peddles than Adam Smith's butcher, baker, or brewer. In essence, many of the critics of economic ideas have paid too little attention to the economics of economics.

The solution to improving the quality of economic literature, then, lies largely in the system of incentives that economists face (Earl 1983). It is the game itself that is the culprit, not the players.

To elaborate on this argument, a minimal amount of formalism is required. Specifically, consider the population of economists in the world, and define a 'referencing circle' as follows: a referencing circle, for some probability p, is the set of all economists with a certain specialization, such that the probability of any of them being referenced (in economic literature) by anyone else *within* the set is greater than or equal to p. The probability of any of them being referenced by anyone else who is *outside* the set is less than p. Experts in set theory could probably have an enjoyable time proving that such a set could only exist under very special mathematical conditions. Nevertheless, the existence of referencing circles in the economic community is intuitively obvious, even though they may have 'grey borders'. From the simple definition above, it follows that some circles could contain other circles. For instance, the circle of economists in agricultural economics contains the circle of economists studying the economics of food safety.

Criticism of economic literature can now be divided into criticisms from inside the same referencing circle, or from outside the circle. Within-circle criticism is severely constrained by strong disincentives, because one is often published on the basis of good relations with members of one's referencing circle (Earl 1983). Criticism from outside the circle may be recognized by other economists outside the circle, but will usually have little influence on the individuals criticized, for the same reason — incentives dictate that they answer only to colleagues within their own circle. The result of this fragmentation of economists is, therefore, an unresponsiveness of the entire profession to criticism. Moreover, to avoid criticism or controversy within the referencing circle, i.e., to make everyone in the circle happy, economists have learned to expand their knowledge and impress their colleagues in the one area that no one has any qualms about, mathematics.

Hence, it is questionable whether referencing circles evolve for the better, or whether they wander off, carried by their own momentums, idiosyncrasies, and pathways of least resistance.[5] Certainly, society's overall demand for useful knowledge helps push referencing circles in the proper direction. On the other hand, that push may not be enough to counterbalance certain harmful idiosyncrasies of referencing circles that tend to drive them on their own course. In the worst cases, memberships in referencing circles that are heavily influenced by unproductive idiosyncrasies could be analogous to the growth of a population of lemmings — eventually there may be nowhere to go but into the sea.

In the long run, then, the idiosyncrasies of referencing circles may be as much a barrier to the quality improvement of economics as the unscientific research orientations that are more often discussed in critical literature. Examples of these idiosyncrasies are provided in Table 8.1, many of which are discussed in Crane (1967), Earl (1983) and Eichner (1983).

The solution to economics becoming more useful may not be a greater appeal to economists to concern themselves with usefulness. Such a solution would be analogous to the policy that

Table 8.1 Examples of idiosyncrasies in economic referencing circles

Nature of the Idiosyncrasy	Idiosyncrasy	Description
Ethical	Apprenticeship	Greater recognition given to authors who have previously worked under, or collaborated with, more senior authors in the circle.
	Homage	Greater recognition to authors who acknowledge and praise the research of others in the circle.
	Cronyism	Greater recognition to authors who enjoy social relations with, work alongside of, or exchange favours with others in the circle; or greater recognition to authors belonging to the same or closely linked institutions.
	Censorship	Exclusion of authors with certain viewpoints, for reasons unrelated to intellectual legitimacy.
	Political bent	Recognition as a function of the political implication of one's findings, independent of analytical validity.
	Prejudice	Recognition as a function of race, sex, sexual preference, religion, ethnicity, income, employer, personality, etc., all else being equal.
	Irresponsibility	Lack of commitment on the part of reviewers to perform their duty to the best of their ability.
	Collaboration	Greater recognition for work by more authors, all else being equal.
	Intolerance	Intolerance toward criticism, regardless of empirical evidence, the logic of one's argument, etc.
Methodological	Formalism	Preference for unnecessary formalism among members.
	Complexity	Reverence for mathematical or literary complexity, independent of the actual usefulness of the research.
	Rigidity	Lack of openness to new ideas, preferred isolation from other reference circles, etc.
Stylistic	Frivolity	Excessive attention to the decorative and showy quality of a research document.
	Superficiality	Lack of interest paid to detail in the evaluation of an author's work.
	Writing style	Undue concern over an author's writing style, as a substitute for addressing economic issues.

the butcher, baker and brewer should be more benevolent in order for the economy to grow faster. In the long run, it is the peer-review process in economics that needs to be revised if there is to be any improvement in the quality of economic literature. In particular, measures should be taken to meet the following intermediate goals:

1. The importance of review within the referencing circle must be reduced, while the importance of review among economists outside the circle enhanced. This change, in turn, will have the following results:
    (a) The idiosyncrasies of referencing circles will have less influence on economists' careers, while the broader appeal of economists' work will have a greater influence.
    (b) This change would tend to interlink economics, and reverse its current trend toward fractionalization (or inbreeding).
2. The review process must be altered in a manner that forces economists to focus on economic thought only, as opposed to all of the other factors that come into play, such as the author's affiliation with other economists.
3. Measures must be instituted such that the kind of commitment to usefulness that so many critics have espoused is actually detectable and rewarded in the community of economists. Conversely, empty formalism, measurement without meaning, etc., must be identified and rejected.

The question, of course, is how these intermediate goals can be achieved.

Before discussing the specific, proposed solution, it must be said, at the outset, that any such solutions would impose greater costs on the reviewing process, which at present utilizes a bare minimum of necessary human resources. However, in the absence of a formal analysis, the benefits would appear to far outweigh the additional costs, especially if those additional costs take the form of voluntary participation by economists.

The proposed solution would be the institution of the following measures by the community of professional economists:

1. Rather than determining who the reviewers should be on the basis of the references that appear in the work, publishers should simply identify a subject category for the work, as, for

example, one of the subject categories used by the *Journal of Economic Literature*. This policy would create a much wider pool from which reviewers could be drawn, and this pool is independent of the author's own listing of references (which may reflect a small circle of his or her associates).

2. Reviewers would be required to sign a form attesting to the fact that they reviewed the material to the best of their knowledge and ability, and without bias. Reviewers should also be required to provide quick responses, and responses that are not influenced by any collaboration with others.

3. The 'double-blind' review method, whereby the reviewer does not know the author and vice versa, must be instituted wherever possible. However, current methods of protecting the author and reviewer's identities in these cases are highly inadequate. Especially in small reviewing circles, reviewers can easily identify the author from the lists of references. Furthermore, the reference list of authors could be unfairly scrutinized by some reviewers for various reasons associated with some of the idiosyncrasies identified in Table 8.1. A proposed solution is for authors to submit their work in a form that actually does not mention any references, but codes references simply as 'Ref. 1', 'Ref. 2', etc., so that reviewers can know when ideas are not original. Besides strongly decreasing the chance of the author being identified, and reducing the chance of idiosyncratic evaluation on the part of the reviewer, this anonymity of references reduces as well the tendency for economists to think of name-dropping as the most important component of their research output.

4. Instead of there being merely two reviewers for a journal article, which makes the game of getting published not far removed from that of roulette, at least three reviewers should be used in the first step of a two-tier process. As suggested above, these reviewers would be drawn from the subject category of the work in question, as opposed to the referencing circle. The second step would involve review by economists who are actually outside the subject category. The three initial reviewers from inside the category could rate the work under a rating scheme that would insure that any one of the reviewers does not have absolute veto power over the work. As part of the second stage, reviewers from outside the subject area could be chosen from within a voluntary pool of highly respected economists, established by the publisher. A similar

method of review in this second stage could then be employed. Finally, work that has passed both stages and has a relatively high score could be published. In this process, it would not be essential that a research piece make everyone happy, but it would be required to make at least some people, including those outside the referencing circle, very happy — and this shift in emphasis would greatly improve the very nature of economic literature.

5.   Finally, a new association or institution should be established, such as the 'Association of Critical Economists' where criticism of economic literature, provided it is in good taste, is welcomed. It would be based on the principle that, if no one can be 'wrong', then there is nothing to be gained from anyone being 'right'. This association could, in part, be a watchdog over the writers, publishers and reviewers of economic literature. It could also draw in critics from other fields, such as the natural sciences, other social sciences, mathematics, and philosophy. To whatever extent possible, this body should be 'paradigm neutral'.

These measures would certainly create some problems of their own. Nevertheless, they would at least represent a start for economists to play an active role in the improvement of their own products, as opposed to the present situation in which they often must scramble to acquire and maintain a respected position within a small, isolated, and hopefully amicable, referencing circle.

NOTES

1. In some cases the humorous discussions are deeply rooted in the philosophical ones. Two examples are:
    An economist, who misplaces his keys, remembers hearing them fall from his pocket while he was walking through a dark alley. However, he chooses to look for them under a street lamp down the road, because the light is better there.
    One economist says to another, 'I have serious doubts about your new method of analysis. Of course, one can easily see that it is intellectually appealing, logistically sound, and extremely useful in practice. But I am sorry to say that it would never work in theory.'
2. See, for example, Blaug (1992), Caldwell (1982), Eichner (1983), Leontief (1971), Mayer (1993), Ward (1972) and Worswick (1972).
3. McCloskey is certainly the chief architect of this perspective — see McCloskey (1983) and Caldwell and Coats (1984).
4. See, for example, Bell (1981), Kuttner (1985) and Thurow (1983).

5. As an example of a pathway of least resistance, one could argue: it is easier to analyse than to hypothesize and experiment; it is easier to read than to analyse; it is easier to count than to read; it is easier to assume than to count; and it is easier to use someone else's assumptions than to create one's own.

9. Conclusion

> Good and bad, I defined these terms
> Quite clear, no doubt, somehow
> Ah, but I was so much older then
> I'm younger than that now
> *Bob Dylan, My Back Pages*

In economics words often serve a different purpose than to convey meaning — they define territory. 'Quality' and 'product innovation' mean the same thing for many practical purposes, but they define distinct territories in economic thought and economic literature. The first territory is controlled by price index economists, and the second by technical change economists. If a technical change economist begins to talk about quality change, he or she is invading the price index economists' territory, and must be fought off, and vice versa for the price index economist who talks about technical change. But what is wrong with this? Why not allow economists to form their own territories and defend them?

The problem lies in the fact that little is being accomplished. Price indices continue to be measured, but only for measurement's sake. Of course, these indices do provide useful purposes, like enabling governments to determine what the minimum wage should be, how much landlords should be allowed to raise rents, etc. But that is all they do. They reflect a great deal of useful and important information about technical change, but they are seldom examined in relation to their own causality. The situation is not unlike that of the comedian, who, when failing to get a laugh, says to the audience, 'Hey, I just read 'em, I don't write 'em'.

In contrast, technical change economists are very committed to understanding the causal factors underlying technological discoveries. They have made substantial progress in identifying what makes firms successful innovators. However, they seem to have paid little attention to an essential question: What causes one innovation to be more important than another? Scientific impressiveness is not the answer, nor are most of the other indicators often used as proxies for technological progress, like the number of patents, R&D expenditure, the number of scientists, etc. Surely, the economic importance of new technology must be defined as the economic value of that technology, i.e., the net economic benefits which that technology provides. In order to address the economic benefits of technological change, one must, sooner or later, deal with quality improvement and cost reduction. These concepts, in turn, are best reflected by price indices, when those price indices are properly measured.

Perhaps the economic importance of technological changes is actually not all that important. There are certainly other concerns — political, ethical, etc. — that society as a whole must address with regard to technological change. But these other concerns are seldom addressed by technical change economists either. Their main concern has been the economic success of the innovative firm.

If the behaviour of firms is what causes technical change to occur, then the importance of prices would be limited. Prices would be important only to the extent that they allow economists to place weights on the relative achievements of firms, which may not change the ordinal ranking of firms, or of innovations, that would otherwise be constructed on the basis of alternative indicators. Thus, the fact that prices do help to convey the economic importance of innovations may not, in itself, be enough to justify a greater interest in prices by technological change economists.

However, another consideration must be taken into account, which is the notion that *different types of goods have their own inclinations toward technical change, which is independent of the firms that produce them.* Cameras have not undergone more quality improvement and cost reduction than shoes because the firms that produce cameras are more innovative than the ones that produce shoes. Cameras have a natural predisposition toward substantial quality improvement and cost reduction, based on the structure of human desires, and the physical nature of photographic reproduction. Surely, one is not likely to believe that, if the firms that produce cameras and those that produce shoes were to reverse their managerial practices and their R&D personnel, the rates of quality improvement and cost reduction observed for these goods would also be reversed.

The evidence is clear: over long periods of time, the *function* of a good or service plays an important, independent role in the determination of that good or service's technological change. The longer the period is, the less significant the role of the firm will be, because the greater the likelihood will be that, within that same amount of time, another firm could have come along and achieved the same success.

One must then ask, if the function of the good or service is what ultimately matters over long periods of time, then what is the causal explanation for the relationship between function and technological change? As suggested, human desires are a major determinant, as are the laws of natural science. Cameras improve in quality faster than gas ranges, because cameras produce much greater (or more influential) sensory stimulation than gas ranges. Information processing undergoes more cost reduction than transportation, because bits of information have no minimum weight or volume requirements, while passengers and cargo do. In essence, it is the *goods and services* themselves that determine their own fates in the long run. The firm, in all of this, is only the messenger.

When Adam Smith (1776) wrote *An Inquiry into the Nature and Causes of the Wealth of Nations*, the prevailing perspective among many of the thinkers of the time was that economic growth was a result of the strength of a nation's armies and the stock of its gold (which were not independent, of course, as armies were often financed by gold, and gold often seized by armies). With the arrival of Adam Smith and the other classical political economists, a new outlook arose: in the broader course of things, armies and chests of gold will come and go, but it is the *productive efficiency* of industries that will make the difference in the long run. Hence, economics and the study of the 'economic system' became prominent. Over the course of time, however, much has changed with regard to the production of goods and services. With the expansion of technological expertise and prowess, along with an increased dissemination of technological information, economic growth can no longer be easily explained in terms of the productive efficiencies of capital and labour units. 'Capital', itself, becomes a hollow term, whose real meaning must depend, in one way or another, on the level of technological advancement that it embodies. The same holds true for labour, or 'human capital', which, similarly, depends much less on the *number* of workers, and much more on their *technological expertise*. In the oncoming information and robotics age, these trends will become even more pronounced. Hence, the old methods of 'bean counting' must give way to new methods of understanding, and these new methods must address the questions of how and why products and processes evolve.

Just as the major players changed in Adam Smith's time from

armies and stocks of gold to capital and labour, the major players in modern times will change again from capital and labour to the specific functions of goods and services. The reason is that these specific functions will follow their own inherent, evolutionary paths of quality improvement and cost reduction, and the development of capital and labour will only follow along for the ride. Humanity may produce goods and services, but in an evolutionary and anthropological sense, it will be goods and services that will *define* humanity.

The economic analysis of these effects surely requires the development of new analytical devices. The representative good approach is one such device, that allows for the analysis of rich sources of historical information, at the expense of some inaccuracy in the comparison of consecutive periods. Across long periods of time the benefits of the RGA far outweigh the costs. Consequently, it opens new doors to the study of technological change, and allows us to take a better look at what economies, and society itself, might look like in the future.

Yet, this new perspective, that *goods and services follow their own evolutionary course*, has a long way to go. Many more experiments will need to be conducted, and many more concepts will need to be developed. The role of the economist will need to change as well. While the evolution of goods is an economic concept, one cannot understand it without also understanding human perceptions and desires, on the one hand, and natural science on the other. In many respects, the evolution of goods and services is larger and more complex than economics itself, precisely because of its dependence on so many other avenues of thought.

If the term quality measurement is, unfortunately, too entrenched in currently-defined territories of economic formalism to be used in reference to the evolution of goods and services, then so be it. Semantics and the territoriality of economic topics are irrelevant here, as they should be in all areas of economic inquiry. What is important is simply that the evolution of goods be realized, and that price linking be accepted as an adequate means, in many cases, of measuring these evolutionary trends. Let us accomplish this realization and acceptance first. Only then will our quibbling over techniques be worthwhile.

Appendix: Raw data from the *Sears Catalog*

G = Type of good: 1-Men's shoes, 2-Sofas and love seats, 3-Gas ranges, 4-Window fans and air conditioners, and 5-Cameras, movie cameras and camcorders
Y = Year ('28' is 1928, etc.)
P = Page appearing in the Spring/Summer Issue of the *Sears Catalog*
$ = Nominal price appearing in the catalog

G	Y	P	$	G	Y	P	$	G	Y	P	$
1	28	259	1.98	1	28	254	3.98	1	28	252	5.50
1	28	259	2.19	1	28	254	3.98	1	28	250	5.50
1	28	259	2.29	1	28	258	3.98	1	28	252	5.75
1	28	258	2.29	1	28	256	4.48	1	28	250	5.95
1	28	258	2.48	1	28	256	4.48	1	28	250	5.95
1	28	257	2.69	1	28	256	4.48	1	28	250	5.95
1	28	259	2.79	1	28	251	4.48	1	28	251	5.95
1	28	228	2.79	1	28	256	4.48	1	28	251	5.95
1	28	478	2.79	1	28	250	4.48	1	33	238	1.00
1	28	254	2.98	1	28	250	4.48	1	33	237	1.19
1	28	257	2.98	1	28	253	4.50	1	33	220	1.39
1	28	255	2.98	1	28	253	4.50	1	33	236	1.49
1	28	257	2.98	1	28	253	4.50	1	33	238	1.49
1	28	255	3.25	1	28	253	4.50	1	33	228	1.49
1	28	257	3.25	1	28	253	4.50	1	33	237	1.49
1	28	256	3.48	1	28	253	4.50	1	33	221	1.59
1	28	255	3.48	1	28	253	4.50	1	33	232	1.69
1	28	254	3.48	1	28	251	4.95	1	33	232	1.69
1	28	257	3.48	1	28	251	4.95	1	33	221	1.77
1	28	254	3.48	1	28	251	4.95	1	33	221	1.77
1	28	256	3.48	1	28	256	4.98	1	33	221	1.77
1	28	257	3.50	1	28	252	5.00	1	33	233	1.79
1	28	255	3.75	1	28	252	5.00	1	33	228	1.79
1	28	256	3.75	1	28	252	5.00	1	33	238	1.79
1	28	255	3.75	1	28	252	5.50	1	33	222	2.00
1	28	255	3.79	1	28	252	5.50	1	33	222	2.00
1	28	255	3.79	1	28	250	5.50	1	33	222	2.00
1	28	254	3.79	1	28	252	5.50	1	33	231	2.00
1	28	254	3.98	1	28	250	5.50	1	33	222	2.00

G	Y	P	$	G	Y	P	$	G	Y	P	$
1	33	236	2.00	1	33	226	3.98	1	38	307	2.95
1	33	222	2.00	1	33	226	4.00	1	38	306	2.95
1	33	220	2.00	1	38	320	1.17	1	38	307	2.95
1	33	220	2.00	1	38	319	1.49	1	38	307	2.95
1	33	232	2.00	1	38	303	1.49	1	38	306	2.95
1	33	221	2.00	1	38	303	1.55	1	38	306	2.95
1	33	237	2.00	1	38	303	1.85	1	38	306	2.95
1	33	222	2.00	1	38	319	1.89	1	38	307	2.95
1	33	232	2.00	1	38	316	1.89	1	38	306	2.95
1	33	220	2.00	1	38	320	1.89	1	38	304	2.98
1	33	228	2.00	1	38	319	1.89	1	38	318	2.98
1	33	220	2.00	1	38	304	1.98	1	38	318	2.98
1	33	222	2.00	1	38	317	1.98	1	38	306	3.19
1	33	236	2.00	1	38	304	1.98	1	38	308	3.48
1	33	233	2.00	1	38	304	1.98	1	38	308	3.48
1	33	221	2.00	1	38	318	1.98	1	38	308	3.48
1	33	228	2.19	1	38	303	1.98	1	38	308	3.48
1	33	228	2.19	1	38	318	1.98	1	38	308	3.48
1	33	233	2.48	1	38	316	1.98	1	38	308	3.48
1	33	223	2.49	1	38	304	1.98	1	38	308	3.48
1	33	230	2.49	1	38	304	1.98	1	38	308	3.48
1	33	232	2.49	1	38	315	1.98	1	38	315	3.49
1	33	223	2.49	1	38	316	1.98	1	38	310	3.65
1	33	223	2.49	1	38	320	2.00	1	38	314	3.69
1	33	233	2.49	1	38	313	2.00	1	38	314	3.79
1	33	231	2.59	1	38	319	2.00	1	38	311	3.98
1	33	231	2.59	1	38	304	2.15	1	38	311	3.98
1	33	233	2.59	1	38	319	2.19	1	38	311	3.98
1	33	225	2.69	1	38	305	2.19	1	38	310	3.98
1	33	225	2.79	1	38	305	2.29	1	38	317	3.98
1	33	231	2.79	1	38	304	2.29	1	38	311	3.98
1	33	225	2.79	1	38	305	2.49	1	38	311	3.98
1	33	224	2.98	1	38	305	2.49	1	38	313	3.98
1	33	224	2.98	1	38	305	2.49	1	38	318	3.98
1	33	224	2.98	1	38	305	2.49	1	38	310	4.25
1	33	224	2.98	1	38	305	2.49	1	38	312	4.25
1	33	225	2.98	1	38	317	2.59	1	38	312	4.25
1	33	225	2.98	1	38	315	2.59	1	38	310	4.25
1	33	224	2.98	1	38	315	2.59	1	38	312	4.50
1	33	227	3.49	1	38	317	2.59	1	38	309	4.69
1	33	227	3.49	1	38	313	2.69	1	38	309	4.69
1	33	232	3.49	1	38	313	2.75	1	38	309	4.69
1	33	230	3.49	1	38	314	2.79	1	38	309	4.69
1	33	227	3.49	1	38	316	2.79	1	38	309	4.69
1	33	227	3.49	1	38	314	2.89	1	38	309	4.69
1	33	226	3.98	1	38	313	2.89	1	38	309	4.69
1	33	227	3.98	1	38	307	2.95	1	43	323	1.77
1	33	226	3.98	1	38	307	2.95	1	43	329	1.85

G	Y	P	$	G	Y	P	$	G	Y	P	$
1	43	329	2.19	1	43	311	3.65	1	43	324	5.00
1	43	328	2.19	1	43	324	3.65	1	43	311	5.00
1	43	328	2.29	1	43	319	3.65	1	43	316	5.00
1	43	320	2.29	1	43	332	3.79	1	43	311	5.00
1	43	321	2.29	1	43	335	3.79	1	43	317	5.00
1	43	322	2.29	1	43	330	3.79	1	43	310	5.00
1	43	322	2.29	1	43	321	3.98	1	43	317	5.00
1	43	328	2.44	1	43	333	3.98	1	43	316	5.00
1	43	325	2.49	1	43	332	3.98	1	43	307	5.50
1	43	326	2.55	1	43	334	3.98	1	43	308	5.75
1	43	323	2.59	1	43	321	3.98	1	43	308	5.75
1	43	320	2.69	1	43	333	3.98	1	43	308	5.75
1	43	323	2.69	1	43	327	3.98	1	43	307	5.75
1	43	323	2.69	1	43	313	4.20	1	43	315	6.20
1	43	322	2.69	1	43	313	4.20	1	43	315	6.20
1	43	322	2.69	1	43	313	4.20	1	43	315	6.20
1	43	323	2.69	1	43	313	4.20	1	43	315	6.20
1	43	320	2.69	1	43	314	4.20	1	43	315	6.20
1	43	322	2.69	1	43	324	4.20	1	43	307	6.45
1	43	322	2.69	1	43	314	4.20	1	48	466	3.29
1	43	322	2.69	1	43	313	4.20	1	48	468	3.98
1	43	323	2.69	1	43	324	4.20	1	48	454	4.49
1	43	322	2.69	1	43	314	4.20	1	48	454	4.49
1	43	331	2.77	1	43	312	4.20	1	48	464	4.49
1	43	320	2.79	1	43	311	4.20	1	48	468	4.49
1	43	321	2.79	1	43	313	4.20	1	48	466	4.65
1	43	329	2.85	1	43	314	4.20	1	48	466	4.75
1	43	330	2.97	1	43	311	4.20	1	48	454	4.89
1	43	325	2.98	1	43	312	4.20	1	48	454	4.89
1	43	331	2.98	1	43	311	4.20	1	48	454	4.89
1	43	326	2.98	1	43	310	4.20	1	48	454	4.89
1	43	334	2.98	1	43	334	4.35	1	48	448	4.98
1	43	325	3.35	1	43	335	4.59	1	48	464	4.98
1	43	327	3.39	1	43	307	4.59	1	48	464	5.49
1	43	333	3.39	1	43	309	4.60	1	48	465	5.49
1	43	328	3.39	1	43	309	4.60	1	48	468	5.49
1	43	325	3.49	1	43	309	4.60	1	48	460	5.89
1	43	310	3.65	1	43	309	4.60	1	48	448	5.98
1	43	318	3.65	1	43	309	4.60	1	48	449	5.98
1	43	318	3.65	1	43	309	4.60	1	48	455	5.98
1	43	320	3.65	1	43	334	4.75	1	48	464	5.98
1	43	318	3.65	1	43	333	4.87	1	48	468	5.98
1	43	307	3.65	1	43	334	4.88	1	48	449	6.45
1	43	319	3.65	1	43	332	4.98	1	48	455	6.45
1	43	321	3.65	1	43	308	4.98	1	48	455	6.45
1	43	319	3.65	1	43	317	5.00	1	48	455	6.45
1	43	320	3.65	1	43	317	5.00	1	48	455	6.45
1	43	319	3.65	1	43	316	5.00	1	48	460	6.49

G	Y	P	$	G	Y	P	$	G	Y	P	$
1	48	462	6.49	1	48	457	9.75	1	53	392	5.95
1	48	468	6.49	1	48	457	9.75	1	53	392	5.95
1	48	469	6.49	1	48	457	9.75	1	53	392	5.95
1	48	463	6.75	1	48	449	9.95	1	53	393	5.95
1	48	465	6.75	1	48	457	9.95	1	53	393	5.95
1	48	448	6.98	1	48	461	9.95	1	53	393	5.95
1	48	449	6.98	1	48	460	9.98	1	53	394	5.95
1	48	455	6.98	1	48	467	9.98	1	53	394	5.95
1	48	463	6.98	1	48	450	10.95	1	53	397	5.95
1	48	465	6.98	1	48	450	10.95	1	53	401	5.98
1	48	469	7.45	1	48	451	10.95	1	53	402	5.98
1	48	463	7.49	1	48	451	10.95	1	53	400	6.45
1	48	463	7.49	1	48	451	10.95	1	53	403	6.49
1	48	449	7.65	1	48	451	10.95	1	53	401	6.69
1	48	449	7.65	1	48	451	10.95	1	53	403	6.79
1	48	449	7.65	1	48	451	10.95	1	53	392	6.85
1	48	452	7.65	1	48	451	10.95	1	53	392	6.85
1	48	452	7.65	1	48	451	10.95	1	53	392	6.85
1	48	452	7.65	1	48	461	11.45	1	53	393	6.85
1	48	453	7.65	1	48	458	11.95	1	53	393	6.85
1	48	453	7.65	1	48	458	11.95	1	53	393	6.85
1	48	453	7.65	1	48	459	11.95	1	53	393	6.85
1	48	453	7.65	1	48	459	11.95	1	53	401	6.89
1	48	453	7.65	1	48	459	11.95	1	53	382	6.95
1	48	453	7.65	1	48	459	11.95	1	53	382	6.95
1	48	453	7.65	1	48	461	11.95	1	53	400	6.98
1	48	453	7.65	1	48	467	11.95	1	53	401	6.98
1	48	453	7.65	1	53	383	2.69	1	53	399	7.49
1	48	467	7.65	1	53	403	3.29	1	53	400	7.49
1	48	456	7.95	1	53	383	3.98	1	53	401	7.49
1	48	456	7.95	1	53	403	3.98	1	53	401	7.49
1	48	456	7.95	1	53	403	4.39	1	53	381	7.65
1	48	456	7.95	1	53	402	4.49	1	53	382	7.65
1	48	456	7.95	1	53	403	4.69	1	53	398	7.69
1	48	460	7.98	1	53	403	4.69	1	53	382	7.85
1	48	460	7.98	1	53	394	4.98	1	53	383	7.85
1	48	461	7.98	1	53	394	4.98	1	53	396	7.95
1	48	470	7.98	1	53	394	4.98	1	53	396	7.95
1	48	457	8.45	1	53	402	4.98	1	53	396	7.95
1	48	457	8.45	1	53	403	5.39	1	53	396	7.95
1	48	467	8.49	1	53	400	5.49	1	53	396	7.95
1	48	448	8.75	1	53	402	5.49	1	53	396	7.95
1	48	467	8.75	1	53	402	5.79	1	53	399	7.98
1	48	459	8.85	1	53	403	5.79	1	53	399	7.98
1	48	449	8.95	1	53	380	5.95	1	53	403	7.98
1	48	462	8.95	1	53	382	5.95	1	53	399	8.49
1	48	469	8.95	1	53	383	5.95	1	53	403	8.49
1	48	459	9.45	1	53	389	5.95	1	53	403	8.49

G	Y	P	$	G	Y	P	$	G	Y	P	$
1	53	381	8.85	1	58	482	3.77	1	58	497	7.97
1	53	382	8.85	1	58	485	3.77	1	58	495	8.64
1	53	383	8.85	1	58	485	3.77	1	58	478	8.70
1	53	383	8.85	1	58	498	3.97	1	58	479	8.70
1	53	389	8.85	1	58	498	4.27	1	58	480	8.70
1	53	389	8.85	1	58	485	4.67	1	58	481	8.70
1	53	389	8.85	1	58	485	4.77	1	58	482	8.70
1	53	390	8.85	1	58	485	4.77	1	58	496	8.70
1	53	390	8.85	1	58	498	4.77	1	58	495	8.94
1	53	390	8.85	1	58	497	4.97	1	58	477	8.97
1	53	391	8.85	1	58	498	4.97	1	58	477	8.97
1	53	391	8.85	1	58	498	4.97	1	58	477	8.97
1	53	391	8.85	1	58	482	5.00	1	58	478	8.97
1	53	391	8.85	1	58	487	5.00	1	58	478	8.97
1	53	391	8.85	1	58	498	5.47	1	58	480	8.97
1	53	391	8.85	1	58	487	5.54	1	58	481	8.97
1	53	391	8.85	1	58	482	5.74	1	58	481	8.97
1	53	387	8.95	1	58	497	5.74	1	58	497	8.97
1	53	387	8.95	1	58	482	5.97	1	58	500	9.70
1	53	397	8.95	1	58	487	5.97	1	58	500	9.70
1	53	397	8.95	1	58	487	5.97	1	58	476	9.77
1	53	398	8.98	1	58	487	5.97	1	58	476	9.77
1	53	403	8.98	1	58	487	5.97	1	58	476	9.77
1	53	382	9.95	1	58	496	5.97	1	58	476	9.77
1	53	387	9.95	1	58	498	5.97	1	58	477	9.77
1	53	383	10.95	1	58	478	6.77	1	58	477	9.77
1	53	388	10.95	1	58	479	6.77	1	58	477	9.77
1	53	388	10.95	1	58	482	6.77	1	58	478	9.77
1	53	388	10.95	1	58	483	6.77	1	58	478	9.77
1	53	388	10.95	1	58	483	6.77	1	58	481	9.77
1	53	397	10.95	1	58	483	6.77	1	58	481	9.77
1	53	397	10.95	1	58	494	6.77	1	58	486	9.77
1	53	399	10.98	1	58	494	6.77	1	58	486	9.77
1	53	384	11.95	1	58	480	7.70	1	58	486	9.77
1	53	385	11.95	1	58	481	7.70	1	58	492	9.90
1	53	385	11.95	1	58	500	7.70	1	58	493	9.90
1	53	385	11.95	1	58	479	7.74	1	58	488	9.97
1	53	385	11.95	1	58	482	7.74	1	58	488	9.97
1	53	385	11.95	1	58	487	7.74	1	58	488	9.97
1	53	386	11.95	1	58	487	7.74	1	58	489	9.97
1	53	386	11.95	1	58	487	7.74	1	58	480	10.60
1	53	386	11.95	1	58	487	7.74	1	58	495	10.70
1	53	386	11.95	1	58	487	7.74	1	58	491	10.90
1	53	386	11.95	1	58	487	7.74	1	58	492	10.90
1	53	397	11.95	1	58	494	7.74	1	58	500	10.90
1	58	484	2.83	1	58	495	7.74	1	58	492	11.70
1	58	498	3.57	1	58	494	7.97	1	58	495	11.70
1	58	485	3.67	1	58	497	7.97	1	58	497	11.74

G	Y	P	$	G	Y	P	$	G	Y	P	$
1	58	500	11.90	1	63	530	8.70	1	63	545	11.74
1	58	489	12.67	1	63	530	8.70	1	63	545	11.74
1	58	489	12.67	1	63	532	8.70	1	63	524	12.70
1	58	492	12.70	1	63	533	8.70	1	63	524	12.70
1	58	493	12.70	1	63	535	8.70	1	63	524	12.70
1	58	493	12.90	1	63	535	8.70	1	63	539	12.70
1	58	493	12.90	1	63	537	8.70	1	63	542	12.70
1	58	489	13.67	1	63	547	8.70	1	63	544	12.70
1	58	474	14.00	1	63	547	8.70	1	63	545	12.70
1	58	474	14.00	1	63	547	8.70	1	63	548	12.70
1	58	474	14.00	1	63	543	8.97	1	63	527	13.70
1	58	474	14.00	1	63	529	9.77	1	63	544	13.70
1	58	474	14.00	1	63	529	9.77	1	63	544	13.70
1	58	474	14.00	1	63	529	9.77	1	63	539	13.97
1	58	475	14.00	1	63	529	9.77	1	63	539	13.97
1	58	475	14.00	1	63	531	9.77	1	63	539	13.97
1	58	475	14.00	1	63	531	9.77	1	63	542	14.70
1	58	486	14.00	1	63	531	9.77	1	63	545	14.70
1	58	489	14.00	1	63	532	9.77	1	63	527	14.97
1	58	493	15.90	1	63	532	9.77	1	63	539	14.97
1	58	473	19.00	1	63	532	9.77	1	63	525	15.70
1	58	473	19.00	1	63	532	9.77	1	63	525	15.70
1	58	473	19.00	1	63	532	9.77	1	63	525	15.70
1	58	473	19.00	1	63	532	9.77	1	63	544	16.70
1	63	547	4.77	1	63	532	9.77	1	63	545	16.70
1	63	546	5.57	1	63	533	9.77	1	63	526	16.97
1	63	547	5.57	1	63	539	9.77	1	63	526	16.97
1	63	537	5.77	1	63	547	9.77	1	63	527	16.97
1	63	547	5.97	1	63	547	9.77	1	63	527	16.97
1	63	536	6.77	1	63	548	9.77	1	63	527	16.97
1	63	536	6.77	1	63	545	9.97	1	63	527	16.97
1	63	536	6.77	1	63	548	9.97	1	63	527	16.97
1	63	537	6.77	1	63	532	10.70	1	63	531	16.97
1	63	537	6.77	1	63	547	10.74	1	63	531	16.97
1	63	543	6.77	1	63	548	10.74	1	63	539	16.97
1	63	546	6.77	1	63	547	10.79	1	63	539	16.97
1	63	534	6.97	1	63	528	10.97	1	63	526	17.70
1	63	534	6.97	1	63	538	10.97	1	68	510	6.97
1	63	534	6.97	1	63	538	10.97	1	68	522	7.88
1	63	534	6.97	1	63	538	10.97	1	68	517	7.97
1	63	534	6.97	1	63	538	10.97	1	68	517	7.97
1	63	534	6.97	1	63	538	10.97	1	68	523	7.97
1	63	537	7.74	1	63	538	10.97	1	68	522	8.88
1	63	543	7.74	1	63	538	10.97	1	68	522	8.97
1	63	546	7.74	1	63	543	10.97	1	68	523	8.97
1	63	547	7.74	1	63	548	11.70	1	68	517	9.88
1	63	547	7.74	1	63	528	11.74	1	68	517	9.88
1	63	530	8.70	1	63	529	11.74	1	68	517	9.88
				1	63	542	11.74				

G	Y	P	$	G	Y	P	$	G	Y	P	$
1	68	510	9.97	1	68	513	15.88	1	73	327	14.99
1	68	515	9.97	1	68	515	15.88	1	73	327	14.99
1	68	516	9.97	1	68	516	15.88	1	73	328	14.99
1	68	521	9.97	1	68	521	15.88	1	73	321	15.99
1	68	521	9.97	1	68	525	15.88	1	73	322	15.99
1	68	522	9.97	1	68	518	16.88	1	73	326	15.99
1	68	510	10.88	1	68	518	16.88	1	73	331	16.97
1	68	511	10.88	1	68	519	16.88	1	73	323	16.99
1	68	511	10.88	1	68	520	16.88	1	73	323	16.99
1	68	511	10.88	1	68	519	16.97	1	73	327	16.99
1	68	511	10.88	1	68	515	17.77	1	73	324	17.99
1	68	514	10.88	1	68	515	17.77	1	73	324	17.99
1	68	514	10.88	1	68	508	19.75	1	73	324	17.99
1	68	518	10.88	1	68	510	19.77	1	73	330	17.99
1	68	519	10.88	1	68	519	19.88	1	73	324	18.60
1	68	520	10.88	1	68	507	19.97	1	73	328	18.69
1	68	521	10.97	1	68	507	19.97	1	73	331	18.69
1	68	523	10.97	1	68	519	19.97	1	73	321	18.99
1	68	525	11.97	1	68	509	20.75	1	73	324	18.99
1	68	525	11.97	1	68	509	20.75	1	73	326	18.99
1	68	513	12.88	1	68	509	20.75	1	73	326	18.99
1	68	513	12.88	1	68	509	20.75	1	73	329	19.29
1	68	518	12.88	1	68	509	20.75	1	73	331	19.79
1	68	518	12.88	1	68	509	20.75	1	73	319	19.99
1	68	519	12.88	1	68	510	20.97	1	73	321	19.99
1	68	520	12.88	1	73	320	7.97	1	73	321	19.99
1	68	507	12.97	1	73	320	7.97	1	73	324	19.99
1	68	507	12.97	1	73	320	7.97	1	73	325	19.99
1	68	520	12.97	1	73	332	10.69	1	73	330	19.99
1	68	523	12.97	1	73	327	10.90	1	73	330	20.59
1	68	525	12.97	1	73	322	10.99	1	73	331	21.77
1	68	516	13.88	1	73	332	11.29	1	73	319	21.99
1	68	525	13.88	1	73	332	11.79	1	73	328	21.99
1	68	507	13.97	1	73	323	11.99	1	73	329	21.99
1	68	507	13.97	1	73	323	11.99	1	73	329	22.29
1	68	507	13.97	1	73	323	11.99	1	73	331	22.29
1	68	518	14.88	1	73	323	11.99	1	73	330	22.97
1	68	518	14.88	1	73	322	12.99	1	73	324	24.99
1	68	518	14.88	1	73	322	12.99	1	73	319	25.00
1	68	519	14.88	1	73	332	13.39	1	73	319	25.00
1	68	520	14.88	1	73	319	13.99	1	73	319	25.00
1	68	520	14.97	1	73	322	13.99	1	73	325	25.70
1	68	512	15.88	1	73	332	14.19	1	73	325	25.70
1	68	512	15.88	1	73	331	14.67	1	73	325	25.70
1	68	512	15.88	1	73	321	14.99	1	73	325	25.70
1	68	512	15.88	1	73	321	14.99	1	73	330	26.97
1	68	513	15.88	1	73	322	14.99	1	73	324	26.99
1	68	513	15.88	1	73	323	14.99	1	73	325	26.99

G	Y	P	$	G	Y	P	$	G	Y	P	$
1	73	325	26.99	1	78	333	28.99	1	83	391	29.99
1	73	329	32.97	1	78	333	28.99	1	83	394	29.99
1	78	331	10.97	1	78	334	28.99	1	83	399	29.99
1	78	331	10.97	1	78	335	28.99	1	83	399	29.99
1	78	332	13.99	1	78	321	29.99	1	83	402	29.99
1	78	337	13.99	1	78	321	29.99	1	83	388	32.99
1	78	327	15.99	1	78	322	29.99	1	83	394	32.99
1	78	331	15.99	1	78	322	29.99	1	83	399	34.99
1	78	331	15.99	1	78	336	29.99	1	83	399	34.99
1	78	331	15.99	1	78	336	30.99	1	83	389	36.99
1	78	332	15.99	1	78	336	30.99	1	83	389	36.99
1	78	337	15.99	1	78	338	30.99	1	83	389	36.99
1	78	337	15.99	1	78	338	30.99	1	83	389	36.99
1	78	325	17.99	1	78	334	31.99	1	83	389	36.99
1	78	325	17.99	1	78	334	32.99	1	83	391	36.99
1	78	325	17.99	1	78	336	32.99	1	83	394	36.99
1	78	325	17.99	1	78	338	32.99	1	83	388	39.99
1	78	325	17.99	1	78	321	34.99	1	83	388	39.99
1	78	325	17.99	1	78	322	34.99	1	83	388	39.99
1	78	331	17.99	1	78	322	34.99	1	83	394	39.99
1	78	331	17.99	1	78	327	34.99	1	83	394	39.99
1	78	334	19.97	1	78	336	34.99	1	83	398	39.99
1	78	324	19.99	1	78	322	37.99	1	83	398	39.99
1	78	324	19.99	1	78	339	38.99	1	83	401	41.99
1	78	331	19.99	1	78	323	39.99	1	83	398	43.99
1	78	331	19.99	1	78	323	39.99	1	83	390	44.99
1	78	340	19.99	1	78	323	39.99	1	83	390	44.99
1	78	327	21.99	1	78	331	39.99	1	83	390	44.99
1	78	327	21.99	1	78	333	39.99	1	83	390	44.99
1	78	331	21.99	1	78	320	41.00	1	83	390	44.99
1	78	331	21.99	1	78	320	41.00	1	83	394	44.99
1	78	331	21.99	1	78	320	41.00	1	83	398	44.99
1	78	340	21.99	1	78	320	43.00	1	83	401	44.99
1	78	324	22.99	1	83	398	19.88	1	83	401	44.99
1	78	324	24.99	1	83	389	19.99	1	83	401	44.99
1	78	326	24.99	1	83	391	19.99	1	83	398	46.99
1	78	331	24.99	1	83	391	19.99	1	83	398	46.99
1	78	331	24.99	1	83	394	21.99	1	83	399	46.99
1	78	337	24.99	1	83	399	21.99	1	83	398	48.99
1	78	321	25.99	1	83	389	24.99	1	83	388	49.99
1	78	326	26.99	1	83	391	24.99	1	83	388	49.99
1	78	336	26.99	1	83	391	24.99	1	83	393	49.99
1	78	321	27.99	1	83	391	24.99	1	83	393	49.99
1	78	326	27.99	1	83	399	24.99	1	83	393	49.99
1	78	326	27.99	1	83	402	27.99	1	83	393	49.99
1	78	326	27.99	1	83	388	29.99	1	83	393	49.99
1	78	336	27.99	1	83	390	29.99	1	83	393	49.99
1	78	337	27.99	1	83	391	29.99	1	83	402	49.99

G	Y	P	$	G	Y	P	$	G	Y	P	$
1	83	401	53.99	1	88	349	44.99	1	93	367	60.00
1	83	400	54.99	1	88	349	49.99	1	93	367	60.00
1	83	400	54.99	1	88	351	49.99	1	93	364	63.00
1	83	400	58.99	1	88	351	54.99	1	93	364	63.00
1	83	402	59.99	1	88	351	54.99	1	93	364	63.00
1	83	393	64.99	1	88	351	54.99	1	93	365	65.00
1	83	393	64.99	1	88	351	54.99	1	93	365	65.00
1	83	393	64.99	1	88	340	59.99	1	93	367	65.00
1	83	393	64.99	1	88	340	59.99	1	93	364	68.00
1	83	393	64.99	1	88	340	59.99	1	93	372	69.99
1	83	393	64.99	1	88	340	59.99	1	93	372	69.99
1	83	393	64.99	1	88	340	59.99	1	93	373	69.99
1	83	393	64.99	1	88	340	69.99	1	93	366	70.00
1	83	393	64.99	1	88	340	69.99	1	93	366	70.00
1	83	400	64.99	1	88	340	69.99	1	93	367	70.00
1	83	400	64.99	1	88	340	69.99	1	93	364	73.00
1	83	400	64.99	1	88	340	69.99	1	93	372	74.99
1	83	393	69.99	1	88	340	69.99	1	93	365	75.00
1	88	342	24.99	1	88	340	74.99	1	93	366	75.00
1	88	357	24.99	1	88	340	74.99	1	93	367	75.00
1	88	355	29.88	1	88	340	74.99	1	93	372	79.99
1	88	355	29.88	1	88	340	74.99	1	93	365	80.00
1	88	355	29.99	1	88	340	74.99	1	93	365	83.00
1	88	355	29.99	1	88	338	79.99	1	93	373	88.99
1	88	343	29.99	1	88	338	79.99	2	28	721	24.85
1	88	343	29.99	1	88	338	79.99	2	28	721	34.75
1	88	343	29.99	1	88	339	79.99	2	28	721	38.50
1	88	343	34.99	1	88	339	84.99	2	28	721	51.75
1	88	342	34.99	1	88	339	84.99	2	28	716	53.75
1	88	342	34.99	1	88	339	84.99	2	28	718	62.50
1	88	342	39.99	1	88	353	84.99	2	28	720	63.75
1	88	342	39.99	1	93	366	36.00	2	28	717	64.50
1	88	344	39.99	1	93	374	40.00	2	28	717	76.85
1	88	344	39.99	1	93	366	42.00	2	28	718	79.50
1	88	344	39.99	1	93	366	45.00	2	28	719	82.85
1	88	341	44.99	1	93	374	48.00	2	28	717	83.85
1	88	341	44.99	1	93	374	48.00	2	28	719	84.95
1	88	341	44.99	1	93	370	49.99	2	28	718	86.85
1	88	348	44.99	1	93	370	49.99	2	28	717	94.75
1	88	348	44.99	1	93	370	49.99	2	28	718	94.95
1	88	348	44.99	1	93	370	49.99	2	28	720	96.85
1	88	348	44.99	1	93	371	49.99	2	28	719	101.95
1	88	348	44.99	1	93	371	49.99	2	28	719	117.95
1	88	348	44.99	1	93	371	55.00	2	33	527	22.50
1	88	349	44.99	1	93	371	55.00	2	33	525	26.00
1	88	349	44.99	1	93	371	55.00	2	33	526	26.50
1	88	349	44.99	1	93	373	59.99	2	33	524	26.95
1	88	349	44.99	1	93	366	60.00	2	33	525	29.00

G	Y	P	$	G	Y	P	$	G	Y	P	$
2	33	527	30.95	2	48	677	79.95	2	73	880	226.95
2	33	525	31.85	2	48	677	89.95	2	73	880	229.95
2	33	524	32.95	2	48	677	99.95	2	73	880	232.00
2	33	526	33.50	2	48	676	110.40	2	73	880	249.95
2	33	525	34.85	2	48	677	119.95	2	78	1224	129.95
2	33	525	35.85	2	48	675	124.00	2	78	1225	129.95
2	33	527	36.95	2	48	677	129.95	2	78	1225	139.95
2	33	526	37.50	2	48	677	129.95	2	78	1225	159.95
2	33	526	40.50	2	48	676	149.50	2	78	1213	179.95
2	33	525	46.85	2	48	677	149.95	2	78	1225	179.95
2	38	494	16.00	2	48	675	159.00	2	78	1224	199.99
2	38	494	18.95	2	48	674	162.00	2	78	1224	279.95
2	38	494	21.00	2	48	674	215.00	2	78	1214	339.85
2	38	493	24.95	2	53	695	109.50	2	78	1213	389.85
2	38	493	26.85	2	53	695	114.50	2	78	1212	399.85
2	38	493	27.95	2	53	694	119.50	2	83	1229	299.99
2	38	493	29.95	2	53	695	164.50	2	83	1231	349.99
2	38	493	33.85	2	58	825	62.95	2	83	1231	349.99
2	38	490	34.95	2	58	825	94.95	2	83	1229	359.99
2	38	492	34.95	2	58	820	169.95	2	83	1231	389.99
2	38	493	42.95	2	58	821	189.95	2	83	1231	389.99
2	38	489	45.95	2	63	1324	41.95	2	83	1230	499.99
2	38	484	46.00	2	63	1319	69.95	2	88	899	149.98
2	38	488	47.95	2	63	1313	79.95	2	88	900	239.98
2	38	486	50.95	2	63	1319	119.95	2	88	902	299.98
2	38	487	52.95	2	63	1319	149.95	2	88	903	399.99
2	38	490	53.95	2	63	1317	175.00	2	93	752	349.00
2	38	492	53.95	2	63	1318	180.00	2	93	757	379.00
2	38	484	58.00	2	63	1317	180.00	2	93	757	379.00
2	38	488	64.95	2	63	1318	215.00	2	93	757	399.00
2	38	484	65.00	2	63	1316	265.00	2	93	757	399.00
2	38	489	65.95	2	68	1351	59.95	2	93	749	449.00
2	38	483	69.85	2	68	1351	59.95	2	93	750	449.00
2	38	486	73.95	2	68	1351	69.95	2	93	752	449.00
2	38	487	73.95	2	68	1351	75.95	2	93	751	479.00
2	38	483	79.95	2	68	1351	99.95	2	93	749	499.00
2	38	484	81.00	2	68	1351	119.95	2	93	750	499.00
2	43	695	25.75	2	68	1359	139.95	2	93	751	499.00
2	43	693	28.95	2	68	1358	159.95	2	93	756	499.00
2	43	694	32.95	2	68	1359	169.95	2	93	756	599.00
2	43	693	36.85	2	68	1358	179.95	3	28	765	23.50
2	43	695	37.95	2	68	1359	189.95	3	28	766	24.85
2	43	693	39.85	2	73	881	149.95	3	28	765	25.50
2	43	693	39.85	2	73	881	154.95	3	28	765	32.85
2	43	693	56.85	2	73	880	174.95	3	28	765	48.50
2	43	693	69.75	2	73	881	194.95	3	28	765	56.50
2	43	691	77.85	2	73	882	194.95	3	28	764	72.50
2	48	677	64.95	2	73	880	209.95	3	28	767	77.85

G	Y	P	$	G	Y	P	$	G	Y	P	$
3	28	764	80.50	3	63	1224	189.95	3	78	949	459.95
3	33	580	11.95	3	63	1225	189.95	3	78	949	479.95
3	33	581	25.85	3	63	1231	209.95	3	78	949	634.95
3	33	580	49.50	3	63	1231	259.95	3	78	949	974.95
3	38	565	8.35	3	63	1231	329.95	3	83	764	309.99
3	38	565	10.35	3	68	1231	89.95	3	83	762	329.99
3	38	565	29.95	3	68	1228	99.00	3	83	764	359.99
3	38	565	39.95	3	68	1228	111.00	3	83	764	359.99
3	38	564	49.95	3	68	1231	129.95	3	83	762	389.99
3	38	564	62.50	3	68	1228	159.00	3	83	764	409.99
3	38	565	69.95	3	68	1231	159.95	3	83	762	459.99
3	43	NA	NA	3	68	1231	189.95	3	83	762	489.99
3	48	NA	NA	3	68	1229	199.00	3	83	762	559.99
3	53	825	62.88	3	68	1227	199.95	3	83	762	689.99
3	53	825	69.95	3	68	1232	199.95	3	83	762	789.99
3	53	825	104.95	3	68	1229	219.00	3	83	765	859.99
3	53	826	114.95	3	68	1231	239.95	3	88	713	259.99
3	53	825	134.95	3	68	1230	299.95	3	88	713	289.99
3	53	826	149.95	3	68	1232	309.95	3	88	713	299.99
3	53	825	169.95	3	68	1233	479.95	3	88	714	329.99
3	53	826	199.95	3	73	807	143.95	3	88	713	339.99
3	53	827	239.95	3	73	806	149.50	3	88	714	369.99
3	58	929	64.95	3	73	807	192.50	3	88	713	399.99
3	58	929	74.95	3	73	806	204.95	3	88	713	429.99
3	58	928	79.95	3	73	807	224.95	3	88	710	499.99
3	58	929	89.95	3	73	807	254.95	3	88	713	499.99
3	58	930	89.95	3	73	806	274.95	3	88	715	509.99
3	58	928	109.95	3	73	808	316.95	3	88	712	549.99
3	58	930	119.95	3	73	807	319.95	3	88	712	559.99
3	58	930	139.95	3	73	806	344.95	3	88	717	599.99
3	58	928	149.95	3	73	807	364.95	3	88	714	609.99
3	58	927	159.95	3	73	806	394.95	3	88	714	659.99
3	58	928	169.95	3	73	806	460.95	3	88	717	669.99
3	58	930	169.95	3	78	948	164.95	3	88	710	709.99
3	58	928	184.95	3	78	950	189.95	3	88	710	789.99
3	58	927	209.95	3	78	948	204.95	3	88	716	799.99
3	58	930	219.95	3	78	950	309.95	3	88	717	869.99
3	58	929	239.95	3	78	950	319.95	3	88	711	889.99
3	58	927	259.95	3	78	948	329.95	3	93	1512	229.99
3	58	931	269.95	3	78	950	339.95	3	93	1504	299.99
3	63	1225	79.95	3	78	948	359.95	3	93	1512	309.99
3	63	1224	109.95	3	78	950	379.95	3	93	1504	409.99
3	63	1224	119.95	3	78	948	399.95	3	93	1512	429.99
3	63	1225	119.95	3	78	948	399.95	3	93	1512	449.99
3	63	1224	159.95	3	78	941	419.95	3	93	1512	449.99
3	63	1224	169.95	3	78	948	439.95	3	93	1512	479.99
3	63	1224	169.95	3	78	950	439.95	3	93	1512	479.99
3	63	1231	169.95	3	78	941	449.95	3	93	1512	489.99

G	Y	P	$	G	Y	P	$	G	Y	P	$
3	93	1504	559.99	4	53	835	394.50	4	68	1244	374.95
3	93	1511	559.99	4	58	1220	19.50	4	68	1244	429.95
3	93	1512	559.99	4	58	1220	29.50	4	73	1062	134.95
3	93	1514	599.99	4	58	1220	39.95	4	73	1062	164.95
3	93	1511	609.99	4	58	1220	57.50	4	73	1062	177.95
3	93	1511	659.99	4	58	1220	62.50	4	73	1062	194.95
3	93	1511	659.99	4	58	1220	67.50	4	73	1062	256.95
3	93	1504	709.99	4	58	912	164.95	4	73	1062	256.95
3	93	1511	739.99	4	58	912	164.95	4	73	1063	307.95
3	93	1511	759.99	4	58	913	189.95	4	73	1063	349.95
3	93	1515	769.99	4	58	912	194.95	4	73	1063	399.95
3	93	1515	799.99	4	58	912	204.95	4	73	1063	459.95
3	93	1511	849.99	4	58	912	234.95	4	78	920	114.00
3	93	1504	899.99	4	58	912	249.95	4	78	920	144.95
3	93	1511	899.99	4	58	912	249.95	4	78	920	184.95
3	93	1515	999.99	4	58	912	254.95	4	78	921	189.95
3	93	1515	1069.99	4	58	912	259.95	4	78	921	199.95
4	28	573	2.75	4	58	913	289.95	4	78	920	214.95
4	28	573	3.25	4	58	913	329.95	4	78	920	224.95
4	28	573	4.45	4	58	913	379.95	4	78	921	229.95
4	28	573	4.75	4	63	1248	18.88	4	78	921	269.95
4	28	573	6.95	4	63	1248	42.95	4	78	923	269.95
4	28	573	7.85	4	63	1248	62.95	4	78	922	279.00
4	28	573	9.95	4	63	1250	169.95	4	78	921	309.95
4	28	573	13.45	4	63	1250	189.95	4	78	921	309.95
4	28	573	22.15	4	63	1250	199.95	4	78	923	339.95
4	28	573	26.45	4	63	1250	219.95	4	78	922	349.00
4	33	607	4.75	4	63	1250	239.95	4	78	923	369.95
4	33	607	7.85	4	63	1250	239.95	4	78	923	389.95
4	33	607	17.50	4	63	1250	269.95	4	78	923	439.95
4	38	618	4.98	4	63	1250	269.95	4	78	923	439.95
4	38	618	6.35	4	63	1250	299.95	4	78	923	499.95
4	38	618	14.75	4	63	1250	299.95	4	78	922	519.95
4	43	NA	NA	4	63	1250	349.95	4	78	922	599.95
4	48	1001	18.95	4	68	1404	10.95	4	83	1009	34.99
4	48	1001	47.50	4	68	1404	29.95	4	83	1009	54.99
4	53	897	24.50	4	68	1244	127.95	4	83	1009	59.99
4	53	897	42.50	4	68	1244	147.95	4	83	1009	79.99
4	53	897	49.50	4	68	1245	204.95	4	83	1009	139.99
4	53	897	52.50	4	68	1245	214.95	4	83	1009	179.99
4	53	897	57.50	4	68	1245	224.95	4	83	1008	194.95
4	53	897	59.95	4	68	1245	234.95	4	83	1008	254.95
4	53	897	59.95	4	68	1245	244.95	4	83	1008	264.95
4	53	897	66.95	4	68	1244	269.95	4	83	1008	264.95
4	53	897	66.95	4	68	1244	284.95	4	83	1008	274.95
4	53	835	274.50	4	68	1244	309.95	4	83	1007	294.95
4	53	835	314.50	4	68	1244	334.95	4	83	1008	294.95
4	53	835	324.50	4	68	1244	374.95	4	83	1008	294.96

G	Y	P	$	G	Y	P	$	G	Y	P	$
4	83	1008	314.95	4	88	123	399.99	4	93	965	519.99
4	83	1008	314.95	4	88	123	399.99	4	93	971	537.99
4	83	1008	349.95	4	88	126	399.99	4	93	965	539.99
4	83	1008	349.95	4	88	123	419.99	4	93	961	549.99
4	83	1008	379.95	4	88	123	429.99	4	93	961	559.99
4	83	1006	389.95	4	88	123	439.99	4	93	965	559.99
4	83	1008	389.95	4	88	118	449.99	4	93	968	569.99
4	83	1008	419.95	4	88	126	449.99	4	93	965	579.99
4	83	1006	429.95	4	88	118	469.99	4	93	961	589.99
4	83	1006	439.95	4	88	118	489.99	4	93	965	589.99
4	83	1006	449.95	4	88	119	489.99	4	93	965	599.99
4	83	1008	459.95	4	88	123	489.99	4	93	967	599.99
4	83	1006	479.95	4	88	126	499.95	4	93	963	674.99
4	83	1006	489.95	4	88	119	539.99	4	93	961	699.99
4	83	1006	519.95	4	88	119	569.99	4	93	965	699.99
4	83	1006	559.95	4	88	119	599.99	4	93	967	699.99
4	83	1005	579.95	4	88	121	599.99	4	93	968	699.99
4	83	1006	589.95	4	88	123	599.99	4	93	968	799.99
4	83	1005	659.95	4	88	119	639.99	4	93	963	824.99
4	83	1006	689.95	4	88	121	639.99	4	93	963	899.99
4	83	1006	719.95	4	88	119	729.99	4	93	963	999.99
4	83	1006	719.95	4	88	120	779.99	5	28	559	0.89
4	83	1007	819.95	4	88	120	879.99	5	28	559	1.25
4	83	1007	839.95	4	93	955	24.99	5	28	559	1.39
4	88	130	39.99	4	93	955	44.99	5	28	559	1.85
4	88	130	49.99	4	93	955	49.99	5	28	559	2.25
4	88	130	49.99	4	93	955	139.99	5	28	558	2.29
4	88	130	89.99	4	93	971	157.99	5	28	559	2.65
4	88	127	139.99	4	93	971	234.99	5	28	558	3.19
4	88	130	149.99	4	93	971	239.99	5	28	559	3.60
4	88	117	194.99	4	93	959	249.99	5	28	558	3.98
4	88	117	194.99	4	93	959	349.99	5	28	558	4.00
4	88	126	199.99	4	93	971	349.99	5	28	559	4.25
4	88	117	244.99	4	93	959	359.99	5	28	558	4.45
4	88	117	254.99	4	93	959	389.99	5	28	558	4.49
4	88	117	274.99	4	93	971	407.99	5	28	558	5.85
4	88	117	274.99	4	93	959	409.99	5	28	559	5.98
4	88	117	294.99	4	93	971	439.99	5	28	558	6.75
4	88	118	294.99	4	93	961	469.99	5	28	558	7.50
4	88	117	314.99	4	93	965	469.99	5	28	558	8.15
4	88	117	334.99	4	93	961	479.99	5	28	558	8.25
4	88	122	359.99	4	93	965	479.99	5	28	558	8.95
4	88	118	369.99	4	93	965	489.99	5	28	558	8.95
4	88	118	389.99	4	93	959	499.99	5	28	558	10.85
4	88	118	389.99	4	93	961	499.99	5	28	558	11.25
4	88	122	389.99	4	93	965	499.99	5	28	558	11.65
4	88	117	399.99	4	93	967	499.99	5	28	558	12.00
4	88	122	399.99	4	93	971	499.99	5	28	558	12.55

G	Y	P	$	G	Y	P	$	G	Y	P	$
5	28	558	13.45	5	38	662	9.75	5	48	591	9.95
5	28	558	14.35	5	38	661	10.55	5	48	591	13.90
5	28	558	15.25	5	38	661	12.25	5	48	590	37.58
5	28	558	16.15	5	38	663	12.29	5	48	590	58.08
5	28	558	16.15	5	38	661	12.75	5	48	597	66.65
5	28	558	16.25	5	38	661	13.45	5	48	590	69.63
5	28	558	18.95	5	38	661	14.25	5	48	597	74.50
5	28	558	20.65	5	38	661	14.65	5	48	590	74.71
5	28	558	20.65	5	38	663	14.95	5	48	597	77.50
5	28	558	22.50	5	38	661	15.45	5	48	591	82.90
5	28	558	25.50	5	38	661	15.75	5	48	590	87.54
5	28	558	26.50	5	38	661	16.48	5	48	591	99.50
5	28	558	28.00	5	38	663	16.95	5	48	597	99.50
5	28	558	62.00	5	38	661	17.65	5	48	597	110.00
5	28	558	89.00	5	38	663	18.95	5	48	597	127.50
5	33	463	0.79	5	38	661	18.98	5	48	591	137.92
5	33	463	1.49	5	38	663	19.45	5	48	597	152.50
5	33	463	1.79	5	38	662	19.75	5	48	591	171.70
5	33	463	3.98	5	38	661	19.95	5	53	466	2.79
5	33	463	6.95	5	38	663	19.98	5	53	466	4.79
5	33	463	7.98	5	38	662	23.95	5	53	466	5.69
5	33	463	8.89	5	38	663	24.45	5	53	466	7.15
5	33	463	8.95	5	38	662	26.95	5	53	467	7.20
5	33	463	9.85	5	38	663	26.95	5	53	467	9.49
5	33	463	9.95	5	38	663	26.95	5	53	466	9.50
5	33	463	10.65	5	38	663	29.95	5	53	466	13.95
5	33	463	11.45	5	38	663	31.95	5	53	467	14.50
5	33	463	11.45	5	38	662	31.98	5	53	467	15.95
5	33	463	12.95	5	38	663	33.75	5	53	467	15.95
5	33	463	13.25	5	38	662	36.95	5	53	467	17.49
5	33	463	14.95	5	38	661	39.95	5	53	467	17.95
5	33	463	14.95	5	38	662	39.95	5	53	467	22.30
5	33	463	28.45	5	38	663	39.95	5	53	466	24.50
5	38	660	1.55	5	38	663	39.95	5	53	467	26.25
5	38	660	1.79	5	38	662	39.98	5	53	467	29.50
5	38	660	1.79	5	38	661	43.75	5	53	467	34.95
5	38	661	1.84	5	38	662	44.95	5	53	467	39.95
5	38	660	2.25	5	38	663	49.95	5	53	471	42.50
5	38	660	2.39	5	38	663	51.95	5	53	467	48.65
5	38	660	2.59	5	38	662	55.00	5	53	471	49.50
5	38	660	2.66	5	38	663	75.95	5	53	470	49.95
5	38	660	2.98	5	38	663	169.50	5	53	471	49.95
5	38	660	3.06	5	43	438	2.97	5	53	471	72.50
5	38	660	3.75	5	43	438	23.45	5	53	470	89.50
5	38	661	7.98	5	43	438	34.88	5	53	471	97.50
5	38	661	8.39	5	43	438	69.50	5	53	471	112.50
5	38	661	8.98	5	48	590	7.75	5	53	471	124.50
5	38	661	9.19	5	48	590	9.95	5	53	471	150.95

G	Y	P	$	G	Y	P	$	G	Y	P	$
5	53	471	154.50	5	63	818	1.79	5	68	759	168.50
5	53	471	157.50	5	63	818	12.50	5	68	764	179.00
5	53	470	158.50	5	63	818	17.50	5	68	757	194.50
5	58	592	4.47	5	63	816	19.50	5	68	759	197.00
5	58	592	5.77	5	63	818	24.50	5	73	1137	10.75
5	58	592	7.47	5	63	818	26.50	5	73	1137	17.50
5	58	593	7.50	5	63	808	43.95	5	73	1137	49.00
5	58	592	8.47	5	63	816	44.47	5	73	1143	49.50
5	58	592	9.97	5	63	808	56.88	5	73	1138	53.50
5	58	592	10.50	5	63	816	64.22	5	73	1143	79.50
5	58	593	13.97	5	63	816	64.22	5	73	1143	134.00
5	58	595	21.47	5	63	813	69.90	5	73	1138	149.50
5	58	599	23.96	5	63	808	69.95	5	73	1143	157.00
5	58	594	29.00	5	63	808	78.88	5	73	1138	187.50
5	58	593	29.50	5	63	817	83.95	5	73	1143	187.50
5	58	595	31.97	5	63	813	88.88	5	73	1138	246.00
5	58	599	39.60	5	63	817	98.95	5	78	1034	13.50
5	58	593	42.50	5	63	809	127.50	5	78	1034	17.50
5	58	594	47.96	5	63	813	129.88	5	78	1034	24.50
5	58	595	49.97	5	63	817	138.50	5	78	1034	34.50
5	58	594	55.50	5	63	809	147.50	5	78	1034	39.50
5	58	594	56.50	5	63	813	148.88	5	78	1035	79.50
5	58	598	57.50	5	68	761	4.19	5	78	1035	149.50
5	58	593	58.20	5	68	761	4.95	5	78	1036	159.50
5	58	595	66.00	5	68	760	12.75	5	78	1035	189.50
5	58	599	67.80	5	68	760	19.75	5	78	1036	369.50
5	58	594	72.50	5	68	757	23.44	5	83	667	99.99
5	58	598	72.50	5	68	764	24.44	5	83	669	109.99
5	58	593	75.60	5	68	760	29.75	5	83	667	129.99
5	58	598	76.50	5	68	760	32.50	5	83	667	169.99
5	58	595	77.50	5	68	764	39.50	5	83	666	199.99
5	58	598	82.50	5	68	764	56.50	5	83	666	219.99
5	58	593	87.96	5	68	760	57.50	5	83	666	259.99
5	58	594	97.50	5	68	698	62.97	5	83	666	269.99
5	58	595	98.50	5	68	758	64.50	5	83	666	284.99
5	58	598	101.50	5	68	757	67.88	5	83	666	319.99
5	58	599	125.00	5	68	760	78.50	5	83	666	324.99
5	58	598	129.50	5	68	764	78.50	5	83	696	489.95
5	58	595	139.95	5	68	757	86.88	5	83	696	1189.95
5	58	598	149.50	5	68	758	89.50	5	83	696	1499.95
5	58	598	153.50	5	68	760	89.50	5	88	687	39.99
5	58	599	154.50	5	68	764	99.50	5	88	687	99.99
5	58	599	155.00	5	68	757	109.88	5	88	684	199.95
5	58	595	165.00	5	68	759	129.00	5	88	684	339.95
5	58	598	173.50	5	68	764	129.50	5	88	685	429.99
5	58	599	179.50	5	68	757	137.88	5	88	685	449.99
5	58	595	189.00	5	68	759	159.00	5	88	659	1189.99
5	58	595	239.00	5	68	757	164.88	5	88	658	1289.99

G	Y	P	$	G	Y	P	$	G	Y	P	$
5	88	659	1489.99	5	93	1414	229.99	5	93	1417	519.99
5	93	1412	39.99	5	93	1416	249.99	5	93	1458	599.99
5	93	1412	57.99	5	93	1414	269.99	5	93	1417	619.99
5	93	1412	59.97	5	93	1414	299.99	5	93	1459	699.99
5	93	1412	69.99	5	93	1415	319.99	5	93	1458	799.99
5	93	1412	89.99	5	93	1415	319.99	5	93	1460	799.99
5	93	1413	129.99	5	93	1415	339.99	5	93	1458	899.99
5	93	1413	129.99	5	93	1416	339.99	5	93	1459	899.99
5	93	1413	159.99	5	93	1417	389.99	5	93	1460	899.99
5	93	1413	159.99	5	93	1416	419.99	5	93	1459	999.99
5	93	1414	189.99	5	93	1417	419.99	5	93	1459	999.99
5	93	1414	199.99	5	93	1415	439.99	5	93	1460	999.99
5	93	1413	229.99	5	93	1417	499.99	5	93	1460	1199.99

Bibliography

Abernathy, W. and James Utterback (1982), 'Patterns of Industrial Innovation,' M. Tushman and W. Moore, (eds), *Readings in the Management of Innovation*, Cambridge, Mass: Ballinger Publishing Company.

Abrams, M. and H. Bernstein (1989), *Future Stuff*, New York: Penguin Books.

Abrams, M. and H. Bernstein (1990), *Towards 2001: A Consumer's Guide to the 21st Century*, London: Angus and Robertson.

Abrams, M. and H. Bernstein (1991), *More Future Stuff*, New York: Penguin Books.

Adelman, Irma and Zvi Griliches (1961) , 'On an Index of Quality Change,' *American Statistical Association Journal*, 56, 534-48.

Anderson, James L. and Sofia U. Bettencourt (1991), *Using a Conjoint Approach to Model Product Preferences: The New England Market for Fresh and Frozen Salmon*, University of Rhode Island/AES Contribution Number 2678, June.

Baldwin, R.E. (1955), 'Secular Movements in the Terms of Trade,' *American Economic Review*, Papers and Proceedings 45 (2), May, 259-69.

Bartik, Timothy J. (1987), 'The Estimation of Demand Parameters in Hedonic Price Models,' *Journal of Political Economy*, 95 (1), 81-8.

Bell, Daniel (1981). 'Models and Reality in Economic Discourse.' Daniel Bell and Irving Kristol, (eds), *The Crisis in Economic Theory*, New York: Basic Books, Inc., 52-3.

Binswanger, H. and V. Ruttan (1978), *Induced Innovation*, Baltimore: The Johns Hopkins University Press.

Blaug, M. (1992), *The Methodology of Economics or How Economists Explain*, Cambridge: Cambridge University Press.

Bloch, Harry and David Sapsford (1991), 'Postwar Movements in Prices of Primary Products and Manufactured Goods,' *Journal of Post Keynesian Economics*, 14 (2), 249-66.

Blomquist, G. and L. Worley (1981), 'Hedonic Prices, Demand for Urban Housing Amenities and Benefit Estimates,' *Journal of Urban Economics*, 9, 212-21.

Brown, James N. and Harvey S. Rosen (1982), 'On the Estimation of Structural Hedonic Models,' *Econometrica*, 50 (3), May.

Burstein, M.L. (1961), 'Measurement of Quality Change in Consumer Durables,' *Manchester School of Economics and Social Studies*, 29, 267-79.

Cagan, P. (1965), 'Measuring Quality Change and the Purchasing Power of Money: An Exploratory Study of Automobiles,' *National Banking Review*, 3, 217-36. Reprinted in Griliches (1971c).

Caldwell, B. (1982), *Beyond Positivism: Economic Methodology in the Twentieth Century*, London: Allen and Unwin.

Caldwell, B.J. and A.W. Coats (1984), 'The Rhetoric of Economics: a comment on McClosky,' *Journal of Economic Literature*, 22 (2), 575-8.

Chamberlin, Edward H. (1953), 'The Product as an Economic Variable,' *Quarterly Journal of Economics*, February, reprinted in Edward H. Chamberlin, *Towards a More General Theory of Value*, New York: Oxford University Press, 1957.

Coase, Ronald H. (1974), 'The Lighthouse in Economics,' *Journal of Law and Economics*, 17 (October), 357-76 [reprinted in Cowen (1992)].

Court, A.T. (1939), 'Hedonic Price Indexes with Automotive Examples,' in *The Dynamics of Automobile Demand*, New York: General Motors Corporation.

Cowen, Tyler (1992), 'Public Goods and Externalities: Old and New Perspectives,' in Tyler Cowen, (ed.), *Public Goods and Market Failures: A Critical Examination*, Transaction Publishers, 1-28.

Crane, Diana (1967), 'The Gatekeepers of Science: Some Factors Affecting the Selection of Articles for Scientific Journals,' *The American Sociologist*, 2 (4), 195-201.

Cropper, Maureen L., Leland B. Deck and Kenneth E. McConnell (1988), 'On the Choice of Functional Form for Hedonic Price Functions,' *The Review of Economics and Statistics*, LXX (4), November, 668-75.

Deaton, Angus and John Muellbauer (1987), *Economics and Consumer Behavior*, New York: Cambridge University Press.

Denison, Edward F. (1962), *The Sources of Economic Growth in the United States and the Alternatives Before Us*, Supplementary Paper No. 13, New York: Committee for Economic Development.

Dhrymes, P.J. (1971), 'Price and Quality Changes in Consumer Capital Goods: An Empirical Study,' in Griliches (1971c).

Diewert, W. Erwin (1990), 'Comment,' in Ernst R. Berndt and Jack E. Triplett, (eds), *Fifty Years of Economic Measurement: The Jubilee of the Conference on Research in Income and Wealth*, Chicago: The University of Chicago Press.

Dosi, Giovanni (1988), 'Sources, Procedures, and Microeconomic Effects of Innovation,' *Journal of Economic Literature*, **XXVI** (September), 1120-71.

Dosi, Giovanni et al. (1990), *The Economics of Technical Change and International Trade*, New York: New York University Press.

Dosi, Giovanni et al. (1992), *Technology and Enterprise in a Historical Perspective*, New York: Oxford University Press.

Earl, Peter E. (1983), 'A Behavioral Theory of Economists' Behavior,' in Alfred S. Eichner (ed.), *Why Economics is not yet a Science*, Armonk, New York: M. E. Sharpe.

Eichner, Alfred S. (1983), 'Why Economics is not yet a Science,' in Alfred S. Eichner (ed.), *Why Economics is not yet a Science*, Armonk, New York: M. E. Sharpe.

Ellsworth, P.T. (1956), 'The Terms of Trade between Primary Producing Countries and Industrial Countries.' *Inter-American Economic Affairs*, **10** (1), Summer, 47-65.

Ethridge, D.E. and B. Davis (1982), 'Hedonic Price Estimation for Commodities: an Application to Cotton,' *Western Journal of Agricultural Economics*, **7**, 293-300.

Findlay, R. (1984), 'Growth and Development in Trade Models,' R. Jones and P. Kenen, (eds), *Handbook of International Economics,* New York: North-Holland.

Fisher, F. M. and Karl Shell (1968), 'Taste and Quality Change in the Pure Theory of the True-Cost-of-Living Index,' in J. N. Wolfe, (ed.), *Value, Capital, and Growth: Essays in Honour of Sir John Hicks*, Edinburgh: Edinburgh University Press.   Reprinted in Griliches (1971c).

Fisher, Franklin M. and Karl Shell (1972), *The Economic Theory of Price Indices; Two Essays on the Effects of Taste, Quality, and Technological Change*. New York: Academic Press.

Freeman, Christopher (1982), *The Economics of Industrial Innovation*, Cambridge, Mass: The MIT Press.

Gilbert, Milton and Irving B. Kravis (1954), *An International Comparison of National Products and the Purchasing Power of Currencies: A Study of the United States, the United Kingdom, France, Germany, and Italy*, Organisation for European Economic Cooperation.

Gordon, Robert J. (1990), *The Measurement of Durable Goods Prices*, Chicago: University of Chicago Press.

Green, Paul E. (1974), 'On the Design of Choice Experiments Involving Multifactor Alternatives,' *Journal of Consumer Research*, **1**, September, 61-8.

Green, Paul E. and V. Srinivasan (1990), 'Conjoint Analysis in Marketing: New Developments with Implications for Research and Practice,' *Journal of Marketing*, **54**, October, 3-19.

Griliches, Zvi (1964), 'Notes on the Measurement of Price and Quality Changes,' in *Models of Income Determination: Studies in Income and Wealth, Vol. XXVIII*, Conference on Research in Income and Wealth, National Bureau of Economic Research, Princeton, N.J.: Princeton University Press.

Griliches, Zvi (1971a), 'Hedonic Price Indexes for Automobiles: An Econometric Analysis of Quality Change,' in *Price Statistics of the Federal Government, 1961*, General Series, No. 73. New York: National Bureau of Economic Research. Reprinted in Griliches (1971c).

Griliches, Zvi (1971b), 'Introduction: Hedonic Price Indexes Revisited,' in Griliches (1971c).

Griliches, Zvi (ed.) (1971c), *Price Indexes and Quality Change: Studies in New Methods of Measurement*, Cambridge, Mass: Harvard University Press.

Griliches, Zvi, (1990) 'Hedonic Price Indexes and the Measurement of Capital and Productivity: Some Historical Reflections,' in Ernst R. Berndt and Jack E. Triplett, (eds), *Fifty Years of Economic Measurement: The Jubilee of the Conference on Research in Income and Wealth*, Chicago: The University of Chicago Press.

Grilli, E. and Maw Cheng Yang (1988), 'Primary Commodity Prices, Manufactured Goods Prices, and the Terms of Trade of Developing Countries: What the Long Run Shows,' *The World Bank Economic Review*, **2**, No. 1, 1-47.

Halbrendt, C.K., F.F. Wirth, and G.F. Vaughn (1991), 'Conjoint Analysis of the Mid-Atlantic Food-Fish Market for Farm-Raised Hybrid Striped Bass,' *Southern Journal of Agricultural Economics*, July, 155-63.

Hall, Robert E. (1971), 'The Measurement of Quality Change from Vintage Price Data,' in Griliches (1971c).

Jung, C.G. (1953), *Psychological Reflections; an Anthology of the Writings of C.G. Jung*, New York, Pantheon Books.

Juran, J.M. (1992), *Juran on Quality by Design: The New Steps for Planning Quality into Goods and Services*, New York: The Free Press.

Kalecki, M. (1971), *Selected Essays on the Dynamics of the Capitalist Economy, 1933-1970*, Cambridge: Cambridge University Press.

Kelman, S. (1981), 'Cost-Benefit Analysis: An Ethical Critique,' *Regulation*, January/February, 33-40.

Keynes, J.M. (1912), 'Board of Trade Tables for 1900-1911,' *Economic Journal*.

Keynes, J.M. (1920), *The Economic Consequences of the Peace*, New York: Harcourt, Brace, and Howe.

Kindleberger, C.P. (1956), *The Terms of Trade: A European Case Study*, Cambridge, Mass: MIT Press.

Kravis, I.B. and R.L. Lipsey (1974), 'International Trade and Price Proxies,' in N.D. Ruggles, (ed.), *The Role of the Computer in Economic and Social Research in Latin America,* New York: National Bureau of Economic Research.

Kuhn, Thomas S. (1970), *The Structure of Scientific Revolutions*, Chicago: University of Chicago Press.

Kuttner, Robert (1985), 'The Poverty of Economics,' *The Atlantic Monthly*, February, 74-84.

Lancaster, K. (1971), *Consumer Demand: A New Approach*, New York: Columbia University Press.

Lancaster, K. (1977), 'The Measurement of Changes in Quality,' *Review of Income and Wealth*, **23**, 157-72.

Lancaster, K. (1991), *Modern Consumer Theory*, Aldershot, Hants: Edward Elgar.

Larson, Douglas M. (1992), 'Can Nonuse Value Be Measured from Observable Behavior,' *American Journal of Agricultural Economics*, **74**, 1114-20.

Layard, P.R.G. and A.A. Walters (1978), *Microeconomic Theory*, New York: McGraw-Hill.

Leibenstein, H. (1980), *Beyond Economic Man: A New Foundation for Microeconomics*, Cambridge, Mass: Harvard University Press.

Leontief, W. (1971), 'Theoretical Assumptions and Nonobserved Facts,' *American Economic Review*, **61**, 1-7.

Lewis, W. Arthur (1952), 'World Production, Prices and Trade, 1870-1960,' *Manchester School of Economic and Social Studies*, **20**, (2), 105-38.

Lewis, W. Arthur (1978), *The Evolution of the International Economic Order*, Princeton, New Jersey: Princeton University Press.

Lewis, W. Arthur (1982a), *Perspectives on Economic Development: Essays in the Honor of W. Arthur Lewis*, T.E. Barker et al. (eds), Washington, DC: University Press of America.

Lewis, W. Arthur (1982b), *The Theory and Experience of Economic Development: Essays in Honor of Sir W. Arthur Lewis*, Mark Gersovitz et al. (eds), London: Allen & Unwin.

Lewis, W. Arthur (1983), *Selected Economic Writings of W. Arthur Lewis*, Mark Gersovitz (ed.), New York: New York University Press.

Lichtenberg, Frank R. and Zvi Griliches (1989), 'Errors of Measurement in Output Deflators,' *Journal of Business and Economic Statistics*, **7**, (1), 1-9.

Louviere, Jordan J. (1988), *Analyzing Decision Making; Metric Conjoint Analysis*, Newbury Park, California: Sage Publications, Inc.

Lucas, Robert E.B. (1975), 'Hedonic Price Functions,' *Economic Inquiry*, **XIII**, June, 157-78.

Macbean, A. and V.N. Balasubramanyan (1978), *Meeting the Third World Challenge*, London: Macmillan.

Mackenzie, John (1990), 'Conjoint Analysis of Deer Hunting,' *Northeastern Journal of Agricultural and Resource Economics*, 109-17.

MacLeod, R. (ed.) (1986), *Technology and the Human Prospect*, London: Francis Pinter.

Maizels, A. (1970), *Growth and Trade,* Cambridge. England: Cambridge University Press.

Mayer, Thomas (1993), *Truth versus Precision in Economics*, Aldershot, Hants: Edward Elgar.

McCloskey, Donald N. (1983), 'The Rhetoric of Economics,' *Journal of Economic Literature*, **XX1**, June, 481-517.

McMillan, M.L., B.G. Reid and D.W. Gillen (1980), 'An Extension of the Hedonic Approach for Estimating the Value of Quiet,' *Land Economics*, **56**, 315-28.

Meadows, D.H., D.L Meadows and J. Randers (1992), *Beyond the Limits: Confronting Global Collapse, Envisioning a Sustainable Future*, Post Mills, Vermont: Chelsea Green Publishing Company.

Meier, G.M. (1958), 'International Trade and International Inequality.' *Oxford Economic Papers*, **10** (3), October, 277-89.

Messonier, Mark L. and E. Jane Luzar (1990), 'A Hedonic Analysis of Private Hunting Land Attributes Using an Alternative Functional Form,' *Southern Journal of Agricultural Economics*, December, 129-35.

Mill, J.S. (1848), *Principles of Political Economy*, London: John W. Parker, Reprinted in Pelican Classics, Harmondsworth, England, 1970.

Morgan, T.O. (1959), 'The Long-Run Terms of Trade between Agriculture and Manufacturing,' *Economic Development and Cultural Change*, **8** (1), October, 1-23.

Muellbauer, J. (1974), 'Household Production Theory, Quality, and the "Hedonic Technique",' *American Economic Review*, **64**, 977-94.

Nelson, R.R. and S.G. Winter (1982), *An Evolutionary Theory of Economic Change*, Cambridge, Mass: The Belknap Press of Harvard University Press.

Palmquist, R.B. and L.E. Danielson (1989), 'A Hedonic Study of the Effects of Erosion Control and Drainage on Farmland Values,' *American Journal of Agricultural Economics*, **71**, 55-62.

Pareto, Vilfredo (1879), *Cours*, § 714.

Payson, S. (1991), *An Analysis of Long-Run Trends in the Prices of Goods and Services, As a Function of Evolutionary Changes in Quality, Production Costs, and Preferences*, Doctoral Dissertation, Columbia University, New York, Ann Arbor, MI: University Microfilms International.

Pearce, David W. (ed.) (1983), *The Dictionary of Modern Economics; Revised Edition*, Cambridge, Mass.: The MIT Press.

Pisik, B., 'Sears Closes Book on a Retail Legend,' *The Washington Times*, January 26, 1993, pp. A1-A10.

Pollak, R. (1989), *The Theory of the Cost-of-Living Index*, New York: Oxford University Press.

Prebisch, R. (1950), 'The Economic Development of Latin America and Its Principal Problems,' United Nations Economic Conference on Latin America. Reprinted in: *Economic Bulletin for Latin America*, 1962, **7**, 1-22.

Ray, G.F. (1977), 'The Real Price of Primary Products,' *National Institute Economic Review*, (81), August, 72-6.

Ricardo, D. (1817), *Principles of Political Economy and Taxation*, London: John Murray. Reprinted in Pelican Classics, Harmondsworth, England, 1971.

Robinson, Joan (1980), *Collected Economic Papers: Volume Five*, Cambridge, Mass.: The MIT Press.

Rosen, Sherwin (1974), 'Hedonic Prices and Implicit Markets: Product Differentiation in Pure Competition,' *Journal of Political Economy*, **82** January/February, 34-9.

Rosenberg, N. (1982), *Inside the Black Box: Technology and Economics*, New York: Cambridge University Press.

Samuelson, Paul A. (1983), *Foundations of Economic Analysis*, Cambridge, Mass.: Harvard University Press (first printed in 1947).

Sapsford, D. (1985), 'The Statistical Debate on the Net Barter Terms of Trade Between Primary Commodities and Manufactures: A Comment and Some Additional Evidence,' *The Economic Journal*, **95** (September), 781-7.

Schellhardt, T. (1993), 'Closing the Book on an American Tradition,' *The Wall Street Journal*, January 26, p. B1.

Schmookler, Jacob (1966), *Invention and Economic Growth*, Cambridge, Mass.: Harvard University Press.

Schmookler, Jacob (1972), *Patents, Invention, and Economic Change*, Zvi Griliches and Leonid Hurwicz (eds), Cambridge, Mass: Harvard University Press.

Schumacher, E.F. (1973), *Small is Beautiful: Economics as if People Mattered*, London: Blond & Briggs Ltd.

Schumpeter, J. (1934), *The Theory of Economic Development*, Cambridge, Mass: Harvard University Press.

Scitovsky, Tibor (1976), *The Joyless Economy*, New York: Oxford University Press.

Sears Roebuck and Company, *Sears Catalog*, Spring/Summer editions: 1928, 1933, 1938, 1943, 1948, 1953, 1958, 1963, 1968, 1973, 1978, 1983, 1988 and 1993.

Segerstrom, P.S. (1991), 'Innovation, Imitation, and Economic Growth,' *Journal of Political Economy*, **99** (4), 807-27.

Singer, H. (1950), 'The Distribution of Gains Between Investing and Borrowing Countries,' *American Economic Review, Papers and Proceedings*, **40**, May, 473-85.

Smith, Adam (1776), *An Inquiry Into the Nature and Causes of the Wealth of Nations*. Reprinted in A.S. Skinner, (ed.), London: Penguin Books, 1970.

Spraos, J. (1980), 'The Statistical Debate on the Net Barter Terms of Trade Between Primary Commodities and Manufactures,' *The Economic Journal*, **90** March, 107-28.

Spraos, J. (1985), 'The Statistical Debate on the Net Barter Terms of Trade: A Response,' *The Economic Journal*, **95**, September, 789.

Steenkamp, Jan-Benedict E.M. (1989), *Product Quality*, Assen, The Netherlands: Van Gorcum.

Streeten, P. (1974), 'World Trade in Agricultural Commodities and the Terms of Trade with Industrial Goods,' in N. Islam, (ed.), *Agricultural Policy in Developing Countries*, London: Macmillan.

Thurow, Lester C. (1983), *Dangerous Currents: The State of Economics*, New York: Random House.

Torrens, R. (1821), *An Essay on the Production of Wealth*, London: Longman, Hurst, Rees, Orme and Brown. Reprinted by A.M. Kelly, New York, 1965.

Triplett, Jack E. (1966), *The Measurement of Quality Change*, doctoral dissertation, University of California at Berkeley.

Triplett, Jack E. (1969), 'Automobiles and Hedonic Quality Measurement,' *Journal of Political Economy*, **77**, 408-17.

Triplett, Jack E. (1971), 'Quality Bias in Price Indexes and New Methods of Quality Measurement,' in Griliches (1971c).

Triplett, Jack E. (1983), 'Concepts of Quality in Input and Output Price Measures: A Resolution of the User-Value Resource-Cost Debate,' in Murray F. Foss (ed.), *The U.S. National Income and Product Accounts: Selected Topics*; *Studies in Income and Wealth, Volume 47*, Chicago: The University of Chicago Press and the National Bureau of Economic Research.

Triplett, Jack E. (1986), 'The Economic Interpretation of Hedonic Methods,' *Survey of Current Business*, January, 36-40.

Triplett, Jack E. (1989), 'Price and Technological Change in a Capitalist Good: A Survey of Research on Computers,' in Dale W. Jorgenson and Ralph Landau (eds), *Technology and Capital Formation*, Cambridge, Mass: The MIT Press.

Triplett, Jack E. (1990), 'Hedonic Methods in Statistical Agency Environments: An Intellectual Biopsy,' in Ernst R. Berndt and Jack E. Triplett, (eds), *Fifty Years of Economic Measurement: The Jubilee of the Conference on Research in Income and Wealth*, Chicago: The University of Chicago Press.

Ullman, J. (1974), 'Product Innovation — Sources and Limits', in John Ullman, (ed.), *Business and Technical Determinants of Product Change*, Hempstead, New York: Hofstra University, 501-509.

U.S. Department of Commerce (1986), *The National Income and Product Accounts of the United States, 1929-82; Statistical Tables*.

U.S. Department of Labor, Bureau of Labor Statistics (1989), *BLS Handbook of Methods* (Bulletin 2285).

Viner, Jr. (1953), *International Trade and Economic Development*, Oxford: Oxford University Press.

Ward, B. (1972), *What's Wrong with Economics?*, London: Macmillan.

Ward, M. (1976), *The Measurement of Capital: The Methodology of Capital Stock Estimates in OECD Countries,* Paris: Organization for Economic Co-operation and Development.

Wilson, W.W. (1984), 'Hedonic Prices in the Malting Barley Market,' *Western Journal of Agricultural Economics*, **9**, 29-40.

Winer, B.J., Donald R. Brown, and Kenneth M. Michels (1991), *Statistical Principles in Experimental Design; Third Edition*, New York: McGraw-Hill, Inc.

Worsick, G.D.N. (1972), 'Is Progress of Economic Science Possible?', *Economic Journal*, **82**, 73-86.

Young, Allan H. (1989), 'Alternative Measures of Real GNP,' *Survey of Current Business*, **69**, April, 27-34.

Index